COLLEGE OF ALAM

D1118805

LD
1250
L5

Liebert, Robert
    Radical and militant
youth

DATE DUE

MAR 25 '8			
MAR 21 '8			

Radical and Militant Youth

Radical and Militant Youth

A Psychoanalytic Inquiry

ROBERT LIEBERT

Foreword by Robert Coles

PRAEGER PUBLISHERS
New York • Washington • London

PRAEGER PUBLISHERS
111 Fourth Avenue, New York, N.Y. 10003, U.S.A.
5, Cromwell Place, London S.W.7, England

Published in the United States of America in 1971
by Praeger Publishers, Inc.

© 1971 by Praeger Publishers, Inc.

All rights reserved

Library of Congress Catalog Card Number: 78–122091

Printed in the United States of America

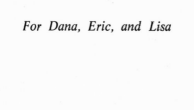

For Dana, Eric, and Lisa

Contents

Foreword

by Robert Coles

Freud's genius to some extent is beyond comprehension. Can we ever really know what accounts for exceptionally gifted men—the artists and writers and thinkers whose vision, whose uncanny sense of things, persists over the centuries, an inheritance for all of us? But, if no psychiatric or psychoanalytic "explanation," even the most "positive" kind, quite does justice to the "mystery and manners" a man like Freud both draws upon and offers to others, we most surely can remark upon the quality of the particular achievement—in Freud's case, volume after volume of strong, clear-headed prose aimed at giving the so-called ordinary reader (Freud was, for most of his life, an outcast among doctors and psychiatrists in Vienna and elsewhere) a jarring and provocative look at the mind's interior.

I mention Freud because Dr. Liebert is yet another observer who has, with good reason, summoned psychoanalysis to the task of understanding how human beings think and feel and act. But I also mention Freud because Dr. Liebert, himself a psychoanalyst, is loyal to Freud in a special way. He writes because he wants to make clear, to himself as well as others, what he has observed and struggled with (and, yes, felt) as a particular kind of clinician, a psychoanalyst with a continuing concern for the young. And, like Freud, Dr. Liebert knows how to respond to the existential rhythm of his own life—hence this book. I would even go further. I would emphasize that Dr. Liebert came to this "inquiry" out of the hazards and dilemmas of both his professional life and his personal life—but I would also hold that a psychoanalyst faced with a challenge to his theoretical and clinical assumptions is in fact a *man confronted,* a citizen forced to think twice, look around more closely, and, in the best sense, doubt himself.

Dr. Liebert needs no one to summarize what he quite carefully and openly and honestly writes about in the pages that follow. In a foreword, one can only offer a few thoughts that one hopes have a suggestive quality to them. One can only invoke a certain tradition—again, that to which Freud belonged. I refer to the uncanny mixture of firsthand observation and theoretical speculation that the founder of psychoanalysis managed to offer his readers in a steady flow of papers and books. Sadly, not all analysts today keep to that example; nor do they demonstrate the lively interest in social and historical developments that comes across in the *New Introductory Lectures on Psychoanalysis, Group Psychology and the Analysis of the Ego, The Future of an Illusion,* or the famous essay "Why War?" Instead (yes, even today, even when fields like "social psychiatry" and "community psychiatry" exist), all too many psychiatrists and psychoanalysts fail to look at themselves as closely as they do at their patients, fail to ask themselves the searching questions Freud insisted are the hallmark of the discipline he founded. I have in mind questions that lead both doctor and patient outside the office, but not too far out. For instance, which people command the time of psychoanalysts, and at what price? How does a theory, however "objective" or "value-free" its proponents claim it to be, fit the needs and mandates of a particular society? Who becomes a doctor, a psychiatrist —that is, which people, from which background, with what set of assumptions? Why, in America, of all places, has psychoanalysis had such continuing acceptance—from upper-middle-class, agnostic, urban intellectuals? These are questions a good social historian must one day ask and try to answer. And there are other questions, too. Do psychiatrists and their particular way of seeing people lend themselves conveniently to the powers-that-be of any political system—be it the Soviet Union's or ours? Do words like "normal," "mature," "antisocial," or "irrational" come to be used not only by judges and politicians and newspaper editors, but also by physicians, as weapons, to be called upon when it is necessary to put down one or another bold, challenging, and unconventional citizen?

Recently we have seen young people all over the world challenge a range of political and economic systems. Again and again, existing institutional injustices have been the target of these youths.

By no means are those rebels who are intent on social change immune to the dangers of messianic self-righteousness, extreme self-centeredness, and cruel zealotry. But all of us, even those who have had years of psychoanalysis and regularly add the letters M.D. to our names, face such dangers every day, and not always do we emerge safe and uncontaminated—as, again, some social historian interested in psychiatric and psychoanalytic sectarianism will one day demonstrate. The issue, then, comes down to this: How does an observer write about radical youth in such a way that he describes what they want, what they aim to do, what actions they take, and how their particular hopes and fears and frustrations and patterns of behavior compare with those of other human beings, including the silent, obedient, compliant men and women, the so-called ordinary ones, who never raise their fists in defiance of established authority, never say no—even, alas, when dictators of one sort or another move into control of a country?

Throughout this book, one feels that Dr. Liebert, a thoughtful, sensitive, intelligent, and compassionate man and doctor, is haunted—not in some melodramatic or hysterical way, but by his own mind's integrity and courageous willingness to face what others in his situation have notably evaded and, if you will, *denied* or *rationalized away* or *suppressed* or *repressed*. And we psychiatrists do indeed call upon those "defense mechanisms," call upon them not only as all human beings do in the face of one or another "private" problem, but also in order to come to terms with our own consciences, which have to be quieted down, made less responsive to the misery and brutality and exploitation all too apparent in this rich and powerful nation, and made less responsive to cries for help or demands for change or charges of bias and deceit and wrongdoing. So it goes for us, the "normal" and "mature," the ones who are in good contact with "reality" and who consider ourselves "sensible" and who are proud to be analyzed and aware and all the rest: In our comfortable homes and apartments, we deplore wars and economic injustice and political persecution—but go on living out our lives, which means insisting that it is for others (*which* others?) to take on directly and actively the social and economic "system," and thereby right the wrongs of this world.

For Robert Liebert, that way of living and looking at things was abruptly confronted in the late 1960's by American college students, particularly those at Columbia College, where he has worked as a psychiatrist. I do not believe I exaggerate when I say that his "psychoanalytic inquiry" is also a testament of sorts, a sharp and touching and candid narrative whose purpose is not to label others with names, and hence be rid of them, but to demonstrate what all of us share, *deeply* share, *unconsciously* share, as citizens of a troubled nation, which has yet to realize the great and important purposes set forth by its rebellious founding fathers.

And, because he is a fair man, a man ready to criticize himself as well as others, a man capable of tolerating complexity, ambiguity, and irony (without getting nervous, hence driven to wordy theories and sweeping, catchy terms), Robert Liebert will no doubt be ignored by those very influential people who always are able to use a middle-aged doctor's words to flail at one or another assertively outraged "group." One can only hope, however, that, quietly and persistently, this book will make its way to other readers, to those young and no longer young Americans who love this country enough to want desperately the same social and political changes dreamed of by some of the men and women Dr. Liebert describes and, more than that, acknowledges as his teachers, his companions in an ethical struggle whose outcome (it has to be said in 1971) is by no means certain.

Preface

If the time when this study began can be pinpointed, it would be about 3:15 P.M. on a Tuesday afternoon, April 30, 1968. Within less than twelve hours, a thousand policemen would clear as many students out of five Columbia University buildings that the students had "liberated" and occupied for almost a week. In cluttered offices at Ferris Booth Hall, the Student Activities Center, where the Strike Coordinating Committee was carrying on the business of running a campus rebellion, I was speaking with one of the members of the Strike Steering Committee, whom I had known before that spring.

We talked of a critical issue in the negotiations—the striking students' demand for "amnesty." The young man believed that the faculty was moving in the direction of recommending amnesty. My perception was that the Ad Hoc Faculty Group grew less inclined to forgive by the hour and that a recommendation of amnesty was increasingly remote. I explained my view and even suggested some motivational explanations for what I thought was a misperception by the students and for the behavior of the faculty. I added a plea for the striking students to leave the buildings at this time, arguing that this action would dramatically demonstrate their good faith, avoid the otherwise inevitable bloodshed, expedite action on their substantive demands, and, just possibly, help to preserve the university as a viable community.

The young man listened attentively without interrupting and, when I had finished, said quietly:

It is you who is misperceiving events. If we compromise now we will go back to *status quo,* and the faculty will go back to *status quo.* . . . If we leave now all will be lost. What started out as a gymnasium and IDA issue [1] became a dream of a thousand people in those build-

[1] The substantive issues in the strike are discussed in Chapters I and II.

ings of a Free University. We may not come back to Columbia, but we now have a dream that is within our grasp. And maybe in the end a thousand of us will walk out to form a new university.

His eyes were bloodshot from the week of little sleep, but he spoke with enormous energy and conviction. I could think of nothing further to say. We shook hands and wished each other well.

As I walked down the corridor, the sounds of the strikers' mimeograph machine and their excited talk faded. I crossed South Field. The long chains of flower beds in the middle of campus were approaching full bloom, lovely and totally incongruous. The college buildings surrounding me were awesome, at once ugly and beautiful. Suddenly, I felt tired and old, and very frightened.

Here I was—thirty-eight years old; married and the father of two children; a fairly prosperous and respected psychoanalyst; a part-time teacher and consultant at an Ivy League college; and more. By the standards of our culture, I was a success. But I felt adrift at that moment between the worlds of strike headquarters and my downtown office.

As I walked to my car, a question kept repeating itself: If the students left the buildings and started a new university, where would I choose to teach—at the old Columbia or the new Free University?

I was bombarded with painful doubts about the relevance of most of my professional activities in the face of the urgent social issues of our time. My "liberal" political gestures and rhetoric seemed weak and futile in contrast to the students' sweeping radical vision and action. My thoughts turned to my children: Which of the two universities would my son and daughter, then aged six and two, eventually choose to attend, and what did I want for them in their life journeys?

In all this, a few things were clear. The students I would be most interested in teaching would be among those at the "new" university. I also knew, however, that the experiences and themes of my own past, coupled with my rootedness, professional and personal, in both the style and content of the life I had come to lead, determined a position for me well short of radical activism.

The explanation of how I resolved this personal disequilibrium cannot be separated from how I came to undertake the present research, an activity remote from my usual professional endeavors. Although I was a relatively peripheral member of the Morningside Heights faculty, I had spent five to fourteen hours a day on campus during the week the buildings were occupied. I had learned a great deal about the sociopolitical structure of Columbia, particularly as regards the process of decision-making; the sources of power; the university's policies toward the neighboring black and Puerto Rican communities growing out of Columbia's need for physical expansion; the nature of some of the university's ties to government, especially regarding research that might be related to the conduct of the Vietnam war; and, finally, the university's attitude toward some of the important needs of its own students. It seemed to me that, in major respects, the struggle in this country was being played out in microcosm at Columbia. The silence of the faculty in recent years had made them, as a body, covert partners in many of these ills. I reached the conclusion that the existing machinery by which students could influence these policies was indeed inadequate.

Events were in motion that plunged the students and the university into turbulence. Campus confrontation has become more commonplace now, but in April, 1968, there were few precedents for what was taking place and none in Columbia's history. Hence, for the vast majority of the college's undergraduates, the crisis produced enormous stress on their adaptive capacities. Overnight, the campus had become an arena for massive protest and counter-protest. During the week of the occupation of the five buildings, virtually all the members of the university community experienced some combination of passion, fear, anxiety, brotherhood, and rage. Uncertainty emerged where certainty had existed, and, significantly, for many, commitment and conviction now took the place of apathy and indecision.

The students who occupied the buildings included some of the brightest and most idealistic of Columbia youth. They had made a commitment to principles in which they believed. The political meaningfulness of their behavior was complemented by something quite lovely and romantic about the communes, symbolized by a candlelight wedding ceremony in one of the occupied buildings. Columbia's Protestant chaplain, who officiated, said, "I now declare you children of a new age." Notwithstanding certain reservations about their critique of the university and about some of the tactics they employed, I was struck by the view these students had of themselves, of their society, and of the university. To them, Columbia had come to represent the training ground for a place in an unacceptable society. These students seemed nothing like my college classmates a generation earlier. So, curious about these youth, as well as about the process by which historical forces interact with individual lives, each affecting and molding the other in ways that make each generation different from the ones that preceded it, I decided to undertake a study of the actors in the events at Columbia in the spring of 1968.

I include this personal note because, in a study such as this, the researcher's attempt to understand the historical perspective of his own life and to develop a model by which others can approach an understanding of these politically committed youth repeatedly and necessarily intersect.

ROBERT S. LIEBERT

New York City
January, 1971

Acknowledgments

The content of this book has been deeply affected by my conversations with many friends, colleagues, and students, but I wish to express my particular indebtedness to a few: to Anthony Phillip, director of the Columbia College Counseling Service, who was always ready to give encouragement, advice, and support; to Paul Lippmann, with whom I spent much of the days and evenings on campus during the 1968 rebellion, and whose capacity to transcend the safe and conventional modes of thought about human behavior has been a source of illumination for me; to Hugh Butts, for his willingness to clarify for me much that was unfamiliar about the black experience at Columbia; to Neal Hurwitz, for sharing his remarkable feeling for the sociopolitical currents at Columbia and his understanding of some of the subtle ways in which they affect the lives of members of the campus community; to Kenneth Keniston, whose own work with radical youth served as a beacon for me again and again, and whose personal encouragement and critique of my initial manuscript have been invaluable; to Robert Michels, who, in criticizing an early draft of the manuscript, forced me to address myself to rigorous questions that I had hesitated to ask myself; to Lucienne Sanchez, for not only typing the manuscript but also helping me so cheerfully with many other aspects of getting the book together.

I shall always be profoundly grateful to my editor, Gladys Topkis, for her faith in me and her dedication to the undertaking, both of which made this book possible. Beyond her technical skills, her humanity is reflected in these pages.

In the total fabric of my life, this book is but one expression of a search, a phase in a life journey that I share with my wife, Lisa. It has thus been sustained by her love and wit and patience, and, throughout, it bears the imprint of her wisdom.

Radical and Militant Youth

I: Introduction

On April 23, 1968, a noon rally of students on the Columbia campus was followed by a march to the building site of the new Columbia gymnasium, where students tore down the fence surrounding the site and otherwise interfered with construction. One student was arrested. The other students then returned to Hamilton Hall, the main classroom and administrative-office building of Columbia College,[1] and began a sit-in, detaining the Acting Dean of the college, Henry Coleman, in his office as hostage for the arrested student, whose release they demanded.

The other demands [2] were as follows:

1. that construction of the gymnasium be stopped
2. that the university's ties with the Institute for Defense Analyses (IDA) be discontinued

[1] In 1754, George II of England granted a royal charter to a group of New York citizens to found Kings College "for the Instruction of Youth in the Learned Languages and the Liberal Arts and Sciences." After the American Revolution, the institution was renamed Columbia College. By 1897, the schools of Law, Engineering, Architecture, and Graduate Faculties had been founded and the several schools moved to their present location at Morningside Heights. In 1912 Columbia was rechartered by the State of New York as "Columbia University in the City of New York."

Today, Columbia College is the men's undergraduate school of liberal arts in Columbia University. With an enrollment of 2,700 students, it is the smallest of the eight "Ivy League" colleges. The college operates with considerable autonomy within the larger university, which has a total of 11,000 full-time and 6,000 part-time students. Columbia College has its own dormitories, administration, and faculty.

Barnard College, with 1,900 female students, has its own campus across the street from Columbia University, its own trustees, administration, and faculty. However, there is cross-registration between Barnard and Columbia for many courses, and a number of extracurricular activities, particularly student political organizations, are coed.

[2] See page 19 for a description of these issues.

3

3. that President Kirk's ban on indoor demonstrations be re-scinded
4. that criminal charges arising out of the protest at the gym site be dropped
5. that disciplinary probation of the "IDA six" (six students involved in a protest demonstration against IDA held in March) be rescinded
6. that amnesty be granted for the present protesters

By sunrise the next morning, the white students had been evicted from Hamilton Hall, and the black protesters—about half the black students in the college—had emerged as a militant political group, with Hamilton Hall established as an all-black protest base. Over the next two days, white students "liberated" and occupied four other university buildings: Avery Hall (the School of Architecture), Fayerweather Hall, the Mathematics Building, and the president's three-room office suite in Low Library. By April 25, approximately 1,000 students were occupying university buildings.

Meanwhile, an Ad Hoc Faculty Committee had been formed to mediate between the students and the administration. In the evening of April 26, the administration decided to call the New York City police to clear the buildings but, later, acceded to faculty pressure and rescinded the decision. Nevertheless, a clash took place between about two dozen police at Low Library and faculty members attempting to bar their entry. On April 28, a group of counterdemonstrators, the Majority Coalition (MC), established a "blockade" around Low Library to bar the entrance of food and of other demonstrators. Faculty formed a cordon around the building to prevent overt clashes between the protesters and MC members.

In the predawn hours of April 30, after a week of stalemated negotiations between the administration and the students, with futile faculty efforts at mediation, the administration summoned the New York City police to clear the five buildings of the student occupants. In the course of this action, 712 arrests were made, and there was violence by the police, directed against, not only protesting students, but also faculty and student supporters and uninvolved bystanders outside the buildings. As a result, 150 people were treated for various injuries and bruises; presumably many more were untreated and unreported.

Among the results of the week of confrontation were: abrupt termination of college classes for the final five weeks of the semester, and cancellation of final examinations; considerable destruction of university property by police and students; at least one major act of vandalism, the deliberate burning of ten years of research notes belonging to a faculty member; the disruption of countless friendships, among students and faculty alike, over political differences; and acute polarization of white and black students.

It gradually became apparent that some of the more radical students were resolved to continue to paralyze the university rather than accept compromises that would allow for restoration of the formal educational process. It also became evident that the top administration was rigid and ineffectual in dealing with the crisis and that real power resided in the trustees, who acted in a manner that seemed calculated further to inflame the situation. General disenchantment characterized the students' view of the faculty and their ability to find an effective means of resolving the conflict. Students, administration, and faculty voiced great uncertainty about their personal futures and the nature of their further relationship to the university.

How does one study the psychological meaning of such an event for the individuals involved? The method is determined, as well as limited, by the purpose of the study, the questions that interest the researcher, the techniques available for obtaining data, and the accessibility and cooperation of the subjects.

I am a psychiatrist trained in psychoanalysis, with a particular interest in the process of crisis and resolution that takes place in the years between adolescence and adulthood—the years of undergraduate college experience. Prior to the rebellion, this interest had led me to teach an undergraduate course in Columbia College and to serve as psychiatric consultant to the College Counseling Service. When the rebellion erupted, I decided to act on the opportunity to explore the students' responses, in part because of my own need to make sense of what had happened, but for other reasons as well.

The current intense interest in the activities of youth and the fate of universities has produced a flourish of armchair literature on student activism. It therefore seemed worthwhile to exploit the availability of empirical data drawn from the students themselves, during a period of maximal personal and community politicization. Although the study was of the 1968 Columbia rebellion, it was my intention to develop principles that had general applicability, not only to many campuses but also to more basic themes of youth and rebellion in any setting, at any time. In studying these young people and their relationship with their world, I hoped to understand more about myself and my time, for we all share a common fate. Yet I know that some conclusions that seem valid at this moment will appear far less certain in only a few months. To appreciate this is not simply a cause for author's humility but an insight into a powerful force, acting in an unprecedented way upon still malleable young people and accounting for behavior that is an adaptation to this flux.

The basic question that concerned me was why particular young men and women, at a particular time and place, engaged in a particular form of radical action. To answer this question required speculation about the process of psychohistory, by which I mean the complementarity and mutual influence of the individual's inner dynamics, the development of his personal "identity," and the existing and changing social conditions. What experiences and symbolic themes are shared by a group of people or a generation that profoundly affect them, making them different in political philosophy, life style, and psychological organization from other groups or generations? This topic will be directly addressed in Chapter XI.

As a psychiatrist, oriented to the psychological interior, I was interested in such problems as: Could different kinds of activists be distinguished on the basis of both manifest behavior and conscious and unconscious motivation? How were the various political positions related to character structure, individual developmental experiences, and family social philosophy? What were the psychodynamic as well as psychosocial implications of the form the political action took—"occupation" of and communal living in university buildings? These questions will be discussed in Chapter IX.

I was also interested in learning about the relationship between the psychological needs of people and the structure and operation of institutions affecting their lives. These considerations are explored in Chapter X.

Chapters II through VIII are concerned with less conceptual aspects of the matter: Why was the university the principal object of youthful protest? How did the nonactivist students respond to the events, and what psychological meaning did the events have for these students? What were some of the background characteristics of the black and white student activists that seem to be related to their becoming militant in their protests? What was the relationship of these radical students to their parents and to the faculty during the crisis? Finally, what psychological significance did the violent police action have for these students? In all these questions, I was interested in the similarities and differences between black students and white students.

This approach is based on my conviction that the political behavior of each student was the outcome of a constellation of interacting forces—character structure, value systems, response to the unconscious as well as conscious meaning of the particular radical action undertaken, and the external reality of the immediate sociopolitical situation.

This study is an example of what has come to be known as "firehouse research"—that is, what takes place when a social crisis erupts unexpectedly and the researcher races out and studies it as best he can, with no prior plan for the project. Further, I was embarking on this effort as a single investigator; the research was not funded or formally supported by any department or laboratory; there were no research assistants or co-investigators. In these circumstances, what techniques could I use in seeking answers to my questions?

The principal sources of data were direct interviews with students, term papers by students, and clinical descriptions of student-patients by therapists other than myself, supplemented by more informal observations and discussions with administrators, faculty, parents, therapists, nonacademic employees of Columbia, and other students. In interpreting these data, I drew on background information on the student activists obtained from college records.

The passage of time has obviously influenced what follows, in that my ideas have evolved over the years of working on this manuscript. Many of my initial impressions have been modified by subsequent experiences and contacts, such as the opportunity to talk with and observe less formally many of the students who were interviewed. In addition, my continuing affiliation with Columbia enabled me to meet with other students who had been at the university in the spring of 1968. Finally, since 1964, I have had a number of Columbia undergraduates in psychotherapy, five of them at the time of the crisis. Some of these students had terminated therapy before the crisis but met with me later and discussed aspects of their participation. Several had occupied buildings.

Although my thinking has obviously been influenced by what I have learned from and shared with these patients, I have not used case material. To have done so would undoubtedly have made for a more interesting, convincing, and comprehensive document, but only at some risk of compromising the confidentiality of the therapeutic relationship. What I have learned in this setting has been invaluable in providing a base for my theoretical formulations, but, since the clinical data are not always presented, I must ask for trust on the part of the reader that at least much in these formulations is based on more than speculation.

Further, my interest in this project has naturally led me into countless discussions with students from all positions on the political spectrum at Columbia and at other colleges (including Berkeley and San Francisco State College) about topics related to this study.

Obviously, what emerges from a study such as this must be balanced by the findings of studies by sociologists, political scientists, economists, urban planners, and other specialists. Yet to shy away from research in this area because of fear of error growing out of theoretical limitations and imperfect methods of study will hardly help us to unravel the complexities of man's sociopolitical behavior.

The psychoanalytically oriented technique presented certain immediate conceptual barriers. My training has been based on a medical model, which emphasizes the study of maladaptive behavior of disturbed people. The systems for description and classification in the discipline, as well as the tradition in the literature, have produced a disposition to view all nonnormative, new, and unusual behavior in a psychopathological frame of reference. But can a science founded on the study of maladaptive behavior help us to understand contemporary social and political group behavior?

It is axiomatic that the laws of intrapsychic operation are applicable to all individual social or political acts. However, before a judgment can be made with regard to the health of the ego governing the action, a concurrent determination must also be made as to the nature and degree of social pathology in the society that the activist is struggling to change. Lives cannot be studied in pure culture, removed from the currents of economic, political, and social forces. Given this thesis, we are faced with the inevitable contaminant introduced into this kind of research by the investigator's own political orientation.

If one bothers to study the protagonists in a confrontation situation, it is because the conflicted issues are of deep personal interest. Therefore, the researcher usually starts with a personal bias, a belief that there are "good guys" and "bad guys," or "moral" and "healthy" versus "immoral" and "mentally ill" participants. As the confrontation is prolonged, this dichotomy solidifies. There is a strong temptation to use psychological description and, particularly, labels of psychopathology in the service of political argument.

This kind of research, then, requires continuous self-searching on the part of the researcher, in order to understand how his own political biases inevitably color *all* phases of the project—the issues selected for investigation, the selection of subjects, the mode of inquiry and data collection, the interpretation of the data, and the conclusions. Because the research and the researcher are inextricably bound, the conclusions will be incomplete unless the relevant data on the researcher himself are included along with his findings on his subjects.

The Interviews

The primary source of data was open-ended, two- to four-hour interviews with fifty students, conducted along "psychoanalytically oriented" lines. I began interviewing late in May and, at the outset, arbitrarily set July 31, 1968, as the target date for completion, in order to capture the students' experience before it was subjected to extensive retrospective change based upon their further political and personal development. Several additional interviews were conducted in the early fall in order to give me some impressions about the students' perspective after the summer hiatus.

The choice of this method was governed not only by the practical considerations mentioned earlier but, more importantly, by the nature of the concerns that interested me. Despite the possibility of selective distortions, the relatively unstructured interview situation has certain unique advantages, in that the subject can be engaged in a collaborative search for the meaning of his behavior in terms of the continuity of his past and present. Apart from the factual information and his conscious explanations for decisions and actions in his life—his associative trend and the quality of the relationship with the interviewer give indications of levels of psychic operation that are less well formulated and accessible to the subject. This method of interview allows for the introduction of relevant material that is unique to the subject, material that the researcher would not have thought to inquire about. In this type of interaction, it is also possible to observe the emotions associated with the material under discussion, as well as to reach conclusions about the more general emotional life of the individual.

The limits of what can be obtained in this kind of interview, however, must also be kept in perspective. How much can be generalized about the flow of a person's life by seeing him at one point in time, after a highly atypical disruption in his usual pattern? Optimally, there should be a series of follow-up observations. Is a systematic distortion introduced by seeing all the subjects at this point in time and compounded by the transient effects of the crisis on the researcher? Further, from the relatively few lives studied in this highly selective population, can we generalize our conclusions about the relationship between individual lives and institutions and between lives and historical events and about new and changing identity patterns?

Of the fifty students interviewed, sixteen were seen in pairs or small groups. The virtue of these small-group interviews was that, in the interaction between the students, both information and emotion emerged that would not have been expressed so readily in a one-to-one interview. In addition, the students often elicited important points from each other that I would not have thought of inquiring about.

The students interviewed, as Table 1 reveals, were drawn predominantly from Columbia College.

TABLE 1

UNIVERSITY AFFILIATION OF INTERVIEWED STUDENTS, BY COLOR

University Affiliation	Black Students	White Students
Columbia undergraduates (all male)	13	25
Barnard undergraduates (all female)	1	6
Columbia graduate students (all male)	0	5
Total	14	36

The reason for focusing on these students was basically two-fold: (1) the college was the primary arena of the crisis and the only division of the university that was effectively closed for the remainder of the semester; therefore, the impact of the crisis was universal and total on Columbia undergraduates; (2) the college had a homogeneous age population, generally from eighteen to twenty-two years old, which made it possible to consider adaptive patterns for this stage of life.

As Table 2 indicates, the white students selected for interview predominantly assumed a radical position during the crisis.

TABLE 2

POLITICAL AFFILIATION OF INTERVIEWED STUDENTS,
BY COLOR AND SEX

Political Affiliation	Black		White	
	Male	Female	Male	Female
Active radical or militant	7	0	21	6
Active antiradical or antimilitant *	0	0	2	0
Nonactivist	6	1	7	0
Total	13	1	30	6

* Students active with the Majority Coalition in blockading Low Library

In speaking of a student "radical," I am generally referring to the *white* student whose perception of social and political reality is such that he no longer believes that the existing institutions and processes provided for social and political reform are capable of correcting the inequities of the society. Concurrent with this outlook is his engagement in tactics aimed at correcting these social ills through confrontation with those in authority by means other than those provided for in existing codes of due process and traditional dissent.

Although the term "black militant" has come to describe rather imprecisely a wide range of political and tactical positions, in this book I define the black student militants by the same structural criteria used to define the white radicals—that is, their view that the existing sociopolitical order is incapable of bringing about necessary reform, and their conviction of the need to use extralegal means. There are nonetheless major differences, which will be discussed later in this book.

The interview subjects were predominantly radicals for the obvious reason that these are the students in whom I, like most people concerned with the college scene today, am most interested. As a basis of comparison, other students, from liberal, moderate, and conservative positions, were interviewed.

Among the blacks who were interviewed, the ratio of militants —that is, those who occupied a building—to the total number of blacks interviewed was the same as the ratio of the militant undergraduates to the total undergraduate black population.

Two of the group interviews—one with six white students who occupied a building and the other with four black students, two of whom occupied Hamilton Hall—were tape-recorded and transcribed. I took handwritten notes during all the other interviews.

The interviews were arranged mainly through a chain of referrals. I reached all but three of the black students through personal introductions by black undergraduates previously known to me. A few of these referred students gave me further names and prepared the way for other prospective interviews. Two interviews were arranged by direct telephone calls to students whom I did not know. Another was arranged by introduction through a white faculty friend of the student. With the white students, similarly, I started with some I knew personally, and they then arranged for me to see friends of theirs. In a few instances, I randomly called names of students I had been told represented a particular group or position. In every case, the students were offered the option of meeting with me at an office on campus, at my private office off campus, at my home, or at their homes. The majority of the interviews were conducted on campus. Interestingly, all of the students who selected either their or my home for the interview were identified with the white radical movement.

Almost all of the white students approached displayed a remarkable willingness, in fact, eagerness, to meet with me. The exceptions were two radical graduate students who refused on the basis that there was no political rationale for their spending time with me for my research purposes instead of on more relevant social or political efforts, one radical leader who simply did not show up for the scheduled meeting, and several conservative students who did not return my calls once they were apprised of my purpose.

In their relation to the "outside" world—the administration, the media, other students, faculty mediators, and researchers—the black students in Hamilton Hall presented themselves as a highly disciplined, unitary organization, with position statements issued only through the four-man Steering Committee. In public appearances, leaders preserved personal anonymity. The Steering Committee took the position that students were not to speak as individuals about the experience in Hamilton Hall, presumably so as to conceal whatever factionalism existed, so that the opposition would be unable to plan a strategy of concessions just sufficient to co-opt some of the black student body; to reduce distortion by the media; and, finally, to generate anxiety on the part of the white establishment, which would be useful in bargaining. With regard to my study, individual members of the Steering Committee ranged from endorsing to disapproving, but the Committee never took an official position.

A result of this policy of the blacks in Hamilton Hall was that many of the students who were there did not feel free to meet with me. Nevertheless, I was able to interview seven of the forty-one undergraduate male students who were in Hamilton Hall. In addition, I formally interviewed six black students who stayed outside of Hamilton Hall and spoke more casually with two others. Given this policy, the seven students who were in Hamilton Hall did not represent a random selection of those who chose to join in the occupation of the building but were at the less militant end of the spectrum of those who participated. Their perception of events is therefore not altogether representative. Knowing of the interdiction against discussing political facets of the life inside Hamilton Hall, I did not inquire into questions of political organization, the decision-making process, or the personalities of the leaders. The students I spoke with outside of Hamilton did not feel constrained in the same way.

Knowing that my study was not "officially" sanctioned or welcome no doubt created some degree of tentativeness in my inquiry. Part of my self-consciousness may also have been a response to the hesitancy and, perhaps, guilt that some of the black students felt in talking to me. But, beyond that, in a first meeting between black student and white psychiatrist, there is inevitably less rapport than in a meeting between the same psychiatrist and most white radical students.[3] The nature of the interviews with blacks was affected by all these considerations.

---

[3] The initial difficulties in establishing rapport between black student and white psychiatrist have been noted by others. Robert Coles, commenting on his work with black students in the early 1960's civil rights movement in the South, says: "Working with these students I have found is not the most conventional psychotherapeutic task. Many of them are profoundly distrustful of outsiders, even those recommended to them by their fellows; and I am white, an obstacle for many Southern Negroes who need

In my interviews with both black and white students, the basis of contact was the reversal of the therapeutic meeting, in that the students had not sought me out because of an expectation of benefit from contact with a psychiatrist. Yet many of the questions I asked were similar to those that would be posed in the usual clinical meeting. In the opening minutes of all the interviews, therefore, the student manifested guardedness, coupled with intense scrutiny of my reactions to him.

For the reasons mentioned, the establishment of trust and rapport was more difficult to achieve with the black students, although there were marked variations in the level of communication achieved. Some interviews were essentially mechanical information-gathering. In others, a high level of personal rapport was reached, and the several hours together were mutually quite pleasurable.

A few patterns in the interviews might be generalized. At the time of the interviews, most of the radical students had criminal charges pending against them. Hence, there was an initial suspiciousness about what would become of the data, and this I had to assuage. I have no doubt that being unfunded and unsponsored made my task easier. Also, I am not sure the project could have proceeded at all without the endorsements of radical and militant students whom I had previously known. That I was a psychoanalyst held special appeal for many students, who regarded the interview as an opportunity for a quasi-clinical consultation. I offered no resistance, with the result that, for some students, the third or fourth hours of talking were barely distinguishable from what commonly takes place during a clinical consultation. This was

---

time and experience to feel even remotely comfortable with any white, even those standing beside them in demonstrations, let alone a watching psychiatrist. Some of these problems of suspicion and aloofness yielded to the slow formation of relationships between many of these students and me." "Social Struggle and Weariness," *Psychiatry*, vol. 27, no. 4 (1964), p. 310.

Two black psychiatrists, William Grier and Price Cobbs, state: "We submit that it is necessary for a black man in America to develop a profound distrust of his white fellow citizens and of the nation. . . . If he does not so protect himself, he will live a life of such pain and shock as to find life itself unbearable. For his own survival, then, he must develop a 'cultural paranoia' in which every white man is a potential enemy unless proved otherwise and every social system is set against him unless he personally finds out differently." *Black Rage* (New York: Basic Books, 1968), p. 161.

mutually beneficial both for the student and for my purposes of trying to understand him at some depth.

The interviews began with my stating my background and my interest in finding out about the student's behavior during the crisis and how his actions might be related to his past, his family, his present, his experience at Columbia, his social relationships, his future, the ways in which he felt changed by the experience, and so forth. In the first fifteen or twenty minutes, the student usually dwelled on and justified his political beliefs and actions, at the same time very carefully watching and measuring my response. While I did not make my own political position explicit, most students sensed my general sympathy for the radical action, and this may account for the greater rapport I experienced with the more "left" students, conducive to their being more trusting and open. Beyond this, however, the radical students were far more eager to talk because they felt transformed, not just politically, but in their whole world view. In the excitement of this moment in their lives, they were eager to convey what had happened, what had changed in them, and where they were now going. The white nonradicals lacked this driving force to communicate their inner experience. In this respect, the black nonmilitants were not comparable to the white nonradicals, since all of the blacks experienced a profound internal confrontation, in which they had to face basic issues of their own identity and then decide on a course of consistent action; for the blacks, the alternative to active protest amounted to "active" nonprotest.

Term Papers

I collected thirty-five term papers by Columbia College undergraduates on their reactions during the crisis and how their feelings and behavior related to their previous history and development. Ten of the papers were by students in my own class; twenty-five were by students who did not know me and who were enrolled in other courses in the Department of Human Development. The papers were all written within five weeks after the original occupation of buildings.

The distribution of political position of the authors of the papers is presented in Table 3.

TABLE 3

POLITICAL AFFILIATION OF AUTHORS OF TERM PAPERS *

Active radical	5
Nonactivist	23
Active antiradical	7
Total	35

* All but one of these students was white; the black student was nonactivist.

The fact that the sample is skewed in the direction of relatively conservative students reflects the characteristics of the students enrolled in these courses.

Most of the papers consisted of five to nine double-spaced typewritten pages. They ranged from simple descriptions of overt behavior and political rhetoric to searching introspective accounts of their author's life at this point in relationship to the crisis.

Clinical Summaries

Five colleagues doing psychotherapy at the University Services or privately gave me descriptions of a total of twenty-five unidentified Columbia undergraduates who were in therapy with them at the time of the crisis. The political positions of these patients during the crisis is presented in Table 4.

TABLE 4

POLITICAL AFFILIATION OF PSYCHOTHERAPY PATIENTS

Active radical	3
Nonactivist	21
Active antiradical	1
Total	25

The therapists were all psychoanalysts, in psychoanalytic training, or otherwise committed to a psychoanalytic orientation. Their political sympathies ranged from moderately liberal to left liberal. In their formulations, they described the behavior, thought, and affect of the students during the crisis and then gave psychodynamic explanations and family and developmental features that were germane.

In the interests of maintaining confidentiality, I will not present any of these clinical descriptions directly. Nor will I supply composite clinical summaries, which tend to involve a degree of selectivity that "proves" the author's hypothesis. As with the patients I myself have treated, my thinking has been greatly influenced by the clinical details, but I must withhold some of the evidence.

In what follows, I will first address the question of why students confront the university. Then, aspects of the students' experience during the crisis will be presented. Finally, I will attempt to construct a psychological model for comprehending student protest.

II: "Why the University?"

It soon became clear to everyone involved that behind the manifest issues of the strike—the students' objection to the proposed new gymnasium [1] and to Columbia's involvement with the Institute for Defense Analyses [2]—was a serious attempt to destroy the existing authority and structure of the university. In pure form, the radical program endeavors, by a series of confrontations, to expose the operations, and their effects, of the vested interest groups that compose the university corporate body and mirror the society at large.

Mark Rudd, President of Columbia's Students for a Democratic Society (SDS) chapter during the rebellion, succinctly stated this relationship between the university and the society:

It's impossible to "restructure" the university without creating a free society. You can't have a free university in an unfree society. And to the extent that everything we're against at Columbia is a

---

[1] During the years 1958–61, the university, through due process, gained the right from the state and the city to construct a new gymnasium on 2.1 acres of land in Morningside Park, a sloping area that separates the university, on a hilltop, from the Harlem community, at the bottom. The gymnasium was to have a swimming pool and other facilities for residents of the area. Throughout the 1960's, there was increasing opposition to the construction plan from members of the Harlem community, who claimed that the community should determine for itself how its park land should be used, that park property should not be leased for private use, and that the community should participate in the planning and operation of a facility they would be using.

[2] The Institute for Defense Analyses (IDA) was established in 1955 by the U.S. Department of Defense to sponsor university research and solicit advice regarding weapons and warfare. Columbia was one of the twelve university "sponsors" of IDA. President Grayson Kirk and a trustee of Columbia, William A. M. Burden, were on both the IDA Board of Trustees and its Executive Committee. The Executive Committee was responsible for authorizing classified projects related to the conduct of the war in Vietnam.

product of capitalist forces, we're not going to be able to do away with these things by forming X number of bipartite committees. In fact, that kind of reform, without a reform in consciousness . . . will lead to co-optation—that's what's already begun.[3]

Following the occupation of the buildings, the political lines of conflict became clearer. On one side was a force embodied in the philosophy expressed by Rudd, which was shared by the majority of the white strike leadership and by some of the black students in Hamilton Hall. The two radical student groups, one of which—the blacks—had some links to the community, were pitted against the central administration of the university, personified by its president, Grayson Kirk. President Kirk drew his strength and support from the Board of Trustees, who, in the main, represented powerful conservative financial and real-estate interests. Given the goals of these two camps, violent collision seemed inevitable, at least in retrospect.

Why do students "confront" universities, which, after all, are among the most enlightened institutions in contemporary American life? Understanding this paradoxical phenomenon depends on recognition of certain aspects of the role of the institution in the life of the undergraduate.

The very word "student" implies an identity that has meaning only in symbiotic conjunction with "university." The quality of this interdependence varies with structural features of the institution—for example, whether it is an urban or a rural campus, a predominantly residential or commuter college, a public or private institution, church-affiliated or secular, a large university with many graduate facilities or a small, homogeneous undergraduate college. But whatever the character of a specific institution, this interdependence always exists between student and college.

Hence, when a student leader responded to the question "Why the university?" by saying, "Because that's where I am," he was simply conveying the impact of having virtually every aspect of his life intertwined with his college. Students enter a residential college like Columbia at age seventeen or eighteen. The great majority have previously lived at home with their parents, and the

---

[3] M. Rudd and P. Spike, "We Don't Want to Be Educated for the CIA," *Evergreen Review*, vol. 12, no. 57 (1968), pp. 53–54.

bonds, conscious and unconscious, with their parents are still strong. This is reflected in the general similarity of values and aspirations between parents and their sons. During the succeeding four years, the students not only use the college and its faculty as a "transitional guide" in the intellectual sphere—in the development from childlike acceptance of "fact" to relative intellectual autonomy, with "active" searching for truth—the college also functions as a protective shelter in which the psychological growth appropriate for this period of life is facilitated.

Away from family, the student's infantile drives and conflicts become subject to ego mastery, and new institutions and groups— both peers and faculty—assume the parental regulatory function with regard to codes and standards of behavior. In particular, there is a loosening of ties to the parents, the early objects of love and hate, and, associated with this, the emergence of a more clearly defined sexual identity. By graduation, after a series of normative crises, the individual may achieve the beginnings of a more autonomous young-adult self.

But where does this "autonomous young-adult self" fit in contemporary society? Away from the family of his past and not yet into the family of his future, the graduate stands disengaged. In the university milieu, he is subjected to what has been described as the "subversive" function of the university:[1] to expose, interrelate, and ultimately question the foundations of the society. Related to this is the function of supporting the student, not only in the task of articulating himself, but also in then relating himself to the processes and institutions of the larger society. In other words, while in college, young people establish the principles and the hierarchy of values and interests that will be the core of their individuality; then, trying to maintain these values, they enter into an interaction with their society in the course of which, one hopes, some satisfactory equilibrium can be achieved. For most youth in elite universities like Columbia, the establishment of such an equilibrium increasingly seems to require a change in the present structure of society rather than changing themselves to "fit in."

The role of the university in its students' struggle concurrently

[4] E. Sampson, "Student Activism and the Decade of Protest," *Journal of Social Issues,* vol. 23, no. 3 (1967), p. 2.

to define themselves and their relationship to society is complicated by the fact that the university itself has evolved into a highly pluralistic institution, with multiple and conflicting purposes. In its early form, it was a "community" where scholars might work together in the pursuit of knowledge and where the students, regarded as "apprentices," joined their elders. Knowledge qua knowledge was valued regardless of its applicability to immediate social and scientific problems. Today's university continues this historic role as preserver and presenter of the humanism and aesthetics of the past and of basic conceptual truths in the social and physical sciences. In universities that are relatively free from religious, political, and economic control, an atmosphere of dialogue and dissent has been a notable accompaniment of this tradition. The faculty in this situation are clearly identified with the "teaching" function—that lovely interaction between the generations in which wisdom is transmitted to the new generation, while, in the ever repeating cycle of courses and tutoring, the teacher remains linked with his own origins, identified with the objects of his nurturing and part of the process of growth, which enables him to advance in years with minimal despair and disdain for the young.

In marked contrast, however, is the increasingly important function of the university as a provider of "expert" and "scientific" advice to government for the development and implementation of the "programs" of that society, that government. The university thus becomes a political body, serving also as a major communications center for our increasingly encompassing technocracy and as a training center for the future managers of the major corporations and government agencies that are the power loci of the society. Many members of the faculty who serve these functions of the university find the "teaching" of undergraduate students a burdensome activity that distracts them from their primary endeavors. Their psychological needs are not fulfilled by contact with the students, particularly with dissenters and humanities majors. Their satisfaction comes from recognition of their influence on and interaction with the sources they serve *outside* the university community.

This dichotomy in the university—a situation that largely distinguishes the university from the smaller liberal arts undergraduate college—potentiates discord among the students who are being affected by both poles and pressured to choose sides, thereby to reduce the anxiety generated by the tugging. The coexistence of these varied and established interest groups, each in a sense having veto power, makes the university necessarily a conservative institution. The successful administrator in the university now must be a skillful mediator and diplomat, not a radical innovator.[5]

In contrast, therefore, to the microcosmic relationship between the adolescent and his family, where mutual accommodation is at least possible and, indeed, is constantly occurring to a more or less satisfactory degree, the relationship between an institution and an individual rarely permits such flexibility. An institution at best can adjust to the needs of a significant body of its constituency. The more decentralized the institution, and the smaller and more homogeneous the population it serves, the more successful and less conflictual the interaction. Thus, at small colleges with a distinctive character—for example, a strongly religious or highly "progressive" rural college—a complementarity of interests and goals tends to exist between school and students.

Although all students are affected in some way by the divisive forces within the large university, they are at the same time profoundly influenced by many other aspects of the university structure not directly related to vocational preparation or formal intellectual enrichment. Colleges, particularly residential ones, are protective islands where students can experiment with defining their own limits with respect to a wide range of matters, with attitudes on the part of university administrators and faculty ranging from covert sanction to active encouragement. Most official policies strongly condemn the use of marijuana, for example, but, in practice, administrators tend to look away, unless a student is using the drug so compulsively and conspicuously that he clearly needs therapeutic intervention. Consequently, the campus has become a *de facto* sanctuary for use, so long as outside authorities are not provoked and the administration is not flagrantly embarrassed. The university community also sanctions a wide range

[5] Clark Kerr, former chancellor of the University of California at Berkeley, makes this point in *The Uses of the University* (Cambridge, Mass.: Harvard University Press, 1963).

of nonmainstream modes of dress and grooming that find acceptance elsewhere only within small pockets in cosmopolitan urban
centers, usually pejoratively labeled "hippie" areas. This shelter
extends to the area of sexuality. Parietal dormitory rules are
rapidly disappearing. Greater tolerance is also reflected in such
trends as official recognition of a student Homophile League on
campus, at Columbia and other universities.

Political protest is also permitted and even encouraged, even
when its thrust is against the university itself. Protest on campus
has become a way of life at some schools, in part because college
administrations are generally far less repressive and punitive than
outside authorities. Fanciful and nonutilitarian scholarly thought
receives encouragement. Even nonthought and sleeping through
classes are acceptable transitory states for students.

Beyond the acceptance of these forms of student behavior, the
university actively provides a host of services designed to guide
the student. In the dormitories at Columbia, for example, each
floor has a "counselor," usually a graduate student, whose job it
is to be a sort of "big brother" and personal adviser to the students in his charge. For problems that exceed his level of competence, counseling and psychiatric services are freely available to
the students, where confidentiality is maintained. The college has
a staff of deans who not only advise students about academic and
personal affairs, but also arrange for loans, grants, scholarships,
paying jobs, and so forth. Among the faculty, particularly the
younger members, there are many who are deeply committed to
the over-all welfare of their students.

Friendships are generally confined to fellow students. Small
quasi-communal living arrangements of students are beginning to
emerge off campus. It is of psychodynamic significance that much
of the food the student eats is prepared by invisible chefs in the
college kitchens, or inexpensive restaurants patronized almost exclusively by college students.

In sum, for eight and a half months of each of the four undergraduate years, there are very few realms of the student's life that
are not in some direct relationship, actual or symbolic, to the college. Since it is both a transitional structure from parent to society, serving to facilitate mastery of certain necessary individual

psychological life tasks, and a socially created institution designed to meet the needs of the social order, the college becomes the recipient, not only of realistic responses to its true nature, but of a full spectrum of irrational and unconscious expectations and attitudes, ranging from rageful resentment at unfulfilled infantile and narcissistic wishes to identification with its power, prestige, and good nurturing.

These generic features of the contemporary university and the students' psychosocial relationship to it are applicable to all universities and all students. However, the relationship of the black student to Columbia—or to any "white" university, for that matter—is still more complex. At the time of the rebellion, most of the black students at Columbia, for a host of reasons, were unable to utilize maximally the educative possibilities of an institution that was steeped in the expectations, intellectual and social customs, norms, and prejudices of white, liberal, upper-middle-class America. Black students, like all others, varied in political view, adaptation to the college, and self-concept. These differences are reflected in the fact that half of the undergraduate blacks "occupied" Hamilton Hall and half did not. Yet all have an identity as black students and as such share significant features of their relationship to the university that serve to unite them as a social unit on any campus.

As recently as three or four years before the rebellion, there were no more than a couple of dozen black students at Columbia. The emphasis was on assimilation into the white socio-intellectual patterns of the college. There was pressure to have white buddies, wear tweeds, enjoy Joan Baez and Bob Dylan, join peace marches, dance standard "rock." The message was clear—"You are special students here and will emerge from this white milk bath cleansed, transformed, ready to take your place in a white world, where you will be accepted." However, in the process of their "rebirth" at the college, before 1967, a very high percentage of black students developed academic difficulties and were on academic probation or suspended for a time.

The experience at Columbia was psychologically devastating—filling them with guilt for the contempt and anger that the process generated in them toward their parents and their black heritage, and with frustration and rage because, despite the promise, they were regarded as second class and unacceptable without special definition. Added to the burden of having to wear a "white mask" and "do well" at college was the expectation that, with the leverage of a position in the black bourgeoisie, they would ultimately help their less fortunate brothers. It is not surprising, then, that this unconscious turmoil was expressed in their poor academic performance—the primary symbol of success in academia. To do well was to submit to this process, and they unconsciously rebelled. Very few of these students could openly acknowledge that the curriculum and social life of the college were in major respects irrelevant to them and to their cultural heritage and personal destiny. Yet, black students continue to come to better white universities—a seeming paradox.

There are several tentative generalizations that can be drawn about the selection of a school like Columbia by a young black. To start with, it represents "Ivy League," the best of establishment institutions. Until, perhaps, the formal turning point of the "black consciousness" SNCC position paper of August, 1966,[6] universities like Columbia were regarded as a possible way out of the pain and petty humiliations of being black in America. This view may be suppressed, but it cannot be completely eradicated by the emergence of a new racial self-concept in midadolescence. Rather, the unconscious conflict is only intensified; the student still carries a residual conviction that a Columbia degree will make him "less Negro."

The conflict of selecting a white prestige university is mitigated for some blacks by its location in New York City, with its large urban black community. For example, a student from another large city said:

The reason we don't feel this alienation thing is that there is all of New York, and what you don't get here you can get in the rest of the city. This differs from Dartmouth, which I had considered.

A student from New York City said:

I'm glad I came to Columbia. It's where the action is. I like the school and the city. The city allows me to feel free, not trapped.

6 *The New York Times*, August 5, 1968.

Another student from a large urban center conveyed his conflict in the following description of his living arrangements:

Changes have always been easy. I had no problem adapting. The first week I wandered around the city and met a lot of people. . . . I was on a great floor at [my dormitory]. At first there were lots of straight, crew-cut kids. That didn't last long. It was fun to mix. I wanted to see Harlem. I wanted to live there, but it cost too much.

In his associative trend, after speaking of the pleasures of integrating, he turns to the wish to maintain the bond with his black brothers in the Harlem community. All three of these students, incidentally, were among the occupiers of Hamilton Hall.

It is interesting that the black students who had come to Columbia from integrated schools and communities saw "color shock" as a problem for those who came from black communities and schools. One said, simply:

Ghetto kids are not at ease. They can't stand seeing so many white faces.

A Barnard girl said:

They are most unhappy they came. They feel inferior and want to quit. But they can't turn down a $4,000 scholarship.

The students from black communities and schools themselves had a different perception. Their emphasis was on the college as an educational facility. One such student, who was in Hamilton Hall, said:

I'm not here to meet white people. I'm not here to meet people. I'm here for an education. I'm not worried about integrating myself into the social structure. I don't need it. I make friends with whom I want to make friends with. So I hang around with black students. . . . It's a great institution and I can get a good education.

Another said:

I don't see this anxiety thing. I saw "Ivy League School." To me that was a good education, and that's all I wanted.

A more conservative student, who opposed the sit-in, said:

I don't see Columbia as a racist university. I see Columbia as an institution that can help me, and I'm willing to use that help.

The view that Columbia is a means to a good education can be translated as good preparation for, and entry into, a specific career. It is pertinent that only 8 per cent of the black students in Hamilton Hall were humanities majors as contrasted with 41 per cent of the white radicals. Among all the black students at Columbia, 15 per cent were humanities majors, markedly below the figure for the college as a whole. The implication of this distribution is that blacks tend to regard the college as a career-preparatory institution rather than as a four-year adventure in intellectual and aesthetic exploration that may, among other things, crystallize in work that is fun, is respected, and pays a good salary. The orientation of most black students is in marked contrast to what a white honors student in philosophy told me, in contemplating his future career as a college philosophy teacher:

Wow, imagine—you teach three classes a week in philosophy, which you love to rap about anyway, to a bunch of kids who are interested in what you have to say. You get four months off every summer. You have most of every day to get stoned, listen to records, read, write, or do whatever you want. For that you get paid $8,000 to $10,000 a year, and your parents and their friends respect you as a college professor.

Among blacks, a high degree of social consciousness is almost universally associated with the possibility of economic-vocational success. Black students usually express the theme that, if they are successful in the system, they will then be in a far better position to help their oppressed brothers. This is another reason for selecting a school like Columbia. Apart from the ethos of helpful brotherhood, which is highly developed in oppressed or minority groups, social consciousness reflects a level of guilt at "making it," whereas their parents and most of their peers could not. This theme—illustrated by the poem reprinted below from a black student publication at Dartmouth—is akin to the guilt of the survivor of concentration camps, Hiroshima, or a black ghetto. For some black youth, the guilt engendered by being able to pack a suitcase and leave the ghetto for the Ivy League acts as an unconscious counterforce to successful academic achievement.

SONG TO MY BROTHER AT DARTMOUTH [7]

Chump!

ya' brothers at home, poisoned
   dyin' in the streets, cop shots, whole
   bodies flyin' through air, bustlin'.
barely makin it.
           sniffin' cocaine
      for quick high—
          That's home bro - ther!

Niggers up at Dart-
mouth "being cool."
   acting "ra-
         tion-
            al,"

  playin'
     the
        role—
Nothin's a game, my bro-
        ther!

War,
     and
        Conflict.

Don't git caught in the enemy's camp,
   eatin' his food, thinkin' his thoughts.
     look out, my bro-
       ther,
     Dyin's for real.

                    GREGORY YOUNG

It follows that to see the college as the educational milieu and fellow black students as the social milieu is the least anxiety-producing attitude possible, and it is the most common. An upperclassman in the college said:

[7] From *Blackout,* vol. 1, no. 2 (1968).

When I got here, Negro students were something out of the ordinary. They [the white college community] saw no barrier to Negro social life. The only possible barrier they could see was open prejudice. I knew this was not true. I came from an interracial high school. When I arrived, I knew black and whites don't mix socially. We are a completely different culture. . . . We have a different idea of what's a good time. What we drink, the music we like, and the dancing we do is different.

In practice, there is a tightly knit black student social community, but this community breaks down in the daily business of academic life. With blacks comprising only 4 per cent of the student body in the school year 1967–68, there were rarely more than one or two in a class. They felt and were conspicuous. White students and instructors regarded them as having a unique contribution to make by virtue of their different backgrounds, but this attitude often carried a strong note of condescension. Black students found that instructors were often less than comfortable with them, and the experience of being confused with other black students was not infrequent. In subtle ways, they felt inadequate—usually because they did not have so broad a fund of prior knowledge to draw on, or were less adept at expressing themselves in the manner valued in academia. In 1967–68, there was one black faculty member at Columbia College, and he was not American born. Courses dealing with such social institutions as "Marriage and the Family"—which I taught at the time—were offered by white instructors and, because of the composition of the class, inevitably ended up addressing themselves to white, middle-class marriage and family life, leaving the few black students in the class feeling excluded or self-conscious about their own family backgrounds and values. There have been overt sources of humiliation, such as campus security guards stopping black students and asking to see their ID cards to make sure they were not burglars from Harlem. This list of unpleasant facets of life for black students at Columbia and other Ivy League schools could be expanded indefinitely.

Most administrators have tried to be helpful to individual students, by arranging tutoring, financial or job aid, flexibility in programming, and so forth. And, if they were not actively recruited, black faculty were certainly not deliberately excluded from the college; it was simply that the traditional criteria of degrees and publications for hiring faculty barred most blacks. Beginning in 1965, there was systematic planning to increase the black enrollment. Within the boundaries of liberal conscience, then, changes were being made. But these changes were often in a direction that had little correspondence with the psychological needs of the blacks. Thus, for example, if blacks suggested an all-black floor in a dormitory, the white liberals felt rejected, bewildered, frightened, and angry. And running counter to the changes taking place on campus was the university's engagement in real-estate practices that dislocated people from the surrounding neighborhoods, most of them Negro or Puerto Rican. The critical issue was the gymnasium, which had moved after several years to the stage of excavation, against the wishes of a sizable segment of the black population and the protests of most black political and community leaders.

Also germane is the conflict the black student experiences between opposing methods of achieving personal advancement— through academic success or political agitation. The student is well aware that the quantum jump in black enrollment at the better white colleges in recent years is the result of agitation by others. He enters with an awareness of unpaid debts to militant fellow blacks who opened the doors for him. He is also aware that, in today's climate, unlike most white students, he need not do particularly well academically to gain admission to a top-flight graduate school. Thus, young blacks find themselves in an intellectual-achievement milieu, but with a new tradition that upward social mobility can be achieved not by good grades, or not only by good grades, but by their blackness, especially as implemented by actual or threatened militant confrontations with the establishment. The effort to resist the temptation to rely on their blackness led many black students to remain outside of Hamilton Hall during the occupation. These students emerged from the crisis stressing a clearer sense of their individuality. In contrast, many in the group that occupied Hamilton Hall later emphasized their heightened personal sense of "black identity."

A black student's commitment to militancy, apart from its broader social and political justification, carries a potential both for resolving conflicts created by the new recruitment policies and for obscuring the boundaries between those problems in his life that are the direct and indirect results of white racism and those that are uniquely his. Yet the historic reality is that, without the militancy, the social order would probably continue to produce psychological damage in every black exposed to it.[8]

The university, then, becomes the object of protest by students not simply because of inequities, questionable policies, and administrative unresponsiveness. These issues are certainly real and far reaching in their effects, but they assume great proportions and intensity because, at the unconscious level, the students are in a profound and enormously complex relationship to this transitional guiding structure at an immensely significant period in their psychological development. But it must also be asserted that the university is not an empty stage on which students of certain character structure, values, and needs act out their psychologically ordained drama of confrontation. Within the broader context of the psychological meaning of university life in 1968, we must look at certain issues that were specific to Columbia University and what these issues meant to the undergraduates who were radicalized in the week following April 23, 1968.

Fewer than 10 per cent of the protesting students, black or white, could have been considered militant or radical before April 23. The political transformation of these students—virtually overnight radicalization for many—closely followed Keniston's

[8] On the relationship of American social pathology and the personality structure of blacks, see H. Butts, "White Racism: Its Origins, Institutions, and the Implications for Professional Practice in Mental Health," *International Journal of Psychiatry*, vol. 8, no. 6 (Dec., 1969); E. Cleaver, *Soul On Ice* (New York: Basic Books, 1968); R. Coles, *Children of Crisis* (Boston: Atlantic, Little, Brown, 1967); P. Cobbs and W. Grier, *Black Rage* (New York: Basic Books, 1968); H. Hendin, *Black Suicide* (New York: Basic Books, 1969); A. Kardiner and L. Ovesey, *The Mark of Oppression: Explorations in the Personality of the American Negro* (New York: World, 1951); J. Kozol, *Death at an Early Age: The Destruction of the Hearts and Minds of Negro Children in the Boston Public Schools* (Boston: Houghton Mifflin, 1967); and C. Pinderhughes, "Understanding Black Power: Processes and Proposals," *American Journal of Psychiatry*, vol. 125, no. 11 (May, 1969).

description of the "process of radicalization" in his brilliant study of young radicals:

> [The] process of radicalization . . . seems characteristically to consist of two related changes. The first is a change in the perceptions of social reality, mediated through personal confrontation with social inequity, and leading through disillusion with existing institutions for social reform to the beginnings of a radical reinterpretation of socio-political reality. Concurrent with this articulation of a radical outlook, a process of personal activation and engagement occurs. The individual's pre-existing feelings of personal responsibility are extended to the oppressed and deprived. . . . The end product of this process is most commonly a growing awareness of the extent of one's radical commitment; a realization . . . that one has changed; the common experience of "finding oneself" acting, reacting, thinking, and feeling in ways that at an earlier stage of life would have been inconceivable.[9]

These two criteria, reinterpretation of social-political reality and personal activation, are clearly applicable to the Columbia militants and radicals. Who these students were and why they occupied university buildings cannot be answered without exploring some of the implications for them of university policies and administrative actions in the few years preceding the crisis. This exploration is necessary if we accept the postulate that all behavior includes inflexible elements of unconsciously driven behavior interacting with flexible elements of conscious behavior. In a well-integrated person, the latter are ascendant in motivating manifest behavior. Such integration involves the perception and understanding of "reality"—a reality that goes beyond the concrete, immediate, everyday experiences in one's life to encompass the institutions of a society and their effects on the perceiver and his fellows. Obviously, the specific nature of the institution will affect the attitude of the well-integrated members of the community affected. That is, constructive institutions evoke positive support, and destructive institutions evoke negative responses.

Would the radical and militant students at Columbia have rebelled against any college they happened to attend? I think not.

---

[9] K. Keniston, *The Young Radicals: Notes on Committed Youth* (New York: Harcourt, Brace & World, 1968), p. 144.

Given the climate in the spring of 1968—the weariness of the country after three and a half years of undeclared war and the resulting internal dissension, urban deterioration, widespread loss of faith in democratic process, racial tensions and the murder of Dr. Martin Luther King, and, for students, the fearful expectation of being drafted—some certainly would have lashed out at their college irrespective of local conditions. But the substantial rebellion at Columbia reflected a moral judgment based on specific activities and policies of the university with regard to the war and ethnic minorities as well as features of student life at Columbia.

Behind the two publicized issues of the gymnasium and Columbia's affiliation with IDA was a history of frustrating interaction between politically concerned students and the administration. Further, although these social-political issues had some practical impact, they were far more important as symbols of the moral attitude of the university.

The students' concern with the moral position of the university perplexes many adults in the mainstream of America, for the ethic of America in this century has been one of pragmatism and practicality. The university's actual involvement with IDA, insignificant by any practical measure, symbolized Columbia's active acquiescence to hated government policies. That the President of the university served on the IDA Board of Trustees and its Executive Committee was highly significant, as was the duplicity of official university spokesmen. In March, 1967, for example, at a faculty smoker, the Dean of Graduate Faculties was asked about Columbia's connection with IDA, and he responded that no connection existed. When, within the following week, the connection was revealed, the Dean was quoted as having stated, "These things are not in the purview of faculty and students. . . . This is a matter for the Trustees of the University to decide." In the view of the students, President Kirk's membership on the board of an institute that included among its functions secret research on war techniques for Vietnam was tantamount to "legitimizing" the government war policy. Further, in the eyes of the students, the attitude of the Dean of Graduate Faculties all too closely mirrored the Johnson Administration's contempt for dissenters.

Critics of the radical disruption have pointed out that Kirk finally did denounce the war in a speech at another university in early April, 1968, and that there were continuous modifications in the policy of giving university support to controversial research. A committee had been set up to make policy recommendations regarding such research. But the strong feeling prevailed that these were hedges, designed to decompress temporarily the vigor of student opposition but in no way to alter the basic moral position of the university. In sum, the IDA issue symbolized not only substantive opposition to the war, but also opposition to the university's hypocrisy and lack of moral integrity.

The issue of the gymnasium was also symbolic. The university, in response to real needs, and in pursuance of a policy that had been legally negotiated with the city and state, proposed to use park land for the building. But the legislative authorization dated from 1958–61, an era of consciousness about community and racial problems different from the climate of 1968. The university proposed to meet the objection that a private institution should not take land in a community recreational area to use for its own purpose by including a $1.4 million pool for use by the community, with a separate entrance.[10] Nevertheless, objections from the community mounted. By 1968, virtually every Harlem leader had protested the proposed form of the gymnasium. But the university continued to act on its unilaterally established policy, without consulting representatives of the community. Thus, the gym became a symbol of institutional racism.

Would the gym have been built if the community had been given a genuine voice in its planning and operation? It seems quite likely that a plant serving the recreational needs of both Columbia and the community could have been brought to fruition. With such collaboration, the gym would have ceased to be an exploitative symbol. Such speculation, however, is academic, because genuine representation was totally out of keeping with the

[10] The two entrances—one for the community at the bottom of the building, and one at the top for university personnel—were given much publicity because of the symbolic implications of dominance. It must be pointed out, however, that these entrances were determined by the fact that the gym was to be built on a slope. The university is at the top of the slope and the community at the bottom.

university's policy and practices in relations with its neighbors at that time. These relations were the source of great resentment on the part of the community and the object of sharp criticism from the Cox Commission.[11]

Faced with the problem of limited space on campus and the ever increasing pressure to expand, the university pursued the traditional American urban-university policy of buying up lots and dwellings in the surrounding area. In the 1960's, Columbia purchased 150 such dwellings, most of them housing Puerto Ricans and blacks. Many were single-room-occupancy buildings, containing a variety of urban social misfits—drug addicts, alcoholics, and ambulatory chronic schizophrenics. In all, some 7,500 people were displaced.[12] At times, when the legal techniques of dispossessing seemed too slow, tenants were coerced into moving by cutting off such services as heat and hot water. Despite an announcement in the early 1960's that the university would help to relocate displaced tenants, such services were only token and often merely directed the tenants to other ghetto areas. The problem is complicated because the housing structure of New York City allowed for no alternative in dealing with such large numbers, unless the university were to build dwellings.

Thus, a sizable segment of Columbia's neighbors, the group least able to fend for itself, was abruptly dislocated. Many did not speak English. Others were too crippled sociopsychologically to do anything but place themselves in the care of the city's Department of Welfare and other community agencies. The result was a pervasive feeling on the part of the community that Columbia was a devouring force that could uproot their lives irrespective of their needs and wishes and against which they were helpless. The gym was a symbol of this perception of the university.

The intense resentment of Columbia by the black community was known to a large segment of the liberal-radical white stu-

---

[11] Other critical evaluations of Columbia's community relations may be found in M. Rauch et al., *Columbia and the Community: Past Policy and New Directions,* Report of the Columbia College Citizenship Council Committee for Research, 1968; and J. Ridgeway, "Columbia's Real Estate Venture," *The New Republic,* May 18, 1968.

[12] About 85 per cent of these were black or Puerto Rican. The entire population of the sixty-square-block area known as Morningside Heights is approximately 60,000. (Data from Ridgeway, *op. cit.*)

dents. Several hundred Columbia and Barnard students had participated in the officially sanctioned Citizenship Council, an organization whose primary activity was to send students into Harlem to tutor black children. As these students encountered increasing resentment and obstruction from black community groups, who were responsible for administering the services, they became enlightened to community attitudes toward Columbia. For the blacks at Columbia, the university's community-relations policy was obviously a much more salient source of pain and conflict.

The students' knowledge of Columbia's real estate operations was, no doubt, limited, but what they did know they regarded as a major example of immoral behavior by the university. It was the students' view that the university not only lacked the right arbitrarily to alter, much less disrupt, the lives of powerless people, but that it had an obligation to use its vast intellectual resources to help the community solve some of its critical problems. This was not to suggest that the university should go into the welfare business but that the urban crises that are threatening to tear America asunder offer a most relevant opportunity for action-learning, a process that would inevitably render useful service to the community.[13]

A third substantive issue of the rebellion can be found in the demands that both the ban on indoor demonstrations and the probation of the IDA six be rescinded.

As at Berkeley in 1964 and Nanterre in 1968, the students' conviction that their right to freedom of speech was being violated was a major precipitant of the Columbia crisis. The origins of this issue go back to a small but disorderly demonstration in May, 1965, at the Navy Reserve Officers Training Corps (NROTC) award ceremonies. Responding to this conflict, Kirk appointed a tripartite committee (administration, faculty, and students) to conduct a "re-examination of existing University policies governing student rights and responsibilities." Two years later, in August, 1967, he received majority and minority reports from this Committee on Student Life. *Both* reports recommended that indoor demonstrations be permitted, but that detailed regula-

---

[13] A program of community-based action-learning is at the core of black and third-world college proposals at San Francisco State, Berkeley, and other schools.

tions be set forth to ensure order and safety. A month later, however, Kirk issued this dictum: "Picketing or indoor demonstrations may not be conducted within any University building." Further, Kirk did not release either report to the university community until seven months later, a week before the occupation of the buildings, and then only because Student Council members had threatened to do so themselves if Kirk continued to ignore their requests.[14]

On March 27, 1968, a month before the occupation, a demonstration organized by the SDS took place inside Low Library, the presidential office building. During the demonstration, attempts were made to hand the administration a petition signed by over 1,500 students and faculty, demanding that the university sever its ties with IDA. The university administration refused to accept the petition but offered to meet three representatives. SDS refused to send delegates in lieu of demonstrating, thereby challenging the legitimacy of the ban. The undergraduate SDS leaders were thereupon summoned to the Dean's office to discuss their roles. The students refused to appear and demanded a public hearing. They were refused and placed on disciplinary probation.

The refusal to grant public hearings tapped the whole issue of disciplinary judicial procedures at the college. The Cox Commission comments:

The request and refusal [for public hearing] focused attention on Columbia's outmoded disciplinary procedure, which provided for no student participation and vested ultimate disciplinary power solely in the President. In a period in which public attention has been focused upon procedural safeguards in criminal proceedings, students have become rightly concerned about procedural safeguards in academic discipline. Their prerequisites as students, and during the current era of selective military service, their status as students, may even attain life-or-death importance.[15]

Encapsulated in the IDA demonstration, then, was the theme

[14] The Cox Commission has commented: "We have been struck, not only by the frequency with which reports of faculty as well as student committees are ignored or overridden but also by the absence of any regular procedure for distribution." Cox Commission, *Crisis at Columbia: Report of the Fact-Finding Commission Appointed to Investigate the Disturbances at Columbia University in April and May, 1968* (New York: Random House, 1968), p. 51.

[15] *Ibid.*, p. 96.

of autocratic exercise of authority by the President of Columbia, with disregard for the participation of faculty and students when their will went counter to his.[16] In this case, it extended from the setting of regulations governing student behavior to the dispensing of punishment if rules were violated. In addition, the demonstration involved what the students regarded as a threat to their right of free expression. The provocations of SDS easily drew so autocratic an administration into a series of responses that exposed the nature of the system.

This autocracy was symbolized in the so-called strawberry statement [17] by the Vice-Dean of the Graduate Faculties. The front-page report of an interview in the college newspaper read:

Herbert A. Deane, Vice-Dean of Graduate Faculties, Friday defended in principle Columbia's membership in the Institute for Defense Analysis, which has recently come under fire from several students and professors.

He also asserted that a consensus of student or faculty opinion should not in itself have an influence on the formation of administrative policy.

"A University is definitely not a democratic institution," Professor Deane declared. "When decisions begin to be made democratically around here, I will not be here any longer."

Commenting on the importance of student opinion to the administration, Professor Deane said, "Whether students vote 'yes' or 'no' on an issue is like telling me they like strawberries." . . .

The administration contended that the model of a political democracy cannot and should not be applied to Columbia.[18]

[16] Dramatic evidence of student perception of the university as nondemocratic was an extraordinary act by the Columbia College Student Council in 1961. The council voted to dissolve itself because it felt powerless to effect significant changes and therefore meaningless. The council decision was sustained in a Columbia College student referendum. Thereafter, Columbia College was without student government.

[17] This was chosen by a Columbia student, James Simon Kunen, as the title for his autobiographical account of the Columbia rebellion, *The Strawberry Statement: Notes of a College Revolutionary* (New York: Random House, 1969).

[18] *Columbia Daily Spectator,* April 24, 1968. The same article went on to say: "Another source high in graduate faculties administration, who requested that his name not be used, also asserted Friday that students should not play too powerful a role in such university decision-making." The request for anonymity in a university community on such an issue could only be viewed as provocative and counter to the tradition of open dialogue.

Deane stated that what he said had been "elliptically" reported by the *Spectator*. However, the "strawberry statement" nakedly expressed the attitude and philosophy of the university administration, as perceived and experienced by the student body.[19]

Because the issues in the student-administration struggle were so intimately related to political concerns beyond the campus, the activist view of Columbia could not be entirely separated from what had happened to and in America since 1964. Lyndon Johnson, the moral as well as political leader of the nation, was a man whom bright Northeastern students could find little to identify with or respect, the man they held primarily responsible for our role in the war in Vietnam. Anxiety-filled awareness of the consequences of white racism had been forced on us by the black power movement; the integrated civil rights movement as a hopeful arena of idealistic commitment for young people had died; the horror of jail or emigration were the alternatives to serving in a war the students regarded as barbarous; the government was prosecuting Dr. Benjamin Spock and Reverend William Sloane Coffin; Dr. King had been murdered (with the alleged assassin then still at large); and we helplessly watched Congress choose guns over butter at every turn. And there was more.

The theme of personal impotence in the university bureaucratic structure was widespread among the strikers; students tended to equate their inability to influence policy at Columbia with their powerlessness in the larger sociopolitical context. Discussing the "frustration of seeing the system fail to produce remedies," one junior said:

My disillusionment started during freshman orientation. All the student organizations seemed remote to me—there did not seem to be any life or verve in them, since the administration had the final word.

[19] For interpretations of events leading to the crisis that challenge the view presented here, see Z. Brzezinski, "Revolution and Counterrevolution (But Not Necessarily About Columbia)," *The New Republic*, June 1, 1968; D. Bell, "Columbia and the New Left," *The Public Interest*, vol. 13 (Fall, 1969), pp. 61–101; L. Feuer, *The Conflict of Generations: The Character and Significance of Student Movements* (New York: Basic Books, 1969), pp. 482–91; and G. Keller, "Six Weeks That Shook Morningside," *Columbia College Today*, vol. 15, no. 3 (1968), pp. 2–97.

Later, when this young man became an officer in a student club, he wrote a long proposal for a broader organization that would bring together people from allied fields, from both the university and the community. The idea had some strong faculty encouragement, but the proposal was ill fated:

Even if my ideas were fuzzy or poorly conceived, one would think that, since my intentions were at least optimistic—to provide a focus for popular interests—I could find one administrator who would talk to me about it. Maybe I went about it all wrong, but my attempt at working within the system was a total fiasco—the only concrete advice I was given was how to dress when meeting [the Director of Student Activities].

It is hardly surprising to learn that this young man was one of those who entered a building and was radicalized during his five days there. He said:

The constant meetings in the building were good. They clarified my thinking. I was doing a criminal act for ideas, not for profit. I was going to take a stand and sacrifice something. That was really good. When Hitler took over, people stood around. We're not going to.

Every one of the students I interviewed who were arrested or spent time in the buildings expressed some anger, agony, sadness, or fear about what had become of America. One student expressed it as follows:

Maybe I am an alarmist, but I fear not only the threat of nuclear war, but also the alienation and dehumanization of man. The Columbia crisis I see as the first installment of a growing revolt against the threatened loss of individuality, the increasing control by slogans, the increasing passivity of the individual who believes himself to be active when he is only "busy," and against the lack of joy and interest in life beyond those of material incentive.

In this connection, it is significant that the President of the university was a man whom virtually no undergraduate met or talked with during his career at Columbia. Kirk's offices were in a different building from the one housing the other officials of the college. The problem was not simply Kirk's unavailability to students but also his personality, style, and point of view, which would have made meetings with students awkward. Ironically, a senior administrator told me:

We discouraged him from going into the dorms to meet students. It would do more damage than good. The kids would then see what he really was like.

The significance of Kirk's remoteness was both real and immediate in that it presented a barrier to communication and hence to the possibility for working out changes, and also symbolic insofar as he unconsciously represented for the students a paternal surrogate. (I shall address this psychodynamic theme at more length in Chapter IX.) Thus a leader in campus activities, who was an idealistic liberal prior to the crisis but became radicalized, said:

Legitimate avenues of redress were attempted. Anti-IDA petitions were presented. Dr. Kirk's answer was, "I cannot respond. The petitions have no return address." . . . The more legitimate channels of recourse, of amendment, were attempted, but our government [Columbia] was unresponsive.

The importance of Kirk's "invisibility" is illustrated in the reactions of three students who occupied his office suite. A sophomore wrote that, upon taking over Kirk's office:

We explore. The temptation to loot is tremendous, middle-class morality notwithstanding, but there is no looting. . . . I restrict myself to a few Grayson Kirk introduction cards.[20]

The selection of Kirk's introduction cards suggests the hunger to "meet" the man.
    Another student said:

Kirk was always present. It was cool. You really felt you got to know the man.

Another student felt that, in living in the President's suite for a week and getting to "know him," they had learned an important political lesson:

All clichés about authority resting in the father dissolve in the corporate system. We found the father to be invisible. For the first time people learned about Kirk—the type of invisible man who runs a system through henchmen. . . . Nobody wanted . . . to break down his life. We just didn't want him to break ours. Kirk is invisible.

[20] S. James [pseudonym of J. S. Kunen], "The Diary of a Revolutionist," *New York*, May 27, 1968.

For some of the students, the remote university President replicated their experience with absent fathers who commuted from suburbia and were, in their eyes, consumed by the need to get ahead in the "system," acquire possessions, and provide "comfortably" for themselves and their families at the cost of being emotionally unavailable to their children. A strong sympathizer of the sit-in conveyed this feeling:

The crisis put a few things in my head. . . . I realized what I didn't want to be—caught up in a hassle about money the rest of my life, of doing what is socially acceptable. . . . My father has had a shitty life, caught up in what I don't want to get caught in. He's a slave.

Would the course of political behavior have been altered if Kirk, instead of moving around campus during the strike through an underground tunnel system, had climbed into the window of his office to talk about their common problems? Although the more ideologically sophisticated students would have seen this behavior as an insidious co-optation, it would have filled a need of many students, interfering with their ripeness for radical commitment. Students' willingness to be "neat and clean for Gene" in the 1968 battle for the Democratic Presidential nomination had represented not simply a political alternative but their support for a man who had allegedly been persuaded to his commitment against the war by his college-aged daughters—that is, a man who talked with and listened to their generation. This may be a rather sentimental basis for political commitment, but such considerations are strong for many young people. Sophomore James Simon Kunen revealed this conflict when, after an interview with the Vice-Dean of Graduate Faculties, he wrote:

God, what am I going to do? I *liked* Dean Deane.[21]

The gulf between President Kirk and the student body was central to the evaluation of the situation by student after student. This feeling is summed up by a student who took no stand in the confrontation:

Perhaps there really is a necessity for revolution in the sense that Kirk and his administration must be overthrown before changes can be made. President Kirk seems to be living in another world. . . .

[21] *The Strawberry Statement, op. cit.,* p. 116.

If he were really in touch with the student body . . . then perhaps all that has happened would never have come about.

The central issues of the strike, as we have seen, were socio-political; yet aspects of student life at Columbia, long a source of grievance, also contributed.[22]

All undergraduates are required to live in dormitories during their freshman year, after which they choose their place of residence. The result is that half of the undergraduates live in the dormitories and the other half in apartments around campus, most of them old, dark, and in ill-kept buildings that frequently house mixed ethnic populations.[23] The nature of these apartments is far more distressing to parents than to the students themselves. Paradoxically, for many upper-middle-class white students, in the process of re-evaluating their accustomed affluent life, there is something quite important about living in close proximity to, and in the manner of, people they have been sheltered from all their lives. To say that these students are driven into private housing by the shortcomings of the dormitories is an oversimplification. Many students elect such housing because of the attraction of being free of supervision.

The situation for the dormitory population is quite different. The dormitories provide a somewhat structured center of living for all freshmen during the critical transitional year of leaving their parents' home. Some freshmen might fare better outside the dorms, but, on balance, it is a desirable arrangement for that year. A significant minority then elect to remain in dormitories for the remainder of their undergraduate careers, for a host of reasons involving convenience, the continuously available camaraderie, greater structure, and a variety of psychological bonds to the

[22] What follows may appear to be a justification of the students' action rather than an "objective" appraisal of Columbia University's problems, needs, alternatives for meeting these needs, and "actual" behavior. It is, in a sense, one "reality," the students' "reality." It is a different "reality" from Kirk's or Vice-President David Truman's, and surely they would tell the story differently. Similarly, the "reality" differed for black and white students.

[23] Columbia is bordered on one side by a park separating it from a black ghetto. On the other three sides, the buildings house students, faculty, and lower-class non-Columbia people, including many Puerto Ricans and blacks.

college. The quality of the dormitory for these students is symbolic of the kind of care the college is taking of them. The Cox Commission report [24] emphasizes conditions in the dormitories as a major underlying cause of the rebellion, quoting the testimony of Dr. Rita Frankiel, who was at the College Counseling Service until 1966. During her tenure, Dr. Frankiel had been asked, as a result of a disturbing rash of student vandalism in the dorms, to examine dormitory conditions and make recommendations for improvements. (The vandalism, incidentally, diminished on those few floors where modifications were made.) Her impressions were recorded by the Commission:

The actual residence facilities for the men were appallingly restricted. Two men would be housed in a room barely adequate for one. . . . Naked light bulbs in corridors, scarred and battered furniture, walls, and floor give the older dormitories the general atmosphere of a rundown rooming house. . . . Frequently students reported a sense that they were being exploited for the financial profit of the University. . . . On individual residence floors there were no social or recreational facilities that would permit a few boys to congregate. . . .
Certainly loneliness, isolation, and social awkwardness are not ordinarily strangers to people of college age. However, it was my impression that the Columbia experience fostered rather than ameliorated such experience.[25]

Most of the undergraduates emerged from their year or more of dormitory living with a sense of embitterment, conscious and unconscious, a feeling of not having been cared for by the institution in a way that they might reasonably expect with regard to elementary comforts of living. This fact assumes heightened significance in the face of talk of millions of dollars for this or that other project. The new building currently in construction for the School of International Relations, for example, has occasioned student protest since it was first proposed, perhaps not only because of the role of the school in the political structure of the society, but also because of the question of priorities in expenditures, in light of the dorms' squalor.

[24] Cox Commission, *op. cit.*
[25] *Ibid.,* pp. 31, 32.

For the blacks, these problems, like the others we have mentioned, were accentuated. Being distributed throughout the dormitory system, arbitrarily separated from those peers who would most naturally be their close friends, deepened their sense of isolation and alienation. Hence, black students were torn between a feeling of social discomfort in the dorm and attraction to the predominately black social group meeting outside. The lack of any black dorm counselors increased the estrangement of black students.

The physical characteristics of dorm life carried over to the classroom. Columbia College's primary classroom building, Hamilton Hall, is a rather dilapidated affair. Inadequate classroom conditions interacted with the highly frustrating relationship the students had with their teachers. Under the heading "Faculty Detachment," the Cox Commission report deals with this subject at length. I will mention only a few salient points.

First, there was no faculty senate or other vehicles for faculty voice in central university policy. Even more disheartening to the students was the manifest disinterest of most faculty members in affecting policy. For the students who protested against the university's position on IDA and the gym, the faculty was like the proverbial "good German" of the Nazi era, who stood by. Many faculty spoke out against the war, and more than 240 signed a Pledge of Support of Draft Resisters, but all but a few were silent with regard to the issue of the military use of Columbia's research facilities.[26]

The faculty's lack of interest in university policy was coupled with apparent lack of concern for the students themselves. The Cox Commission report puts it succinctly:

The faculty's lack of concern for the noncurricular interests and needs of students was all too evident to students themselves. We are not unmindful of the pressures of modern scholarship upon the individual professor, especially when joined with government or private consulting. Yet the scale of priorities at Columbia all too regularly put

[26] One of the targets of the radicals in the fall of 1968 was a psychology professor who had government support for perceptual research that could conceivably be applied to enhance the accuracy of Air Force planes firing at targets. Analogies were drawn between his work and that of the German university scientists during the Third Reich. Under continuous pressure of this kind, the professor canceled this line of research.

the students' problems at the bottom. . . . We are persuaded that the faculty's remoteness from the worries and grievances of students and its lack of vigilance vis-à-vis the Administration were significant factors in the development of an atmosphere in which student unrest could reach the point of combustion.[27]

To this, one could add the general student complaint that senior faculty were unavailable for any kind of contact, including discussion of their own courses or lectures.

For the blacks, again, this problem was more acute, and the fact that there was only one black on the faculty hardly provided a sense of generational continuity between faculty and black students. The faculty's inability to "relate" to them was bitterly commented on by a number of militant blacks. For all students, the emotional unavailability of these idealized parentified figures created a resentment that would not have existed if they were neither so near nor so potentially admirable.

Thus, Columbia University became the object of massive student protest in part because of certain aspects of student life and administrative governance that directly affected all of the students, coupled with issues of university policy and practice that made it appear a contributor to national policies of war and domestic oppression. But university life in general and the climate at Columbia in particular were hardly sufficient stimuli for rebellion. We shall now examine the spectrum of student responses and will then offer a conceptual formulation of student protesters, in an attempt to explain why some students but not others are radicalized, and why, within the generic class of "radical" and "militant," individuals vary in their political behavior.

[27] Cox Commission, *op. cit.,* p. 35.

III: The Nonactivists

The abrupt disorganization of the campus community created the potential for a profound experience of parallel internal disorganization. Disregarding for the moment each individual student's ego strength and unique personality organization, this potential was greatest in students who, prior to the rebellion, had not been committed to any of the organized political blocs but who had identified with, accepted, and drawn sustenance from the structure of the institution.

The relationship between external stability (or instability) and the individual's psychological state was clearly illustrated in the responses of several students in the study. For example, a politically conservative white junior reflected on his dependence on the structure of the college:

I at first saw these events as essentially external to me and involving me only as I was actively participating in or affected by them. I have found, however, that this disintegration of society around me affected me in ways far deeper and more fundamental than I had ever imagined. I have discovered, to my confusion and dismay, that my basic orientation and ways of perceiving things are closely tied to institutions and groups in which I live, and that sudden changes and disruptions could not occur around me without very basically disorienting me in the process. . . .

The . . . loss of purpose and direction which has occurred here can only be described as mass ennui. . . . I had never before seen the basic importance of institutions and strong groups to human behavior and psychic balance.

This young man, whose father died early in his life, had had a very difficult first two years at college. He had initially affiliated with various off-campus artistic groups, while suffering periods of transient depression, largely surrounding his conflicted sexual identity. By his junior year, considerable resolution of the anguish followed his identification with and reliance on the structured routine of classes, assignments, and traditional college life.

A similar response was expressed by a white senior reared in a blue-collar community. He had managed, in his years at college, to liberate himself from what he considered the repressive and authoritarian ethic that had prevailed in his home community. Now he observed:

I had come to rely upon the educational community as my most immediate source of identity. The ultimate destruction and restructuring of this community, therefore, also signaled an inevitable destruction and restructuring of the self, if restructuring was at all possible.

He had regarded himself as a liberal but experienced great conflict during the occupation in that he agreed with the strikers' attitudes toward the issues of the strike but not with their tactics. Feeling the need to act, he joined the Majority Coalition blockade for a while but found that he could not fully accept the MC position either. In the early stage of the crisis he wrote:

Neither the administration nor the demonstrators would yield. Each group called upon tactics that would breed ultimate destruction; each . . . failed, but each continued to wage indiscriminate war, letting the consequences fall on me. Education and language no longer held any meaning. "Liberation" meant "occupation." Moral right was converted to complete license. My only recourse was to rear back, dazzled and uncomprehending. I felt a need to reassess myself but could find no method; order, self-respect, and unity had been destroyed; the community lay in shambles—factioned. I was sure of one thing: Situations were not reasonable—none of us would ever be the same.

A freshman from a protective, small-town background described the need to do something in an attempt to resolve the turmoil and fear that the disruption engendered in him. He too joined the Majority Coalition blockade.

I had to choose one side. I did: I was part of a mob. I was without identity, yelling and clapping for our speakers.

He went on:

Every home in my town has a flag riding a holiday's breeze: It goes well with apple pie. Am I happy I left that isclated niche? For the sake of my improvement—yes; for the destruction, bloodshed, and bitterness I've seen and felt—no. If life is so full of rude awakening, it might have been better to sleep uninterrupted.

A rather shy and constricted mathematics major, who played no active role during the week of occupation but strongly opposed the tactics of the radicals, dramatically concluded:

What I have witnessed on this campus is a nightmare, and, like all bad dreams, it will leave a permanent scar on my mind. I will never forget what has happened to me. . . . I only hope that my scar will not become malignant and do me severe damage. In June, I will graduate from Columbia, and then and only then will I say "Good-bye, Columbia!" and mean it.

These are graphic descriptions of psychological disequilibrium. While they represent the experience of a large number of students, such reactions were by no means universal. Whether a particular social or political situation is psychologically stressful depends not only on the interaction of the manifest characteristics of the situation (that is, the external stimuli) and the general psychological strength and adaptive capacities of the individual, but also on the personal values—in this case, sociopolitical values—that are being challenged. Thus, the response of disequilibrium occurred in students who did not have the necessary defense mechanisms or the possibilities for effective action to be able to integrate the confrontation as a positive event in their lives. It is significant that almost all the students who described this kind of upset to me were politically to the right of center, apparently because of the over-all political definition of the situation—that is, forces on the "left" were successfully disrupting the harmony of the established, more conservative authority. These more conservative students were witnessing the disruption of a system that not only was ideologically congenial to them but also was a source of security because of its familiarity and their confidence in the protective wisdom of the university leadership. For them, what was happening was "bad" and threatening, and, therefore, they experienced unpleasant feelings.

The campus situation had high potential for creating anxiety in every member of the Columbia community. In general, being an active participant, as a member of one of the adversary or mediating groups, was among the most effective modes of managing this anxiety. Although the student groups that received the most publicity were the radicals occupying buildings and the Majority Coalition members blockading buildings, there were organized "activities" appropriate to just about every point on the political spectrum.

Yet there were also hundreds of students who can only be described as passive wanderers, not only unable to take a political stand but also unable to do school work or anything else constructive during that period. They wandered around campus day and night, watching, talking among themselves, and listening to the campus radio station. Their attitude was suggestive of the apprehensive passivity characteristic of some young children during heated confrontations between other members of the family. All of these students were white. As we shall see, the nature of the social structure among the black students made this passive orientation far less likely for them.

How did these nonactive, politically uncommitted students master the anxiety, anger, and fear engendered by the crisis? Since they did not resort to personal activity, which, among other results, would have allied them with fellow students, they had to rely on intrapsychic operations to retain their equilibrium. Among these students, three mechanisms of defense were widely employed: withdrawal, isolation, and denial.

The following description by a junior clearly demonstrates the dynamics of withdrawal:

I am the man in the middle, without representation. The only way to stop the strike now would be to resort to violence as they had [done], and this is, very simply, not the way I choose to live. . . . My overwhelming urge now is not to smash Mark Rudd in the face but simply to get away from campus as quickly as possible.

This statement conveys the central conflict of many conservative students—their frustration and powerlessness to do anything about what they perceived as an encroachment on their rights ("in the middle without representation"). These feelings lead to the impulse toward aggressive violence. The student attempts to suppress this unacceptable impulse with a general ethic ("not the way I choose to live"), but he has trouble containing the violent fantasy ("to smash Mark Rudd in the face"). Unable to sublimate

his aggression effectively, he resorts to the only route left open—
"to get away . . . as quickly as possible."

Many students with similar conflicts did go home. One student,
with an unusually strong defense against the emergence of aggression, who could rarely speak out his clear opinion in a controversial discussion, responded in the following manner:

I simply did not wish to get involved. I have my own business to
attend to and prefer to conscientiously do my own work while the
campus radicals are busy stirring up trouble and dissension. . . .
Friday [the third day of the sit-in], I left for home. I wanted no
part of violence on campus.

I am aware that I have implied that for a student to withdraw
and thereby remove himself from the scene was a less healthy
response than to take a position consistent with his sociopolitical
values, wherever they fell on the political spectrum. This, most
certainly, is a debatable point. But I would argue that, if one's
own community—in this case, Columbia—is in open conflict, a
characteristic of satisfactory ego development would be social
responsibility—the capacity to concern oneself effectively with
more than just managing one's own anxiety and fear.

The Columbia situation allowed for many more responses than
occupying a building or blockading those who did. There were
gradations of noninvolvement short of going home. Some students
became "observers," placing themselves outside the events by the
mechanism of isolation. By this psychological technique, events
and ideas that are threatening to the individual's security are
realistically comprehended; however, the intellectual understanding has become separated from any emotional response, and the
individual lacks appropriate intensity of feeling. For example:

I felt a certain aloofness. I was walking around the grounds, not so
I could feel more intimately concerned with my friends who had
taken positive action, but rather so I could tell my children and
grandchildren that I had been at Columbia during the days that
shook the city.

This student tries to undercut his alienation and inability to react
by just thinking about the high drama of the situation that he will
exploit to excite people yet unborn. His fantasy transports him
to the safety of another era. By thus projecting himself into the
future, he denies the threat of the present.

Other students who were apparently very little affected by the crisis employed the defense of denial—that is, they prevented the emergence of anxiety and fear by organizing their thoughts, concerns, and activities "as if" nothing of any significance was occurring. Thus, a highly self-preoccupied senior, who, shortly before the outbreak, had achieved his primary goal—being accepted at a professional school—was concerned during the occupation of the buildings only about his girlfriend's intention to break up with him and what preventive steps he should take. His principal concern about the college pertained to whether he should study and take letter grades or close the books and take pass-fail grades (an option that came into being as a result of the cessation of classes). Several other therapists described obsessional-borderline patients who were so consumed with their inner preoccupations that they seemed almost unaware of external events at the college.

It is an oversimplification to dismiss the behavior of the large numbers of students who roamed around, seemingly uninvolved, as mere apathy. Manifest noninvolvement for many students served as a kind of safety valve, cutting off unmanageable conflicts generated in the situation. This pattern is illustrated in the behavior of a sophomore:

I dug going around campus alone, talking with no one. The battleground outside corresponded to the battleground inside. I felt a harmony. I pretended I was a traveling reporter—a Norman Mailer. . . . One night I went inside Low to get arrested . . . to get fucked—relieved of all responsibility and commitment. But I didn't feel I fit. I had on slacks; they had on blue jeans. I didn't have my moustache yet. I spent the night there but didn't talk with anyone. I felt very alienated. I was tired the next day and left. . . . I was looking for something, by myself. I don't know what, maybe a chick. But then again I wasn't talking with anyone. . . . The only one I spent time with was T. P. He's a sensitive, artistic soph. I told him I was going out to get arrested. I felt I wanted a daddy to go to ask. Maybe I wanted to see—could I act myself?

Here I will briefly examine the behavior of this student in a more technically psychoanalytic way than is employed elsewhere in this section of the book, because he illustrates well how, for adolescents with fluid and poorly crystallized adaptive patterns, events of this magnitude can overwhelm the ego. In this state, their behavior comes to be more in the service of the compulsive repetition of unresolved unconscious conflicts than a functional or consensually validated political action.

This poignant picture of wandering, alienation, self-destructive impulses, and searching reflected pressure in the campus situation that unleashed a much more primitive level of functioning than was characteristic of this student (ordinarily, he maintained a group of active, close friendships). His remark that the "battle-ground outside" corresponds to the "battleground inside" indicates the symbolic equation of the external events on campus to his inner, private themes, conscious and unconscious. His behavior derived from unresolved feelings relating to the sudden death of his father during the student's pre-adolescence. As oldest son, he moved into his father's place well before he had negotiated resolution of his Oedipal conflicts. Thus, his choice of Low Library was significant because it was the President's office, the quarters of the symbolic paternal authority figure. However, to displace the President was intolerable. He had felt compelled to act out, with group support, what he unconsciously experienced as the "murder" of the father. He could not sustain his occupation of the office, because of its unconscious meaning. He was then preoccupied with getting himself arrested—that is, expiating the unconscious crime. The sequence of his associations—(1) "to get arrested," (2) "to get fucked," (3) to be "relieved of all responsibility"—represents the unconscious fantasy of being castrated because of his impulse to rebel against and displace the father-president. (It should be noted that, in this action, his political commitments were minimal.) He then goes through the reparative maneuver of wanting "daddy to go to ask." It may be postulated that his uncharacteristic behavior of not talking with anyone on campus reflected his realization that others would constitute concrete reality forces that, if permitted to do so, would intrude and disrupt the dreamlike quality of his unconscious scenario.

The Black Students

The psychological experience of confronting the authority of the university was manifestly very different for the black students in Hamilton Hall than for the white students who occupied other buildings. Similarly, the situation for the black students who remained outside Hamilton differed from that of the white students who did not enter buildings. All the black students at Columbia and Barnard were part of a small subculture where everyone was known to everyone else. Despite possible personal antagonisms, with few exceptions they felt an overriding fraternal bond. With the entry into Hamilton, action became the standard; to stay out was not nonaction but action of a different kind, that was seen and judged by all the other members of the brotherhood. Whatever his specific reasons for doing so, every one of the black undergraduates who stayed out had to justify, to himself and others, the fact that he had chosen not to join the group that identified itself, and was identified by the outside black and white communities, as the defender of black people against the injustices perpetuated by the establishment.

Although those blacks who stayed out rejected the tactic of occupying a university at that time, they nonetheless played an active supportive role that they divorced from the politics of the confrontation. They saw this role as related to the bond to their brothers that transcended ideological differences. Just about all helped on the outside, by purchasing food, running errands, and so on. When there were threats that the Majority Coalition would invade Hamilton to remove the black occupants physically, they took positions in front of the building as the first line of defense.

Nevertheless, by withstanding the pressure to join actively in the rebellion, they felt by and large that they had experienced important growth of a different order than the students inside. The theme that they stressed was a firmer sense of their "individuality" resulting from resisting peer-group pressure. Thus, one student who stayed outside said:

It [staying out] solidified my feelings about my individuality. I know where I'm at now, and I can't go for the black tyranny. I go for myself. I feel I'm more for my people than many of them.

Another stressed his greater sense of autonomy:

I was testing my ability to reason for myself. I like the results. . . . Columbia is more than buildings to me now. . . . Now you see it is made up of students. It's like a community now—a whole new idea.

Even blacks who did not enter the buildings felt that they were politicized by the events and opened further to the realities of the racial struggle. One such student, who had previously associated freely with the whites, said:

I realize now that in the white community I was no better than any other Negro. I could now work with them, but never be friends.

A Barnard student said:

Protest is still hard for me. I'd rather follow the crowd. But I lost my innocence. I can never go back, rationalize, and blindly follow the establishment.

The more militant wing of the black student body had committed itself to confrontation with the administration, with all the possibilities of massive violence (with Harlem as Columbia's near neighbor), police action, criminal records, disruption, and possibly termination of the participating students' further college study. Every black student had to make an immediate choice.

There were four main areas of *conscious* concern involved in the decision to go into Hamilton Hall or not: (1) Was the gymnasium, as planned, a good or bad thing? (2) If the gymnasium was a bad thing, could the tactic of building occupation be justified morally or politically? (3) If the balance of (1) and (2) was in the direction of a militant confrontation, was the issue of such magnitude as to warrant risking the personal consequences? (4) Did the student feel he had to participate in the occupation in order to retain the good opinion of his peers?

All the black students I talked to agreed that, because of the political climate, the gymnasium should not be built. A few acknowledged that, in its original form (which included a pool built for community use) the gym had been acceptable to them personally, but they concurred in the official Student Afro-American Society (SAS) position that the community that used the park and would use the gym should be given an opportunity to decide if they wanted it in the proposed form. Thus a student who occupied Hamilton said:

I did this so the community could get together and stop it if they wanted to. It's up to them now. I have to get back to my career.

Although manifestly arguing for a role for the community in the decision-making process, most of the students had strong personal feelings about the proposed gym. This was typified by a militant student who said:

This represented university intrusion into Harlem and was setting a precedent that had to be stopped.

A student who opposed the rebellion and who felt that the students in Hamilton were pushing their own view of the gym said:

The pressure to go into Hamilton Hall was so strong that the gym issue got blurred. That we, the middle class at Columbia University, will decide, with the politicians, what is good for "the people" disregards the community. Harlem is not made up of black-power people but of a mass of people on welfare and in demeaning jobs.

Again, it must be underscored that the gymnasium was a symbol that became the receptacle for varied resentments—resentment of university expansion, with the attendant uprooting of the lives of people with no means of voicing protest; rage at the physical evidence of white power—the university on top of the hill above a community of slum dwellings; indignation at the daily, subtle forms of racism that inhered in the structure and functioning of any white university in 1968. Some of these feelings are embodied in statements by two members of the four-man steering committee in Hamilton Hall:

I think Columbia University's building of a Jim Crow gymnasium on public park land in Harlem is representative of the most significant issue at stake here: that is, the relationship of an urban university to the community surrounding.

The black students are specifically opposed to Columbia University's use of its position of political strength to take advantage of the powerlessness of the black community. It's our position that insofar as we are able we will either stop this kind of usurpation of power or focus attention on it by dramatizing it in the manner we did.[1]

In formulating the black students' attitude toward the Harlem community, one would be naïve to disregard their ambivalence.

[1] Quoted in S. Donadio, "Columbia: Seven Interviews," *Partisan Review*, vol. 35, no. 3 (1968), p. 376.

Some feel shame (and guilt about feeling shame) and resentment of residents of the ghetto communities, who deviate in style so markedly from middle-class norms, black or white. But this puts them in the highly conflictual bind of identifying with an institution that was aggressing against their "brothers." For some who opposed the black protest against university policy, a force in their resolution of the conflict was the mechanism of "identification with the aggressor." [2]

Given their disapproval of the planned gym, was the tactic of occupying a building and obstructing the formal educative process defensible? My impression is that the black students who occupied Hamilton Hall wrestled much more painfully with the moral justification of this tactic than did the white students who occupied buildings. This is not to say that the whites did not see the decision in moral terms, but they seemed to experience less conflict in deciding that the radical act was highly moral.

A student who was in Hamilton Hall said:

I was concerned with doing the right thing. I was constantly going over—was it right? I still question, was it right? Were the decisions we made right? But, when a moral issue like this is involved, you can't come to absolutes.

Another said:

I still have doubts that perhaps there was another way. At the time I couldn't think of another way.

All the students I talked with seemed ultimately to have found a satisfactory justification, as the following comments indicate:

We had a right to disrupt college after two years of watching people go through the usual channels and hearing that it was "legal" and "fair." I don't think it's fair, and with nothing happening there was

---

[2] "Identification with the aggressor" is a concept formulated by Anna Freud—in *The Ego and the Mechanisms of Defense* (New York: International Universities Press, 1946)—to describe the mechanism of denying the anxiety and fear surrounding a threatening "object" (a person, institution, government, and so forth) by introjecting or identifying with the object. The individual then assumes the attributes of or imitates the aggressor, thereby transforming himself from the threatened to the threatener. This shift from passive victim to active aggressor reduces the unpleasant emotion.

nothing left to do. It was not disruption for disruption's sake but to dramatize the plight of the university.

I had no conflict about disrupting classes. Ten thousand [community residents] [3] had been displaced. There was no conflict. The issue transcended classes. The irony was, there were all the jocks [4] protesting in front of the now nonclassroom building.

I had no conflict about stopping classes. I feel education goes on anywhere, anytime. You don't need classrooms.

The students who stayed outside of Hamilton took a different view of the moral legitimacy of the tactics:

If I have any hope of getting anywhere in this system, getting anything of my own, I want it, and I will want it, to be protected. In order to get it, I must go through "due process," so I will be protected later.

Another told me that he could not endorse "stick-em-up tactics" [5] to gain ends, by mobilizing and playing on the university's fear of violence from the Harlem community.

Was a confrontation over the gymnasium worth the possible personal sacrifice that it might entail? On this question as well as the issue of morality, the black students evidently experienced far more turmoil than most of the white radicals. More than half (55 per cent) of the Hamilton Hall students were from a working-class background, contrasted with only 6 per cent of the white radicals. Over 85 per cent of the black students at Columbia receive scholarship or financial assistance. Well over half of the black students are members of the first generation in their family to attend college. Their being in college is a source of particular pride, fulfillment, and, perhaps, vindication to their parents. In contrast, most of the white students always took going to college

[3] The displaced community residents actually numbered 7,500.

[4] "Jocks" refers to the athletes in the Majority Coalition, with the implication that they were ordinarily less-than-serious students.

[5] This is a reference to a line of LeRoi Jones quoted by Mark Rudd in an open letter to Grayson Kirk dated April 22, the day before the Hamilton occupation. Rudd wrote: "There is only one thing left to say. It may sound nihilistic to you, since it is the opening shot in a war of liberation. I'll use the words of LeRoi Jones, whom I'm sure you don't like a whole lot: 'Up against the wall, mother-fucker, this is a stick-up.' "

for granted; only underachieving or dropping out is noteworthy. Thus, the black students carry an added burden of responsibility for sustaining their parents' pride and, with it, a potential for greater guilt in the event of failure.

If the student is dependent on scholarship or financial aid for continuing in school, he is obviously in an extremely vulnerable position. By transgressing the rules of the institution and challenging the existent authority, he is jeopardizing his future. Suspension or expulsion from Columbia might make it impossible to obtain comparable financial support from any other institution. In the interim before he is placed elsewhere, the student would be subject to the draft. Thus, the scenario could end with administrative retribution that would dash all the hopes and plans invested in obtaining a degree.

The black students were well aware of these dangers. A student who was in Hamilton said:

If you were suspended you were instantly faced with the draft. With the kind of education you had and having no skills, if another college didn't accept you, where would you be?

Another said:

I'm planning a professional career. This will definitely be a blemish on my record, but I felt if I saved myself for the future, every time something came along I'd find a way out.

And another said:

You think it through and accept that your whole career and scholarship are on the line. Once you have passed that barrier, things are easy.

Referring to the black students who stayed out, a student from Hamilton Hall said:

They were more concerned with their own getting ahead than with those who are left behind.

A student who remained outside expressed bitterness at the Barnard girls in Hamilton Hall over this question of consequences:

The women there had nothing to lose. All they have to do is marry the right guy. They become Mrs. So-and-so. They have nothing to lose.

The white students, by contrast, were capable of the facetious remark: "So what if we're all kicked out of Columbia? We'll just all transfer to Harvard."

The difference in the vulnerability of black and white students to administrative discipline was a source of considerable resentment among blacks against the white radicals. It also, as we shall see, contributed heavily to the generally greater fearfulness and anxiety in Hamilton Hall than in the white communes.

A potent counterforce to their awareness and apprehension of the possible consequences of entering Hamilton Hall was peer-group pressure. By April, every black undergraduate knew every other; there was no hiding place. The organized, vocal group was in Hamilton Hall, acting as the spokesman for black students. No comparable organization existed for the black students outside. The emphasis was on the protest as a group action, expressing the will of *the* black student. Thus, two occupants said:

I saw myself not so much as an individual, but as part of a group.

A majority were wrapped up in this black-consciousness thing. "If you're black, you have to be in here—if not, you're just Negro."

Two students who remained out said:

Some confronted me with "Either you're with us or against us." But I didn't go in and for a while would sort of hang my head.

For a black student, because of peer-group pressure, it took more courage to stay out than to go in.

A student who opposed the occupation said, referring to the Steering Committee:

Instead of the white man tyrannizing and brainwashing you, the black man will do it.

A number of black students expressed the view that the good opinion of the black Barnard girls was at stake. A student inside said:

The only pressure you'd get was from the Barnard girls—a manhood sort of thing.

A student who left Hamilton said,

The black man is hung up about being a man, and the girls say, "You're not a man if you leave."

A Barnard student who did not stay in Hamilton said:

It's a man's role to stand with a group and fight for a cause.

Recognizing this pressure, the males also conveyed ambivalence and resentment against the Barnard girls for making them feel that they had to prove themselves as men.[6]

Given all the peer-group pressures on blacks to enter Hamilton Hall, in terms of proving their brotherhood, their masculinity, their moral fiber, the decision not to enter the building was a positive assertion of individualism in a sense that did not apply to whites who stayed outside buildings.

The Majority Coalition

The several hundred undergraduates who affiliated with the Majority Coalition represented a student counterforce to the radical and militant occupants in the buildings. This force within the student body posed a far greater threat to the future of Columbia as a viable community than did outside intervention. Administration and faculty were agreed that every measure should be taken to prevent physical clashes between the two student groups. The most successful achievement of the Ad Hoc Faculty Group was the prevention of violent intramural confrontation.

My data on the MC members are not so extensive as my information on the white and black radical students, for reasons detailed earlier. I introduce my impressions of the members, not simply for the sake of completeness in describing the Columbia

---

[6] This theme of pressure from the Barnard girls and the issue of masculinity is reminiscent of Eldridge Cleaver's letter "To All Black Women, from All Black Men": "I greet you, my Queen, not in the obsequious whine of a cringing slave to which you have become accustomed, . . . but in my own voice do I greet you, the voice of the Black Man. . . .

"I have returned from the dead. . . . For four hundred years you have been a woman alone, bereft of her man, a manless woman. For four hundred years I was neither your man nor my own man. . . .

"Across the naked abyss of negated masculinity, of four hundred years minus my balls, we face each other today, my Queen." *Soul on Ice* (New York: McGraw-Hill, 1968), pp. 205–6.

crisis, but because the coalition, although a small minority at Columbia, represented the prevailing attitudes of Americans across the country—Richard Nixon's neologism, the "silent majority." Hence, in microcosm, the struggle at Columbia represented the struggle between "middle America," on the one hand, and the left-liberal, radical, and third-world groups in this nation, on the other.

It was my initial expectation that the group of students that would experience the least psychological cost in the crisis would be the members of the Majority Coalition. My rationale was that they could identify with the administration stand and would view the police action as a logical and desired intervention. As we shall see, this was not at all the case. I do not have statistics on the composition of this group, but observers agree that it was composed largely (although by no means entirely) of athletes and fraternity members. The attitude of these students was summarized by one young man:

A great university has been brought to its knees, helplessly divided, by a small minority who broke the laws to feed its conscience. Private property was no longer safe, and fear crept into "white" hearts that passed Hamilton Hall.

A focus of special outrage was the fact that Acting Dean of the College Henry Coleman was held as a hostage for the first twenty-four hours of the occupation of Hamilton Hall:

I was outraged to find that the leftists were holding Dean Coleman hostage in his office. I have always admired Henry Coleman, and it struck me as totally unfair to be punishing him for university policies that he did not in any way control.

Another said:

Now I was mad—they had no right to hang those posters in a hall that was as much mine as theirs, or to hold my Dean captive until their demands were met.

The fact that classes had been suspended and the formal educational process halted also elicited outrage:

My right to attend the classes I have paid for supersedes any strike demand, especially when the strike demands are so uncompromising. Changes of this scope . . . need not be made overnight.

Another student said:

My immediate reaction was, "Who the hell do they think they are?" I will certainly agree that anyone has the right to protest anything, just so long as he doesn't interfere with others' rights.

And another:

Basically, I think I can only describe my reaction as anger. I am angry that the school I work to pay for has been virtually destroyed for the semester.

These themes were expressed by most of the MC students.

As for political orientation, most of the members of the Majority Coalition were not at that time opposed to the U.S. role in Vietnam.[7] Few had ever been active in the civil rights movement. Administrators and faculty generally believed that the academic performance of these students was significantly lower than that of the protesters. They have strong respect for and reliance on established authority. They believe in change only by due process. They subscribe to Vice-President David Truman's statement, "Legality determines morality and justice." It is not surprising that, given this orientation, they reacted heatedly to the radical student position, as expressed by Mark Rudd:

We feel this university exists on a broader level than the campus. Whether the gymnasium should be built or not is perhaps not a question that should be open to students—shouldn't it be opened to the people of Harlem? Why should a few kids who happen to come to Columbia have more right to decide on whether weapons research for Vietnam should go on here than the 17 million Vietnamese. . . . Maybe a kid who pays three grand a year to come here has a right to go to classes. But if you weighed the evil of our stopping him against the evil of continuing certain university policies, you find that you have to involve a concept of the lesser evil against the greater evil.[8]

This argument was not congenial to the conservatives. To tell them that their right to go to class is being subordinated to some

[7] It is my impression that many of the 1968 members were active in the November 15, 1969, antiwar protest in Washington. This reflects not only the changing public opinion about the war, but also the effects of acculturation on a campus like Columbia.

[8] M. Rudd and P. Spike, "We Don't Want to Be Educated for the CIA," *Evergreen Review,* vol. 12, no. 57 (1968), p. 54.

greater good, which most of them don't agree is so good anyway, as decided by a minority, evoked immediate rage. One of the founders of the Majority Coalition said:

Initially, I wanted to take matters into my own hands and beat up some "pukes," [9] but I realized that violence would result in trouble.

The urge to fight physically—to go into the buildings and try to beat up the protesters and drag them out—seemed alien to a university community. Many New Left students are veterans at being whacked around by police at demonstrations, but, up to that point in 1968, few had extended their overt aggression beyond shouting obscene epithets. During the few days before the formation of the blockade, however, leaders of the Majority Coalition would come to meetings of the Ad Hoc Faculty Group and state that, although they personally did not want violence, unless the faculty came up with something soon, they would be unable to control their following. Respected coaches and Dean Coleman begged them to "cool it" and leave matters to the administration. The blockade of the students in President Kirk's office (estimated as 100 to 150) was an excellent compromise solution, thanks largely to the line of faculty members who stood in the buffer zone between the hedges and the building ledge, where no students were allowed, reasoning and imploring for nonviolence.

Why did the athletes want so much to fight with the strikers? Their rage and feelings of impotence were quite intolerable, especially because the situation was imposed on them, not by authority, but by renegade fellow students—their siblings, in a sense. These feelings were compounded by the fact that Columbia is not the most comfortable place for students who are accepted primarily for their athletic prowess. We have noted that they are derisively referred to as "jocks." With the exception of basketball, there is little spectator following of teams; except for a handful of football players and the basketball team, then, most Columbia athletes are anonymous jocks. I think it highly significant that only one member of the basketball team was active on the MC. Columbia's 1967–68 basketball team compiled the best record in

[9] The radical students were referred to as "pukes" in the vernacular of the conservative students.

the college's history, was Ivy League champion, and went to the National Invitation Tournament. The team was therefore supported, games were televised, and the players were celebrities on campus. In contrast with members of most other teams, they enjoyed an "identity as athlete" and were highly respected by the community.

Furthermore, most athletes, by family background and prior inclination, are not at home in the community of "intellect" that is Columbia's traditional identity. They are more pragmatic and generally not so much interested in ideas qua ideas as their fellow students and faculty. And they cannot express themselves verbally with the facility of the nonathlete Columbia student (whose average verbal SAT score is slightly over 700).[10] For some, the formal educative process of the college offers continuous exposure to the possibility of embarrassment.

At the outset, the MC clearly placed itself dynamically in relationship to the administration as the "good and loyal son." Members wore ties and Columbia blazers, guarded the President's office, and defended the administration's rights. One member spoke about this filial relationship to the authority:

Late Thursday night Dean Coleman . . . told us no longer to cool it, but to "stay out of it." A hushed crowd left Wollman Auditorium early that morning with a feeling of depression. But we knew that the depression came of wisdom, for just as father had always taken care of problems in the past, so the administration would do so now.

This faith in an omnipotent, omniscient administration could not, of course, be rewarded in the magical terms the students hoped for. Thus, disenchantment was inevitable, expressed by a member of the Coalition as follows:

Thursday night my emotions reached a peak. A lot of jocks blockaded the entrance at 116th and Broadway to prevent some Harlem people from walking across campus. Coleman told us we could do it and he was for us. . . . I didn't want any more outsiders on campus. The blacks tried to break through, but we held them off. Then the cops broke through with the blacks behind them. Coleman led them across Campus Walk, and we all thought that we had been betrayed.

[10] Such a score places the student in the top one per cent of those taking this college application test.

My feeling then, along with most of the other guys, was "Let them have the whole fucking campus! Why should I give a shit? The administration doesn't!"

This student had earlier expressed indignation that "his" dean had been held captive. Given this rebuff by the "father" he had tried to serve, his feelings evolved over the next three days to:

Later on Monday night, down at the Rail [an off-campus restaurant-bar patronized by students], I met a girl whom I shacked up with for a few days. I was really ticked when I realized I missed the bust, but I was glad to see that the administration finally took a stand, even if it was a week late.

One of the MC organizers talked about the same meeting with Dean Coleman:

I felt incensed and frustrated, because the administration had failed to be decisive. No one seemed to be taking action to alleviate the situation, but what could I do?

This feeling of helplessness was in marked contrast to his original feeling when the MC was formed:

For the first time at Columbia I felt part of the school, because I could identify with a group. My emotions were high and I was proud.

By Monday, he had changed: to

My emotions on Monday varied tremendously. At times I joined the MC line around Low, but, after participating for a few hours, I became depressed and left. Since classes had been interrupted, I decided to compensate by studying, and for the next six hours I worked without leaving my room.

As a response to the administration's futile attempt to nego-tiate and its refusal to call the police immediately, a nonathlete moderate-conservative said:

I joined the ranks of the Majority Coalition blockade of Low Library because I felt I could no longer stand aloof and trust Grayson Kirk to handle it.

However, after witnessing the police violence, this student went on to say:

When the police finally did come, I felt nothing but sadness. I knew that this would be the end of something grand about Columbia.

Associated with the initial confidence of the more conservative students that the administration could maintain control and would effectively deal out punishment to the rebels was their conviction that the faculty would be able to effect a resolution to restore the operation of the university to some form resembling its previous nature. What evolved was the loss of blind faith in the ability of the faculty, with its accumulated wisdom, to solve all problems. But it was my impression that the faculty still retained some aura of omniscience, and that their failure to resolve the crisis was simply regarded as further evidence of the intransigence and de-structiveness of the radicals. The onus of failure was placed on the administration and on the radical and militant students.

What disturbed many of the more conservative students was what they saw as the faculty's unwillingness to punish the strikers. One student said:

How can you people in there [Ad Hoc Faculty Committee] even talk of amnesty? If they [the building occupants] aren't punished severely, it will lead to anarchy. I don't, and I doubt that many of you [faculty], care to live under those conditions. If you and the administration aren't clear in this, it's all over.

In sum, the conservative students felt that the students who were occupying buildings were incorrigible and a direct threat to their welfare and that the university would do well to get rid of them; the administration was weak where it had the power to be strong, and thus betrayed them; the faculty was well inten-tioned but had no real power and was, therefore, stymied by the refractory radicals and militants.

These students felt themselves the losers in this struggle. One summed up his feelings during the remaining weeks of the semes-ter, after the buildings had been cleared by the police:

I can feel a great tension building within myself and many of my classmates. I don't, and to the best of my knowledge my friends don't, know what to do about it.

More simply, a conservative student told a colleague of mine, with tear-filled eyes, "They took away my college from me." The feeling was that somehow the administration had allowed it to happen. While the administration did not exactly welcome the protesters as "prodigal sons" in the end, the loyal sons hardly felt rewarded for their service. With no positive cause of their own to fight for and with a "father" they were angry at because of his impotence, they drifted toward apathy. Few felt that the events of the crisis had facilitated any personal psychological growth. Perhaps what they had painfully learned was that there are strong forces at work in a complex world that threaten to disrupt in style and form the values and institutions they had been inculcated with from their earliest years.

IV: Who Were the Rebels?

It was possible to obtain background statistics on over 90 per cent of the white undergraduates and all 41 of the black undergraduates who were arrested in the building occupations. The student's college admission folder supplied the year of his entrance to Columbia, the type of secondary-school education, the vocational background of parents, and the student's major field of academic interest.

The statistics do not clarify any individual's motivations, of course, but they do provide some social and cultural data that help to reveal ways in which certain groups of individuals tend to be influenced.

Year of Entry

The class standing of the arrested students, black and white, is shown in Table 5 by "year of entry." Students were not listed in their records as "freshman," "sophomore," and so on.

TABLE 5

YEAR OF ENTRY OF ARRESTED UNDERGRADUATES
(In Per Cent)

Year of Entry *	Black Undergraduates in Hamilton Hall	Total Black Students at Columbia	White Undergraduates in Buildings
1963	7	†	1
1964	12	9	15
1965	12	21	26
1966	39	35	35
1967	29	33	23

* 1963 and 1964 were seniors; 1965, juniors; 1966, sophomores; and 1967, freshmen.

† Data were not available on black students who entered the college in 1963 or earlier. The number is small but would reduce the percentage slightly for the classes entering 1964–67.

I had originally expected to find a disproportionately high percentage of seniors and first-year graduate students in the buildings because of the despair and rage I had observed among these older students over the draft and the war. The following account, by a politically liberal senior graduating with Phi Beta Kappa honors is, typical of feelings expressed by these students. Although he was quite torn during the crisis, he never entered a building. Nor, in the end, did he attend either the "official" commencement exercises or the radical "counter commencement" exercises. He said:

My opposition to the war, which did not exist in my freshman year, has grown to the point where I refuse to serve in the armed forces while this war is in progress. Clearly, as a result of the current draft laws, my physical condition, and my beliefs about the war, I have a choice of obtaining some sort of occupational deferrent, going to jail, or leaving the country. I have been accepted at law school, but attendance there would assure me of having to choose one of the latter two choices, something I'd prefer not to do. . . . With a large amount of regret and with feelings of frustration and anger, I have postponed such plans [law school and a career in politics] and, in fact, have almost given up on them. Instead, I am seeking employment as a teacher.

With these feelings at this moment in their lives, these are the youths who, given a local "cause," might be expected to become activated.

This hypothesis, however, was not borne out for the white seniors, who constituted slightly less than 15 per cent of this group—a disproportionately small representation. I had no sense that the explanation lay in their disapproval of the tactic of occupying buildings. Most likely, given their despair about their immediate futures and the pain involved in leaving the protective sanctuary for a distasteful alternative—the army, Canada, a stopgap job—a paradoxical "riddance" phenomenon takes place, in which the pain of separation is attenuated by an emotional withdrawal (decathexis) from the place or person left behind, prior to the separation. Hence, an event of great magnitude, such as the strike at their college, has a very different impact on a student five weeks away from graduation than it does on a student for whom Columbia represents his past, his present, *and his future.* By April of a student's senior year, the college tends to be his past alone.

In contrast, sophomores and juniors comprised somewhat over 61 per cent of the white protesters. The sophomore year is often the romantic time in a young mans' life. During freshman year he has done most of the work of emotionally freeing himself from those aspects of his traditional family legacy that he finds alien. More often than not, his future vocation is still unclear, so he has not yet reached the senior-junior stage of apprenticeship in both fantasy and preliminary planning for his role in "the system." The movie that most engaged youth at the time of the Columbia rebellion was *The Graduate*. Benjamin, the sentimentalized hero, is really more of a sophomore than a graduate in his desperate, romantic moment of commitment and freedom from the system. For many of the Columbia sophomores, going into the buildings had a romantic quality of commitment that was less political, in the sense of pre-thought-out ideology, than was true of their older peers. A sophomore (and perhaps only a sophomore could have) said:

The strike was in the context of what is between people screaming out that they do exist. It's not any political meaning that I'll remember but something else, something about the power of time and circumstance.

The class distribution of the black students occupying Hamilton Hall has meaning only when contrasted with the widely varied absolute numbers of blacks in each class. Thus the percentage of freshmen and sophomores in Hamilton Hall—68 per cent of the group—is the same as the percentage of freshmen and sophomores in the total black student body of the college. There were only five juniors (12 per cent), a number too small for a sound, statistically based explanation. Those who had entered in 1963—7 per cent of the protesters—represented three seniors who had spent a year away from college.

In contrast with the peak representation of sophomores and the small number of seniors among the white radicals, there is little significant difference between the composition of Hamilton Hall students and the distribution by class of blacks in Columbia College. The explanation for this probably relates to a difference in the college careers of blacks and whites. The whites were in a transient state, liberated from their past roots and not yet committed to their future fixed roles, which enabled many of them to act out their ideals with less concern for practical consequences than ever before or ever again. The black students more often saw the university as a career-training institution and did not experience so pronounced a separation of past and future. Also, the labile shifts in values and behavior characteristic of white students in their sophomore year are less pronounced in blacks because the blacks are part of a tightly knit subgroup, with shared values, that crosses year-of-college lines. In sum, there is less discontinuity in the black's college career, once at college, than in the lives of the white activist youth.

Type of Secondary-School Education

Table 6 presents the distribution of radical and militant students according to their pre-college education in (1) an urban or a small-town public school; (2) a suburban public school; or (3) a private school.

TABLE 6

SECONDARY-SCHOOL EDUCATION OF ARRESTED UNDERGRADUATES
(In Per Cent)

Type of School	Black Students	White Students
Urban or small-town public school	74	32
Suburban public school	8	33
Private school	18	35

For the white students, no control data are available for suburban, urban, and small-town public high school attendance. The private-school figure of 35 per cent is identical to the percentage of the total Columbia population admitted from private schools from 1963 to 1967. It is my educated guess that, with respect to the preparatory education of the white radicals, they were probably fairly representative of the total white Columbia undergraduate population, except that students from small towns and rural districts may have been underrepresented. In any event, the rebellion was neither a revolt of the private-school elite nor an action that was odious to them. The white radicals as a group had been exposed to superior educational opportunities at the secondary-school level.

No control data are available for the black students who did not occupy Hamilton Hall. What might be noted, however, is the predominance of the public educational background and the relatively few blacks who came from either suburban public schools or private schools. No doubt, many of these urban high schools were not "better" schools. One can conclude that the quality of both the pre-Columbia student life and the academic preparation of many of the black students made for a difficult transition and marked discomfort at college. The intellectual and cultural values and styles at Columbia are a natural extension of the values and styles at private and suburban high schools. Therefore, urban high school blacks are not so well prepared in the style of language, the approach to the acquisition of knowledge, and peripheral "cultural" advantages as white students. Aside from the universal language of athletics, they are also less prepared for and experienced in most extracurricular activities. Thus, for example, few blacks are on the newspaper staffs, because the style of journalism as well as the activities reported are less familiar and relevant to them. This preliminary schooling for many of the blacks, which presents them with such a difficult transition to the Columbia community, enhances their sense of alienation and logically predisposes them to demand changes in the nature of the institution to accommodate their separate needs.

I have not seen the statistics regarding academic performance for rebel and nonrebel students at Columbia, but the general feeling expressed by faculty and administrators is that the strikers represent an academically above-average selection of students. Most studies of radical white students in contrast with nonradical populations at particular campuses have, with one equivocal exception,[1] revealed the radical student to be more intellectually

[1] W. A. Watts and D. Whittaker, "Free Speech Advocates at Berkeley," *Journal of Applied Behavioral Science*, vol. 2, 1966, pp. 41–62.

disposed [2] and with higher academic performance [3] than the non-radicals. In this connection, a top university official regretfully noted to me that no leader had emerged from the conservative students at Columbia who could compare in intellect, articulateness, and charisma with more than a few such leaders on the left.

I know of no published studies of the academic performance of black student activists, but a black student who opposed the occupation of Hamilton Hall told me that the academic performance of the students who did *not* stay in the building was significantly higher. His explanation was that the students who were having a difficult time with their studies used the strike as an excuse to project the blame onto the university.

This student touched on a dynamic that characterized at least a few of both white and black students who were doing poorly because of their own internal conflicts and found relief from the resultant shame and depression by projecting blame onto the college and then, having convinced themselves that they were victims of the college system, felt justified in attacking the institution.

Socio-economic Background

Again, comparative data for the student body as a whole are lacking. But the findings shown in Table 7 are striking in their absolute implications. The students are categorized by the occupation of the parent (usually the father). Families that appeared to be on the border between middle and upper-middle class have been assigned equally to those two categories.

These figures indicate that at Columbia, as far as the white students were concerned, there was a revolt of the privileged, not oppressed or economically deprived youth. This finding is consonant with Kenneth Keniston's observation that, among the group of radicals he studied, "identification with others who are op-

[2] P. Heist, "Intellect and Commitment: The Faces of Discontent," Berkeley, Calif.: Center for the Study of Higher Education, 1965, mimeo.

[3] R. H. Somers, "The Mainsprings of Rebellion: A Survey of Berkeley Students in November, 1964," and H. C. Selvin and W. O. Hagstrom, "Determinants of Support for Civil Liberties," in S. M. Lipset and S. Wolin, eds., *The Berkeley Student Revolt* (New York: Doubleday Anchor, 1965), pp. 530–57 and 494–518, respectively.

TABLE 7

SOCIO-ECONOMIC BACKGROUNDS (SEB) OF ARRESTED
UNDERGRADUATES
(In Per Cent)

Family SEB	Black Students	White Students
Working class	55	6
Middle class	18	15
Upper-middle class	28	79*
(including professionals and academics)		

* Of this 79 per cent, 15 per cent were sons of college or high school teachers.

pressed is [a] far more important motivating force than any sense of personal deprivation." [1] In terms of their manifest status, the white radicals stand in marked contrast to the black militant students. They also are very different from the Marxist students of the 1930's, who usually lived at home with their marginally employed parents. They are different from the traditional revolutionary masses throughout the world who have been economically exploited and politically disenfranchised.

The spirit of this aspect of the rebellion is conveyed in a description by a white, upper-middle-class suburban student of a conversation he had with a policeman shortly before the bust:

"Don't you understand, we're doing this for you? You and your kids are going to profit from what we're doing a hell of a lot more than we are!" But the cop just looked at me and smiled blankly like he didn't know what the hell I was talking about.

The policeman probably did *not* grasp what the student was talking about, for many policemen and skilled union laborers now own their own homes and cars and send their children to college. They may have been materially and socially deprived as children, but what they were deprived of is now seemingly attainable. They feel the "success of success," not the "failure of success," which is the experience of these privileged youth. Keniston describes the

[1] Keniston, *The Young Radicals* (New York: Harcourt, Brace & World, 1968.)

"failure of success" as a "second identity crisis" growing out of the conflict over having achieved enough success, by most standards, to open the doors to the "good things" (that is, property and power) that American society offers its more fortunate adults but finding this prospect unsatisfactory.[5] Having been amply provided with material goods, economic security, and educational opportunity, these students have become increasingly aware that these things do not generate personal fulfillment, inner meaning, or satisfaction.

In contrast, the majority (55 per cent) of the black militant students came from working-class backgrounds. Just as their high school experiences did not prepare them for the intellectual climate at Columbia, so the structure and values of their working-class families did not prepare them for the social climate at Columbia. This discontinuity between family and college contributed to their sense of alienation from the mainstream of life at the college.

A correlate of these figures is that over 85 per cent of the black students depend on scholarships and financial assistance through the university to be able to sustain their studies, and that 72 per cent of the black students are in the first generation of their families to attend, not only an Ivy League college, but any college at all. These two facts in the experience of the black students had far-reaching implications for the decision to take the risk inherent in "illegal" confrontation with the administration by staying in Hamilton.

The marked disparity in the economic backgrounds of the black and white groups also contributed to the antagonism that almost all the black students felt toward the white radicals. This theme is expressed in the following statements by black students:

A white student can say all he wants against the system. He can always shave his beard and join the system. Black students can't. They want to join the system. Every other group has melted in.

It's expensive to be a revolutionary. The luxury of ideas. You can't go back to mother and father for money and go elsewhere. I don't have that luxury.

Black students from the middle class differ in the roots of their

[5] *Ibid.*

militancy from students from the ghetto. The middle-class black student finds himself faced with a dilemma as he enters college, away from family, comparable to the feeling of the white radicals from suburbia who have been, in part, radicalized by the "failure of success" in "the system." E. Franklin Frazier concluded his classic book *Black Bourgeoisie* with the statement:

The emphasis upon "social" life or "society" is one of the main props of the world of makebelieve into which the black bourgeoisie has sought an escape from its inferiority and frustrations in American society. This world of makebelieve, to be sure, is a reflection of the values of American society, but it lacks the economic basis that would give it roots in the world of reality. In escaping into a world of makebelieve, middle-class Negroes have rejected both identification with the Negro and his traditional culture. Through delusions of wealth and power they have sought identification with the white America which continues to reject them. But these delusions leave them frustrated because they are unable to escape from the emptiness and futility of their existence. . . . The black bourgeoisie suffer from "nothingness" because when Negroes attain middle-class status, their lives generally lose both content and significance.[6]

One could question the applicability of Frazier's conclusion today, but to the degree that it is still accurately descriptive of large numbers of middle-class black families, their sons are presented with a model that scarcely attracts them to follow in the parental mold. For some of these sons, to work quietly for their piece of the pie presents a prospect of enduring psychic starvation. They have witnessed the failure of their parents' definitions of success and, like their white radical counterparts, militantly confront and attempt to destroy the system so as to generate new forms and possibilities, not only of economic opportunity but of psychological harmony. These militants from the black bourgeoisie exist with their white radical fellow students as fraternal twins and sibling rivals.

Major Field of Academic Interest

The major fields of academic interest as indicated by freshmen on entering the college are listed in Table 8.

[6] New York: Macmillan, 1957, p. 195.

TABLE 8

FIELD OF ACADEMIC INTEREST OF ARRESTED UNDERGRADUATES
(In Per Cent)

Area of Interest	Black Under-graduates in Hamilton Hall	Total Black Students at Columbia	White Radicals *	Total Student Body at Columbia
Science and mathematics	41	33	18	34
Humanities	8	15	41	35
Social sciences	38	34	41	31
Not indicated	15	18	—	—

* These percentages are based on available records for 80 per cent of the white undergraduates arrested.

The relatively high proportion of white radical students interested in the social sciences and humanities will surprise few. The reasons for this are basically twofold. The first pertains to the general personality structure and defense mechanisms characterizing the students in each of the three interest areas. The other relates to the "relevance" of the student's vocational and intellectual interests to the requirements of the economic-technological order of the society.

The primary objects of concern in a scientist's or mathematician's work are "things" and symbols. The scientist tries to understand the laws that govern the operations of physical and biological phenomena. Perhaps he works in applied areas to bring science to the service of man, but his primary concern is not interpersonal or social. Inasmuch as man's early significant emotional experiences are with people, the turning to science usually represents, in a highly functional way, a model of buffering too much stimulation and consequent anxiety from continuous "people-concern." It is a familiar pattern in medical schools to see some of the best pre-med science majors, who head their class during the first two years of medical school, encounter considerable anxiety and decline in performance when they move into the third and fourth years, where most of their work is at the bedside of live patients. Conversely, the pre-med humanities major usually grits his teeth through the first two years and begins to enjoy school only when the live patients are rolled in. Upon completing training, the former returns to the lab and academic medicine, and the latter hangs out a shingle. In any event, the particular style of intellectualization that scientists and mathematicians have make it less likely that they will experience the degree of empathy with the oppressed that makes it possible to act boldly and impulsively in a radical cause.

Social-science majors are, by definition, interested in the forces and dynamics accounting for the behavior of people—in the present and in the past. Apart from being better informed and more curious about such matters as balances of power, conflicting interests, and the historical evolution of the crisis, they are less likely to retain emotional detachment when it relates to groups of people. Social-science majors are trying not only to understand the forces at play in their particular discipline as pertains to society but also, by so doing, to come to further resolution in an unconsciously parallel way with their interpersonal conflicts, intrapsychic conflicts, and personal historical past.

Some of the correlations between vocational choice and the nature of social involvement are suggested in the following excerpts from the "Application to the Graduate Department of Sociology" of an arrested graduate student who had worked for two years as a chemist before deciding to pursue his studies beyond the bachelor's degree:

. . . I came to understand that society is not necessarily right and good, not something to be taken for granted or passively questioned. With this understanding on my part came a decision to actively involve myself with the betterment of our society. . . .
This development of my attitude took place as I worked as a chemist. I quickly found that my newly developed concerns would find neither sustenance nor implementation within a chemistry environment. . . . I began to read about sociology and saw that this was a profession that would allow for the total scope of my societal interests and my desire to be socially creative.

Certain generalizations can be made about the humanities majors. They are the searchers, the "seekers after truth"; the ones most interested in inner experience, in personal ethic, in making a "personal" statement, and, also, the ones with the most *angst*.

They are least compulsively organized in their work patterns and, more often than the others, live in cycles from personal crisis to personal crisis, from peak experience to peak experience. In this generally affluent group, for some, the interest in humanities represents a conflict in identification with the father's materially successful vocation. It is a "liberation" born out of ambivalence. Out of this more labile affective world and quest for personal identity, one would expect a capacity for empathy with the truly oppressed, more ambivalence toward existing institutions, and more proneness to join a romantic cause, involving rapid change in outlook, style, and rhetoric.

These personality categorizations are, of course, overgeneralized and schematic. They obscure the significant differences between different fields of study under the three major headings of science, social sciences, and humanities. For example, the classical-languages major is classified under humanities but is probably much closer to the physical scientist in character than to an aspiring novelist, who is an English and literature major. Engineering and business-administration students were virtually unrepresented among the rebels. These two groups of students are generally more obsessive-compulsive, less feeling, less impulsive, less romantic, than the striking students. These personality features are, however, subordinated to their perception of the social order.

This theme, which very few of the strikers would dispute, was summed up by one student:

The occupation of the buildings was quite symbolic of protests directed not only toward Columbia University but against that intangible, amorphous structure which we term the "American Society."

Such terms as "invisible president," "loss of individuality," and "irrelevance" pervade all the descriptions of the "enemy" they were fighting. To take a stand in the buildings was experienced by one student as "the fulfillment of dreams—to do and feel and act in one whole."

This lyrical statement is the individualist's cry against the anonymity increasingly imposed by the "technetronic" society. Recognizing this spirit, Erik Erikson called the Columbia rebellion "the humanist revolt against technology." [7] These humanities ma-

[7] Erikson, personal communication to the author.

jors feel terribly alienated. Where does the nonutilitarian thinker, the noncommercial artist, the humanist, find his place in a society moving in the direction of automation and specialization of the work force? The computer becomes the deity and the expert the priest in the new religion of "technetronics."

Against this tide a Columbia rebel cried:

Some plead the cause of a "value-free" university and declare that ties with IDA must be dropped. I must go a step further and ask that certain humanistic values be adopted. . . . I honestly doubt that free, humanistic inquiry and eventual understanding can take place where the enveloping structure is intimately involved and inextricably tied to nonhumanistic endeavors.

Students and university are less and less acting in symbiosis, each capable of profoundly influencing the other. Now the large universities have moved into a symbiotic relationship with power centers of the technetronic world. Hence, although they clearly assign opposite values to what they believe the modern university has become, we hear almost identical descriptions of the new university from such strange bedfellows as Columbia political scientist Zbigniew Brzezinski and and radical historians Christopher Lasch and Eugene Genovese. Brzezinski says:

Today, the university is the creative eye of a massive communications complex, the source of much strategic planning, domestic and international. Its engagement in the world is encouraging the appearance of a new breed of politicians-intellectuals. . . . The university has become a community of organization-oriented, application-minded intellectuals, relating itself more effectively to the political system.[8]

Lasch and Genovese say:

The changes in production that have made young people superfluous . . . have altered the institutional function of the university. . . . It still retains the old functions: it trains professionals and high functionaries of the traditional type, and more important, it trains the managerial elite and performs direct and vital services for the corporations and government. But its most striking function today— apart from the custodial function it shares increasingly with secondary schools—is that of training an army of intellectual workers on which the corporate system depends. . . . The university now trains

[8] Z. Brzezinski, "The American Transition," *The New Republic*, Dec. 23, 1967, p. 20.

men who govern through the application of specialized skills to the solution of technical problems. It also carries on government-financed research that will be directly useful to the corporations and to government, particularly the military. These activities further erode the autonomy of the university. . . . No longer is the university viewed as a place in which to raise philosophical questions about the very premises of the society it serves.[9]

Although both of these statements are oversimplifications of the structure and purposes of the pluralistic university, both capture a growing trend, further differentiating the small liberal arts college, with no graduate schools, and the large university.

Professor Brzezinski, a former member of the State Department policy-planning staff, is cognizant of the threat to the humanities majors:

Some of the recent upheavals have been led by people who increasingly will have no role to play in the new technetronic society. Their reaction reflects both a conscious and, even more important, an unconscious realization that they are themselves becoming historically obsolete.[10]

Contempt for the university humanities community has been articulated clearly by the president of San Francisco State College, S. I. Hayakawa, who told a study team for the National Commission on the Causes and Prevention of Violence:

Central to the problem of violence on campus is the existence of a large number of alienated young men and women who practically take pride in being outside the mainstream of the culture, of being against the establishment. . . . How did they get alienated? Well, besides the usual psychologically neurotic reasons for this alienation there is something else that's going on. I think that they are taught this alienation by professors. Especially in the liberal arts departments, the humanities, English, philosophy, sometimes in social sciences. There's a kind of cult of alienation among intellectuals, among intellectuals in literary fashion such as you find in the *New York Review of Books* or the *Partisan Review*. They sneer at the world the way it's run by politicians, businessmen, and generals. . . . The first great enunciator of this theory was Plato, who believed that philosophers should be kings, and notice that he himself was a

[9] C. Lasch, and E. Genovese, "The Education and the University We Need Now," *New York Review of Books,* Oct. 9, 1969, pp. 22–23.

[10] Z. Brzezinski, "Revolution and Counterrevolution (But Not Necessarily About Columbia)," *The New Republic,* June 1, 1968, p. 25.

philosopher. The contemporary literary critics and philosophers feel the same way.[11]

Kate Millett has cogently argued that there is cultural programming in education toward a division between "masculine" and "feminine" subject matter.[12] The fields that directly serve the interests of patriarchal power in industry, government, and the military, such as science, engineering, law, and business, are "men's" fields. In contrast, humanities and certain social sciences that are remote from centers of political power (particularly anthropology, psychology, and sociology) are open to females. Because they are not exclusively male, they suffer in prestige.

Thus, these youth, whose interests, life style, and vocational aspirations render them vulnerable to condemnation as "irrelevant" and "obsolete," accurately perceived the growing incompatibility of their identity and destiny and the identity and destiny of the university. This feeling found expression in the standing ovation offered by the junior faculty and the humanities faculty to the young historian Jeffrey Caplow following his speech in support of the student strike at the full faculty meeting the morning after the police cleared the buildings. Caplow concluded by crying out Sartre's words, "I detest people who love their executioners!"

So, apart from the psychodynamics and character structure that are unique to each individual protesting student, these youth are profoundly influenced by their discordant relationship, as a "minority group," with the mainstream of America. With their knowledge and the perspective that comes from being outside the system, they feel increasingly helpless before the politicians and university administrators who wield the power that expresses the will of large corporate interests. Many felt that they had no choice but to pursue their careers in universities as quasi sanctuaries in an alien society, but now they perceived themselves as unheard and ineffectual in their own university.

Conversely, the relative scarcity of scientists, mathematicians,

---

[11] Quoted in *Shut It Down! A College in Crisis: San Francisco State College, October, 1968–April, 1969.* A Staff Report to the National Commission on the Causes and Prevention of Violence, prepared by William H. Orrick, Jr., June, 1969, p. 56.

[12] K. Millett, *Sexual Politics* (New York: Doubleday, 1970).

and engineering and business students in the radical student movement, regardless of their character structure and other psychodynamic forces, is inevitable, since the aspirations, skills, and self-images of the students in these groups are wedded to the perfection of the technetronic era.

Table 8 reveals that significantly fewer black students in the college were interested in the humanities. Further, there were disproportionately fewer of these students in Hamilton Hall. The difference between the percentage of black and white humanities majors at Columbia reflects several factors. First is the trend among black students to use their college education as preparation for a "tangible" career, which will not only yield satisfaction for themselves but also fulfill a felt responsibility to place themselves in a position where they can effect changes for the black community. With a group psychology of the disenfranchised, they want admittance to the system, not membership in a different disenfranchised group—university intellectuals. Further, the content of the areas of study in humanities has little relevance to their past heritage, their parental values, and the political-economic struggles of oppressed minorities. Thus, in terms of the sociological forces motivating militancy in black students, the relationship of their academic and vocational identity appears to be very much subordinated to their identity as an oppressed minority.

Morality and Student Activism

The question of the "morality" of student activists has been the subject of major research and writing. To place Columbia in perspective with what has been found at other universities that have been centers of student activism, a review of some of the related literature is necessary.

The whole issue of civil disobedience in protest over social injustice, in a society that defines itself as "democratic"—that is, that has the legal machinery to redress wrongs—is one of the central dilemmas of the student radical movement. We consider men like Gandhi and Martin Luther King "moral leaders" in our century. They pursued a commitment to ethical principles that violated the law of the land. At the same time, we are deeply concerned lest a minority of radicals and militants, under a banner of moral righteousness, will encroach on the rights of the majority. At Columbia, conservative students said, in essence, "I worked to earn money for tuition, and now they [the radical minority] prevent me from going to classes that I want to attend, because of issues over which I may or may not agree with them." The radical and militant students said in effect: "Unless we dramatize the situation by disruption, the injustices (which are of greater significance than missing class for a few days) will continue."

The morality of the radical movement and its relation to family background has been the subject of an important study by Haan and her colleagues,[13] who based their work on Kohlberg's classification of the levels and stages of development of moral judgment.[14]

All individuals are presumed to progress through a sequence of stages of moral development to whatever level they ultimately reach. The developmental stages, according to Kohlberg, are as follows:

1. "Obedience and punishment" orientation, in which the individual defers unquestioningly to superior power or prestige
2. "Instrumental relativism," an egocentric orientation in which the action regarded as "right" is that which instrumentally satisfies the self's needs and occasionally those of others
3. "Personal concordance"—a "good boy" orientation in which action is in the service of gaining approval from others by pleasing and helping them
4. "Law and order," in which orientation the individual believes that the code of the existing authority and social order should be adopted and followed
5. "Social contract"—a contractual, legalistic orientation, in which behavior is guided by rules and established tradition
6. "Individual principled"—an orientation that emphasizes

[13] N. Haan, M. B. Smith, and J. Block, "Moral Reasoning of Young Adults," *Journal of Personality and Social Psychology,* vol. 10, no. 3 (1968), pp. 183–201.
[14] L. Kohlberg, "Moral and Religious Education and the Public Schools: A Developmental View," in T. R. Sizer (ed.), *Religion and Public Education,* (Boston: Houghton-Mifflin, 1967).

conscience as a directing agent and stresses mutual respect and trust

Haan classified 214 experimental subjects on the basis of their responses to a series of stories posing classic moral dilemmas to determine the involvement of the various types in the 1964 Berkeley Free Speech Movement sit-in. No students were classified in the "obedience and punishment" stage. This suggests that students with conventional moral reasoning do not tend to vigorously question the *status quo*. Hence, they do not participate in illegal protest activities.

The FSM protest attracted large proportions of students at the extremes of the developmental scale of moral reasoning. Haan explains the presence of large numbers of "instrumental relativists" (IR's) by the student's need to

. . . reject the status quo since it often does not comply with his egoistic view of his relationship to others and society and with his personally reversed definition of the good. His self-view does not permit him to see or take the roles of others including those in authority. . . . Since the IR's concern about society is personally referenced, a generally politicized milieu is undoubtedly required for the IR to protest, and his ultimate criterion would often be whether it would work or not. Political protest itself is likely a fine expression of the politicized IR's personal battles with a society which is seen as ungiving rather than immoral.[15]

Haan then discusses the high likelihood that the "individually principled" person (IP) will partake in such a protest as the FRM sit-in:

The principled individual is not automatically limited by the extant characteristics of a specified social order or arrangement. . . . [His] allegiance in a moral confrontation will be to universal and logically consistent ideal principles of justice which necessarily include existing social agreements, but his principles will be primary if these two considerations should conflict. . . . One cannot reject a social contract on the basis of individual principles without first understanding the essential contractual nature of social orders and human affairs. The IP takes the role of others in a most inclusive, abstract, and ideal sense.[16]

[15] Haan *et al., op. cit.*, p. 199.
[16] *Ibid.*

Keniston has attempted to account for the existence of these two very different modes of moral thinking in a movement that is manifestly based on commitment to ethical principles, not personal gain or protection. He draws a distinction between "ethicality," on the one hand, and "destructive moral zealotry," in which a man, in pursuing his own principles, will disregard the rights of all who stand in his way. Drawing on Anna Freud's discussion of the integration and harmony of "developmental lines"—that is, evenness or unevenness in the progression of intellectual, motor, affective, perceptual, psychosexual, and other sectors of development —Keniston proposes:

Whether the highest stages of moral reasoning lead to destructive zealotry or real ethicality depends upon the extent to which moral development is matched by development in other sectors. The critical related sectors of development, I submit, are those which involve compassion, love, or empathic identification with others.[17]

With the knowledge from the Berkeley study of the great potential for participation in a college sit-in of students at the low and high ends of the morality scale, the tantalizing question is raised: What percentage of the students who did sit-in fell into each category of moral reasoning? No such data exist for Columbia, but we do have a study by Smith of "protesting" and "nonprotesting" students at Berkeley and San Francisco State College.[18] The 109 protesters participated in actions ranging from "illegal" protest (for example, the FSM sit-in) to "legal" peace marches and picketing, within or outside the university. The 284 nonprotesters had never participated in political protest, although many had engaged in social-service activities (for example, tutoring underprivileged children). All these students were classified on the basis of Kohlberg's three levels of moral judgment, as follows:

1. The "pre-moral" level, in which moral value is determined unsystematically by the events, individual needs, and emo-

[17] K. Keniston, "Moral Development, Youthful Activism and Modern Society," paper delivered at American Psychiatric Association meetings, Bal Harbour, Fla., May 7, 1969.
[18] M. B. Smith, "Morality and Student Protest," paper delivered at Psychological Association meetings, San Francisco, Calif., 1968.

tions of the moment, rather than by any constant social or ethical standards

2. The "conventional" level, in which moral value resides in performing "good" or "right" roles, in maintaining the conventional order and expectancies as defined by others

3. The "principled" level, in which moral value resides in conformity to shared or sharable standards, rights, or duties— that is, to an ethical code rather than to the expectancies of others [19]

The percentage of students at each of these levels of moral reasoning is summarized in Table 9.

TABLE 9

LEVEL OF MORAL REASONING IN PROTESTING AND NONPROTESTING STUDENTS

Level of Moral Reasoning	Protesting Students (N = 109)	Nonprotesting Students (N = 284)
Premoral (preconventional)	10	3
Conventional	34	85
Principled (postconventional)	56	12

We see that the composition of the protesting group is heavily skewed in the direction of postconventional morality. Thus, there is a very great likelihood, as Haan has shown, not only that any postconventionally moral individual will join a protest movement but also that the movement itself will consist preponderantly of postconventionally moral students.

It must be borne in mind that the "protesters" in Smith's study included participants in "legal" and "illegal" protests, nondisruptive as well as disruptive, and protest directed against nonuniversity institutions as well as against the university. We can assume that as the protest becomes more radical—that is, illegal—and directed against their own college, the percentage of "conventionally" moral participants will decrease.

[19] Kohlberg, *op. cit.*

In evaluating these findings, we must keep in mind the distinction between the "moral content" and the "moral style" of students. These studies measure primarily moral content. Therefore, the distinction between "ethicality" and "destructive moral zealotry" in actual conduct may not be accurately determined by the Kohlberg scale. Many liberal adults in the university community would argue that the radicals and militants are following the "wrong" principles for the "right" reasons, whereas the conventional students are following the "right" principles for the "wrong" reasons. In any event, in speaking of moral values we are talking of "values" and not inherent "good" and "evil."

To understand the development of "principled morality"—a major theme in the college New Left movement as well as a characteristic of a significant body of its membership—we must look beyond the political and social views of parents. My data (see Chap. VI) and those of others demonstrate that the members of the New Left are by no means simply the sons and daughters of the Old Left. Child-rearing practices and the family dynamics of the radicals influence the character of "morality," but their impact is subjected to continuous modification by extrafamilial influences.

Keniston [20] has suggested a number of factors that are accelerating moral development in youth today, among them the changing nature of the university system. With vastly more students attending college, not only in the United States but abroad, and greatly increasing numbers of students going on to graduate-student status well into their 20's, the result has been what Keniston terms "disengagement from adult society." The postponement of job, marriage, and children militates against an early foreclosure of nonconventional modes of thought and behavior. In a more positive sense, the college experience allows for "confrontation with alternate moral viewpoints." The composition as well as the climate of college is changing. The elite colleges have become more "democratized." Admission policies are changing, and campuses have many more black, third-world, and scholarship students. It is my impression also that a greater percentage of parochial secondary-school graduates are going to secular colleges. All this leads to

[20] Keniston, "Moral Development . . . , *op. cit.*

contact, even confrontation, between students with differing points of view and value systems. This confrontation of ideologies is possible with the change in the climate of dissent on campuses, from the "silent" era of the Eisenhower 1950's to the present open forum for expression of the whole range of antitraditional and antiestablishment views.

The findings at Berkeley and San Francisco State are in accord with my conclusion that the radical and militant students at Columbia were a heterogeneous group. In Chapter IX, I will introduce a classificatory scheme for radicals and militants, from "idealistic" to "nihilistic." The correlation between "principled morality" and "idealistic" radicalism or militancy and between "pre-morality" and "nihilistic" radicalism or militancy, is high. Like the student radicals at Berkeley and San Francisco State, the activist groups at Columbia were composed predominantly of students who may be characterized by their "principled morality."

V: The Communes

The first afternoon and night of the occupation, black and white students together sat-in at Hamilton Hall. At 5:30 the following morning, the black students established themselves as a separate political entity and, by coercion or agreement, depending on what version of the events one accepts, took over Hamilton Hall from the predominantly white student group and established it as an all-black protest base.[1] Initially the black group included not only students but residents of the surrounding community. In and out of the building moved such dignitaries as psychologist Kenneth Clark, Borough President Percy Sutton, Human Rights Commissioner William Booth, State Senator Basil Paterson, and militant leaders H. Rap Brown and Stokely Carmichael. However, the nonstudents moved out within a day or two, leaving Hamilton Hall occupied exclusively by Columbia and Barnard blacks. The four white "communes" were occupied by Columbia and Barnard students plus a few significant outsiders such as Tom Hayden, a founder of SDS and a leading figure in the New Left movement, and a small number of young alumni.

The experience of occupying a university building was different in each building. But almost all of the students, black and white, felt that it was one of the most significant moments of their lives.

The variables determining the quality of experience in the four white "communes" included: the relative homogeneity of the occupants with regard to age, stage of schooling, and position on the political spectrum; the relative freedom of entry and exit from the building; the physical characteristics of the building and the organization of daily life; and the quality of leadership.

[1] The best account of the internal political maneuvers during the crisis is to be found in a book by the student editors of the *Columbia Spectator:* J. Avorn *et al., Up Against the Ivy Wall* (New York: Atheneum, 1968).

It is essential to distinguish between aspects of the experience attributable to the commitment to activism and those resulting from communal living itself, bearing in mind that the two are largely fused since the style of life in the buildings to a great extent represented a political statement.[2]

The four buildings occupied by whites were as follows:

1. President Kirk's three-room office suite in Low Library. This was the first area taken over when the rebellion became separatist. There were approximately 100 occupants, of whom 79 were arrested, including 39 Columbia undergraduates and a few Barnard undergraduates. As a result of the Majority Coalition blockade, there was virtually no entry or exit for the last four days. One student, Tony Papert, emerged as the leader and commanded considerable respect from the communards. Living conditions were cramped. There was only one bathroom, with continuous long lines. Low was the building that received the most attention from the media.

2. Mathematics building. This was the last building occupied, on April 26th. Of the 203 students arrested, 67 were Columbia undergraduates and there were a few Barnard girls. Entry and exit were permitted but markedly restricted. People were not allowed in unless they agreed to stay for six hours, and it was decided to limit the group in size. Frequent movement out was discouraged. This group tended to be politically more homogeneous—that is, radical—than the others. There was very skillful and respected leadership in the person of Tom Hayden. Since Math was a large classroom building, with faculty offices, there was some opportunity for privacy.

3. Fayerweather Hall. Of the 286 people arrested, 83 were Columbia undergraduates. There was a broad spectrum of political outlook represented, from liberal to radical. This building contained the largest number of outsiders since entry and exit were unrestricted; people dropped out and new people joined along the

---

[2] Chapter IX presents a more theoretical discussion of the effects of the particular form of the group radical action—seizure of a building and communal living—on the individual's psychodynamic constellation of needs, impulses, and defense mechanisms.

way. No clear leadership ever emerged. The size of the building provided ample opportunity for privacy.

4. Avery Hall. In the School of Architecture building, forty-two students were arrested, only nine of them Columbia undergraduates. The majority were graduate students from the Department of Architecture and the Urban Planning Program. They were the least militant. There was no single leader as strong as those in Low and Mathematics, but nonetheless leadership was stable. Entry and exit were not rigidly controlled, and the building offered privacy when desired.

Of the three buildings containing the most undergraduates, the communal experience in two—Low and Math—was exhilarating for most, but in Fayerweather it was, on balance, largely unpleasant. Low and Math were in congenial rivalry. The students at Low felt that, by virtue of occupying President Kirk's office, they were the symbolic center of the struggle; those at Math felt that they were the spearhead of the rebellion because they were the most radical and the best organized. In both buildings, nearly all the undergraduates I spoke with described a closeness and openness with their fellows that they had never before known. They were united for a cause, an ideal, as they saw it, that could bring them no personal material gain in the usual terms of the culture; they were facing the common danger of arrest, beatings (possibly having the chemical mace used against them), and perhaps expulsion from college; and, at a deeper level, they were sharing a common anxiety, the fear that, regardless of their motives in participating, they might be responsible for triggering a sequence of events that would blaze out of control. Specifically, they feared that the community might be incensed enough to move against the university, perhaps burning it [3] or unleashing exchanges of gunfire.

Addressing himself to a new kind of interpersonal experience, a student who had previously been very absorbed by his creative activities said of his experience in Low:

I get melancholy if there are more than ten at a party. I've always

[3] H. Rap Brown threatened that the university would be razed if disciplinary action was taken against the black students.

felt like "a man without a peer group." Here I did belong. I was overwhelmed by the suddenness that I could function in a group. . . . It was the beginning of a new vocabulary—"brother," "friend"—a vocabulary of comaraderie, where people didn't talk before.

Another typical feeling was voiced by a freshman who, having been valedictorian of his suburban high school class, drifted into chronic low-grade depression at Columbia, had lost interest in his classes, and was contemplating taking a leave of absence before the crisis arose. He had held strongly liberal views but did little about them. One of his few pleasures was his increasingly frequent use of marijuana. In discussing his heightened sense of human contact in Low, against this background of his freshman year, he said:

Being in Low was like a "trip." You realized the way things should be but aren't going to be very often unless things change a lot.

In connection with his metaphor, it should be noted that there was virtually no use of drugs in any of the buildings, not only because the students agreed that it would be politically unwise to have stores of marijuana in the buildings in the event the police came, but also because they had virtually no desire to "turn on." There was no need for any external agents in order to come alive. A Barnard student in Math said:

You were so turned on, so psyched up about what was going on, you didn't need anything.

It would lead us far afield at this point to enter into a discussion of the function of marijuana in the lives of some of these students and the relationship between pot-smoking and radical activism. But one aspect is germane here—the popular student view that marijuana provides an escape from overwhelming external realities. This was articulated by another striker, talking about his freshman year, before he had become radicalized:

Things at Columbia did not seem right to me anymore. I could not get myself to study, and I could not find any interest in my courses. In looking around me, I saw many in the same shape. Some of my friends seemed lost in a hazy world of beautiful smoke. It was only in this bizarre but wonderful world that they could be at peace with themselves and the world. It was only in this dream that they could escape the grim realities of poverty, racism, Vietnam, and many other issues.[4]

Marijuana is thus described as the palliative for the helplessness of these young students, which manifests itself in their passive retreat.

In the buildings, the exhilaration of being part of a continuous, affectively shared experience involved a paradoxical anonymity. Although people did disagree on both ideology and tactics, there was great stress on accepting the right of others to hold divergent opinions. Students reported relatively little reaction to the specific characteristics of fellow communards, either negative or positive. There was a kind of codified camaraderie. One student said, "There was no time for 'What's your name, what's your major?' You just saw someone and went up and talked with them." Another said, "There was this compulsion to talk with anyone." The essence of this kind of contact was touched on by a student who said:

We were always in a crisis situation. There was such urgency that right away we got to the nitty-gritty.

In this respect, there is a parallel between the subjective experience of pot, the illusion of heightened contact and emotional interchange, and what happened between people in the communes. People were sharing a peak here-and-now affective experience. This was felt by all; any student could turn to almost any other, and each would convey a "I know what you feel" validation of the other's feeling. Who they were beyond that was almost irrelevant. A number of romances grew out of the meeting of boy and girl in the communes, but none that I have heard of survived the return to a more "normal" life routine after the "bust." One undergraduate girl, who had been going "happily" with a boy from another school for a year before the crisis, was very dis-

---

[4] In students who are daily and compulsive users of marijuana, this helplessness before the chaos of the outside world, while perhaps reflecting a valid political and social appraisal, is an externalization of intrapsychic turmoil, in which the ego is overwhelmed. The drug-user neutralizes his unacceptable impulses by a characterologic passivity. This produces the chronic and painful conscious experience of "boredom," from which he seeks relief via the marijuana "high."

turbed because of her behavior in such a brief romance. In the building, she said she found herself "much more physically turned on to people." She had a passionate affair there, but, after the occupation, there was little to hold the couple together, and they parted. She resumed her relationship with her old boyfriend but was quite shaken by the ease with which she had entered into so short-lived an affair, fearing that this might portend a pattern of promiscuity.

The theme of "participatory democracy" was important to these new radicals. Every one of the buildings had daily meetings running for hours and sometimes several meetings in a day. The character of the meetings was to let everyone say anything and everything he had to say, respecting his right to assume any position. There was an implicit understanding that consensus would be arrived at. In certain areas, individualized actions were condoned. For example, when the police came, each student could do as he personally decided to do, from walking out voluntarily to sitting in an open area to barricading himself in a room. With regard to this kind of decision-making, a student said:

I felt I was an essential individual there. Living on campus day to day, you don't make decisions. You're not important. Inside the commune, your own head went forming along with all the arguments, and by the time the meeting was over a consensus was reached.

Each building also sent delegates to the Central Strike Steering Committee, which refrained from taking any action until all four of the buildings agreed. The open-ended quality of the meetings, with everyone allowed to have unlimited say, and the requirement of unanimity among the buildings necessitated six and eight hours of meetings a day. One meeting lasted thirteen hours. The meetings became the fulcrum of the communal life.

Despite the role of the meetings per se, the leadership in the buildings was of profound importance and influence. In these protracted meetings, the leaders did not assume an air of superior experience or wisdom but, rather, clarified the themes, relating the discussion to the immediate issues that demanded a position be taken and, most importantly, catalyzing the participants' sense of having a meaningful part in the decision-making process.

A student in the Math building said:

We had a really superb leader in Tom. If we hadn't had Tom, we would have ended up like Fayerweather. At the beginning, some splits were very, very deep.

Hayden was also called "a really cool head," "calm, with a sense of humor," "a smart person." The feeling was symbolized in one striker's reaction—that the leader had a "fatherly" quality, not in the traditional authoritarian connotation, but, rather, in the sense that he was a wise "resource" person who assists others to actualize what is in themselves.

A similar situation obtained in Low Library with a similar kind of leader. A generally difficult-to-please striker labeled him a "genius."

The climate in Fayerweather differed dramatically. I was told that an envoy came from Fayerweather to Math to appeal for a leader to come to talk to the people in Fayerweather, at a point when anxiety was highly manifest. One rather stable and reliable student described life in Fayerweather:

[It was] like a mob encaged in a box and left to live together. The people in Math were more homogeneously radical, plus Hayden. At Fayerweather, there was constant division and strain—battles for leadership; the question of who would represent Fayerweather. There were accusations of "liberal," "cop-out," "sell out." There was a tremendous amount of distrust. . . .

Another student from Fayerweather said:

Each liberated area was different, ours being wracked with political debate, wrangling and tensions. . . . Anyone who wanted could have left.[5]

Fayerweather alone had a fist-fight growing out of political disagreement at a meeting and hysterical outbursts of crying and fist-pounding at other meetings. A student who felt politically committed to staying said that he avoided the meetings and spent that time in the building's attic, writing. Clean-up, food, and other such committees were difficult to organize.

The contrast between Fayerweather, with its fragmentation and unpleasantness, and Low and Math, with their communal spirit,

_____

[5] As quoted in F. W. Dupee, "The Uprising at Columbia," *New York Review of Books,* Sept. 26, 1968, p. 36.

is largely attributable to the difference in leadership. This factor again underscored the students' need for leadership that they can respect. The whole form of their lives can vary with a leader who allows them a sense of real participation in decision-making, while providing some guidance and structure, and who is in touch with their hopes and frustrations. This reverberates with a major area of grievance that contributed to the evolution of the rebellion— the invisible, insensitive, and unresponsive leadership of the university.

At Avery Hall, with its largely graduate-student population, several leaders emerged early. But, with this older population, the quality of leadership and the personality of the leaders were not nearly so important as to the younger undergraduate rebels.

Efforts to create *leaderless* organizations in many radical and revolutionary groups have had only illusory success. Some members, by virtue of their "natural" qualities of leadership, naturally act as leaders, although they are not formally designated as such. In order to conform to the principle of leaderlessness, then, the participants must deny their perception that there is indeed a spectrum from leaders to followers. Many such groups dissolve because the members are confused as to whether they should respond to the actuality or the mythology of the group. If leadership does not emerge, groups frequently splinter because of lack of organization, planning, and differentiation in function of members —all of which are essential to the continued existence of any group.

Many people—particularly conservative and older people—feel that the hard-core SDS leaders in Low and Math, as well as the members of the Strike Steering Committee, manipulated hundreds of relatively innocent young idealists. The students in the buildings would agree that they were influenced by SDS, but they would insist that the influence was in the direction of helping them to translate their ideals into effective action.

The question of manipulation was raised frequently by the occupiers of Avery, with its more politically moderate composition. A student from Avery said:

At times during the sit-in there was a lot of distrust of SDS. We questioned whether we were being used. In retrospect, we were in agreement. *The bust made everything come true.* All you heard about Grayson Kirk—it all symbolically came true.

His comment touches on the remarkable unconscious dance that Kirk and SDS engaged in, with each responding, in part, to their fantasies of the other.

One's final judgment concerning SDS "manipulation" probably depends on one's political position. For those who conclude that the occupation was a good thing, the view will be that the strikers were shown the truth. For those who conclude that the occupation was bad, the concept that they were duped makes it more palatable. What is clear, however, is that there was no duping in the sense that radical leaders pretended to be liberals and espoused a liberal platform of reform while tricking their following into supporting tactics that would facilitate revolutionary confrontation. The radicalizing was explicit and open. The political critique and goals of SDS were not secret. Most of the white students in the buildings considered themselves to have been radicalized during that spring and not inspired simply to act on behalf of a liberal cause, such as working for Senator Eugene McCarthy, as many previously had done.

In addition to the lack of adequate leadership, other factors made life in Fayerweather relatively disagreeable. Whereas Low and Math had relatively stable populations, Fayerweather, with its open-door policy, had a constantly changing composition The population fluctuated, according to one source, from 150 to 300. The open door served as a safety valve for those in the building, allowing them to leave at peaks of anxiety. Most of the students liberally exercised this option. It also served to dilute markedly the level of communal feeling, which in Low and Math was largely a function of people's helping each other work through their mutual anxieties. At Fayerweather there was no sense of being part of a small group of comrades that shared every moment from beginning to end. Thus one student in Fayerweather said, "I didn't feel ties with everyone else; it was more that we broke into small groups." Another reported that by the third day he was deeply depressed and bewildered. He therefore left and went to a museum with his girlfriend. Once outside the building, he came to a resolution that permitted him to go back far more comfortably at the end of the day. This mode of "outside resolution" was not possible at Low or Math. Problems had to be worked through with the group in an explicitly political milieu. The inevitable result in the closed milieu was a subjective sense of clarity about the issues and, therefore, heightened political commitment.

Avery's students were also allowed to move in and out, and they recognized the decompressing function that this practice served. The conscious and unconscious need for the communal "high" was far less pronounced among the students at Avery than with the younger rebels. In contrast with the undergraduates, they were virtually all committed to a chosen career (although they express great discontent with traditional architecture, traditional teaching of architecture, and the large firms that most of them join after graduation). They also had more stable relationships in their lives than their younger fellows; many more were married or engaged. One twenty-six-year-old summed up the communal experience as:

. . . an extraordinarily fantastic thing—seventy people engaged in this intense experience with a good deal of apprehension and fear. I don't know that I felt "high" emotionally; it was more intellectually —but I really enjoyed it.

A twenty-four-year-old student from Avery related:

The atmosphere was very subdued, but not serious. The average age was older and we wanted to get away from the kids. The days passed very quickly. I didn't read anything. We spent most of the time lolling around—sitting on the ledge. There were no parties, no drugs, no fucking. Some people were uptight about the bust and some about the feeling of being led by SDS. There was no overt attempt at proselytizing, but people knew they were becoming radical. The next demonstration will start with 1,000, not end with 1,000.

The mood in the buildings was enormously labile, from periods of merry abandon to near-panic. For example, in Math, a "Pied Piper" who played bagpipes led everyone in a chain dance through the building. At Fayerweather, there was a dance with a light show shortly before the bust. A student at Low referred to the "popcorn, pleasure orientation." The mood, however, followed a day-night rhythm. A student in Low said:

Every day we would have rising expectations that we would win. Every night there would be a great panic, with people flying around the room not knowing what to do. They had to be calmed.

The anxiety related to the prospect of the police action and was based, in part, on the belief that if and when the police came, it would be at night. Also, one striker explained, during the day, their support on campus was visible; at night, they felt alone. Another major factor was the rising sense of passivity and help-lessness normal before going to sleep. By and large, sleep patterns were disturbed; many students reported sleeping much less than usual and having many disruptive unpleasant dreams, usually pertaining to police beatings or punishment.[6] Although the amount of anxiety varied, the vast majority of the students in the buildings initially felt considerable anxiety about the police bust. Discussing the first day in Math, a girl talked about the preoccupation with a police bust and the posture the occupiers should assume when the bust came:

That caused the biggest amount of dissension of all the arguments at the meetings—the question of violent or nonviolent resistance. Because those who wanted to use violent tactics were really strong about it. [T]he majority of people . . . didn't consider the best tactic; they were just scared of getting their head busted.

This changed quickly as the students accommodated to their new quarters and their peer group and lost their doubts about the legitimacy of their cause and their tactics. Also, the students were allowed to choose various positions, from cooperation with the police in the arrest process to forms of marked passive resistance, so that each of the strikers felt he had an opportunity for some personal choice in handling this experience.

By the time the police did come, most of the students described minimal fear of the prospect before them, alternating with considerable detachment. A relatively small minority felt afraid of

[6] An interesting incidental observation, evidence of the general imprint of the experience in the building, comes from Dr. Howard Roffwarg. In his Sleep Research Laboratory (which is not affiliated with Columbia), he recorded the content of three to five dreams a night, for twelve nights, of a student who was in a building for five days. Over 80 per cent of the student's manifest dream content consisted of material from the sit-in and related campus political activity.

being beaten, although it was expected that such a fear would be widespread. What elicited the greatest fear was the anticipation that the police would use mace or tear gas. The prospect of being beaten was familiar. It was on a psychological continuum from their childhood experience of spanking. However, the idea of chemical immobilization terrified them. It was totally unfamiliar to their past. Significantly, it meant that they would lose control— a universal fear experienced by those under stress—and be at the mercy of the vengeful authority. Furthermore, many of the students had become seasoned protesters at demonstrations where there were clashes with police. They had assimilated this aspect of protesting in a way that is not very different from the acceptance of a lineman on a football team that every Saturday afternoon, in the course of playing the game, he will sustain a few lacerations and contusions but rarely a fracture or a concussion. The prospect of injury has become similarly matter-of-fact with regular New Left protesters. To allay anxiety, they constantly reiterate the litany that the police are carefully trained not to hurt people so badly that hospital in-patient care will be required. (Whether or not police are formally trained in this manner, the belief has, with occasional exceptions, empirical basis.)

In Avery, the level of apprehension was more constant, but without outbreaks of stark fear. It has often been said that the SDS leadership wanted a violent police bust to horrify the liberal middle ground of observers of the crisis and thereby gain their support. Whether or not this is true, for most of the rebels, the police bust was an end that was unconsciously sought, despite the anxiety—both manifest and revealed in dreams. This unconscious wish, observed by therapists working at the time with radical students, was a required component of the students' psychological drama, and the bust was to serve as a highly integrative event. Very few of these young men and women could carry on a relatively successful rebellion, dispossess the President of the university, hold a dean hostage, go through the President's files, dislocate the lives of their nonrebel sibling-students, and exasperate the majority of the mediating faculty, without feeling some unconscious guilt and the expectation of retribution stemming from their individual histories of Oedipal and sibling conflict.

Their dreams showed that, to them, the anticipated bust, with the prospect of their being clubbed, would provide the "punishment" and "expiation" they sought, in a form that would also confirm the righteousness of their cause by exposing the brutality of the enemy—police and administration.[7]

For the students in Low and Math, the bust brought to a close a week filled with a greater sense of their humaneness, of purpose, of the heroic than they had known previously. A sophomore in Low said, simply:

I take my place with seven others at the front barricade. . . . We sing "We Shall Not Be Moved" and realize that something is ending. The cops arrive.[8]

The students had great difficulty accepting the fact that life could not continue to be as it was that week. The people from each building had daily reunions on campus in the days after the police came. While the meetings were ostensibly political in purpose, they were much more a vain attempt to recapture the feelings they had experienced in the buildings. The people from Math erected a huge tent in front of the building for a reunion. A girl from Math said:

There was this nostalgia for the experience afterwards—the tent. People were going around saying there's going to be a Math reunion. The same people would tell the same people 300 times. It was a *"let's all get together"* thing.

A young man who, in his usual life, manages to exist by friction with most people, peers as well as authorities, said:

It would be great if we could stay there forever. I just didn't want to leave the building.

As the rebellion became increasingly successful in terms of the number of students behind barricades and the paralysis of the university, the motivation to see the radical point of view as the only legitimate one increased. This was another mode of attenuating the students' guilt over the effective disruption. They

[7] Further aspects of the police bust are discussed in Chapter VIII.

[8] S. James [J. S. Kunen], "The Diary of a Revolutionist," *New York,* May 27, 1968.

could not tolerate the possibility that anyone connected with the administration or policy-making was not wholly malevolent.[9] If a faculty member was not *for* them in every respect, he was ideologically *against* them. When, at an Ad Hoc Faculty Group meeting, a leader of the strike was asked, "Is there any redeeming aspect to the university?" the student could not reply. Rather than tolerate the possibility that they were wrong—that is, "bad" —the students needed to deny this intolerable concept totally by seeing the parent-university as all bad. In this climate, acts of vandalism become "reasonable" tactics for certain individuals. The demand for amnesty by the strikers, in addition to its political-moral justification, represented psychologically a plea that they should be treated as having done no wrong, only good. Yet the word "amnesty" implies that one has done wrong but should not be punished—which more accurately represents their preconscious feeling. Reciprocally, the administration could not grant amnesty, because that would convey doubt about the absolute legitimacy of *its* position.

I have mentioned earlier the conviction on the part of the Strike Steering Committee, as the sit-in progressed, that they were progressively enlisting support of faculty and other intermediaries in their demand for amnesty. My perception was that this was wishful thinking, in that the faculty—unable to persuade the strikers to follow their recommendations, after expressing understanding of the students' frustrations—acted like a teenager's "progressive parents" who, having permitted a limited degree of rebellion, talk reason and then are enraged when their youngster continues to rebel. At the time of the police action the faculty was actually moving *away* from feeling that amnesty should be granted.

The radical philosophy is extremely well accommodated to the

[9] This position draws theoretical support from Herbert Marcuse's essay "Repressive Tolerance" (in Marcuse, B. Moore, Jr., and R. Woolf, *A Critique of Pure Reason,* Boston: Beacon Press, 1965), which argues the moral justification of acts by a "militantly intolerant" minority against majority forces that "tolerate destruction and suppression." In the Columbia situation, Marcuse's thesis translates into active confrontation with advocates of any position that does not support the immediate termination of the university's community-expansion policy and war-research ties.

need of student rebels to deny any guilt related to their unconscious destructive impulses toward authority. It must be emphasized that this does not mean that the rebellion was motivated by unresolved Oedipal or destructive impulses. Rather, because of the students' psychodynamic development and psychological fluidity at this point in their lives, the symbolic meaning of the administration, and the function of the university for them, such a rebellion will interact with currents of unconscious thought common to many. This is analogous, in the psychoanalytic theory, to the event in the day-residue of a dream becoming the focus of an unresolved infantile neurotic conflict that resonates unconsciously with the symbolism of the dream. Because of some of these conflicts in the rebellion, radical philosophy was practiced rigidly by some to exclude the possibility that other systems or divergent people could be honorably intentioned or legitimate. Disagreement with ends or means evoked accusations of "counterrevolution."

In contrast to the four white student communes, stood Hamilton Hall and the experience of the black students there. The differences were many and significant, reflecting differences in political goals and tactics, in relationship to the university, in personal backgrounds and personalities.

For reasons detailed earlier, I have little information about how the organization of Hamilton Hall evolved, how it was worked out that whites and then community people would leave, how policies were set and decisions were arrived at. Leadership was exercised by the Steering Committee, composed of two undergraduates, a law student, and a graduate student in government. Each was charismatic in his own right, but no one dominated the scene or claimed to be the primary spokesman.

Some black students outside of Hamilton expressed deep resentment at the authority of the Steering Committee. In fact, this was one of the major reasons for leaving Hamilton among students who had originally occupied the building. One such student went so far as to say, "The first night was like reading the totalitarianism of Hitler." However, for the students who remained in Hamilton, especially during the first few days of confusion, the

Steering Committee's strength, apparent clarity of thought, and ability to organize functional living arrangements greatly moderated anxiety, as well as socially unifying and politicizing their constituency.

The fact that the Steering Committee was the sole liaison with the outside powers and communicative channels was of enormous importance in making the group at Hamilton cohesive and allowing the great anxieties generated in the situation to remain manageable. This meant that the views and decisions of individuals inside the building were all based on data given to them by the Steering Committee. The Committee organized the communards for cooking, cleaning, and other such functions. There were even schedules for showers. The high degree of organization conveyed the sense that the Committee really knew what it was doing and provided great comfort for those who remained in the building. The policy of limited entry and exit was also important in that it forced the students to work out all aspects of their common experience together, rather than diffusing it outside.

From the outset, the potential for fear and anxiety was much greater in Hamilton than in the buildings occupied by white students,[10] for two principal reasons: The personal consequences of dismissal from the university were realistically much greater for the blacks than for the white radicals, and the associations that young blacks, particularly those raised in ghetto communities, have for policemen are very different from, and far more fearful than, those of whites. This greater potential for fear and anxiety itself contributed to the more centralized and authoritarian process of leadership in Hamilton Hall.

One student said:

My first reaction [in the first day, before the white students left Hamilton Hall] was very confused. I knew why I was there but didn't really know what was happening or what I was following. The whole thing wasn't real. It was a picnic. There was very much a carnival atmosphere. As soon as the blacks moved in, there was a radical change. We were serious, and afraid, because we took the

[10] The interviews I conducted reflected the views of the more moderate students occupying Hamilton. It is likely that the more militant students had a qualitatively different experience, in which their radical commitment mediated their anxieties and guilt.

consequences seriously—the realities that could happen. The possible consequences affected our life more than any whites. Most of us have no money for another school, and we would lose scholarship possibilities if expelled for radical activities. Also there was the possibility we would get killed by the cops or very messed up.

Other students expressed the same themes:

Most black students are in terror of the police. They know what they can do. For the whites the bust was an awakening. The policeman is for them "your friend." You go to him when you're lost. The blacks had no illusions.

All white students on pot are paranoid about the police. That's not as true with blacks. They live with the reality of the policeman all the time. They build a feeling of being more intelligent than the cop. He [the black] knows the reality of cops—what [the cop] does and does not do.

It was a different feeling with just us in there. All of a sudden it became serious. The festive atmosphere disappeared. There was more tension, and I wondered how it would end, what the police would do, about my future career. . . . I got little sleep because of the anxiety. It was the most anxious period of my life.

Everyone felt impending doom—administrative reaction, police record, suspension—the uncertainty about which, if any, would happen. Everyone acted cool but inwardly was uptight.

Being beaten [by police] is like trying to imagine death. You know it's going to come, but you don't think of it. . . . The policemen wanted to beat us but wouldn't because Harlem was so close. I think if I were white, I'd want to beat a few black heads. There's something about it—go home and tell your wife. It's more a conquering thing if its white on black.

This last student, in his whimsical fantasy about being a white policeman, demonstrates his "identification with the aggressor," the result of a lifetime of fear and helplessness before urban police. Almost all of the students, in or out of Hamilton, asserted that they knew what the police could do, particularly to blacks.

The Steering Committee at Hamilton gave specific attention to the prospect of the police action, recognizing the potential for panic on this issue. A member of the Steering Committee stated:

The students in Hamilton Hall . . . conducted daily drills on how to deal with tear gas and mace, and things like this add, I think, to people's confidence, and consequently minimize the chances of panic.[11]

When the police did come into Hamilton Hall, the students had lawyers there advising them on the arresting process and were prepared to act in a prescribed manner. The students all agreed that they found this preparation anxiety-reducing.

One student described a countermyth that spread through Hamilton Hall early in the sit-in, which was related to a myth outside. It was rumored on campus that the black students were armed and ready to die in the defense of Hamilton Hall; the rumor inside Hamilton was that the police had the building surrounded with weapons and might open fire on the students inside. I asked whether it had occurred to him, while he was in there, that, given the delicate balance of race relations in New York City and the university's proximity to Harlem, it was quite unlikely that violence or harsh administrative punishment would be inflicted on the black students without extreme provocation. He said this was perfectly clear in retrospect but not at the time. Apparently, the roots of fear, based on the conditions of life for blacks in America, are so deep as to defy realistic modification in situations of great stress. Beyond this, however, is a more general anxiety connected with taking a position of forceful challenge and confrontation with the white power structure. Thus, one student wrote:

All the time you were in there you knew what you were doing was wrong, but sort of morally right. There was the constant pressure of what kind of action the university was going to put on you. Would you be suspended or expelled? Are the cops going to come in and beat you up? And the pressures outside. You think that you would rather be outside than inside, and you are wondering what your parents think. You read the newspapers—all these lies—and everyone outside is reading it as truth—so they are against you. The constant pressures—the decisions, decisions. Just the scope of the thing. It was really big. That was a big demonstration, and I'd sit there and think, "Gee, I'm part of this."

This student went on to say:

[11] S. Donadio, "Columbia: Seven Interviews," *Partisan Review,* vol. 35, no. 3 (1968), p. 378.

I was constantly nervous throughout the whole thing. I started to smoke although I had never smoked before. I was in constant fear.

These reports by the students of their great manifest anxiety surprised Professor Immanuel Wallerstein—the one faculty member permitted access to Hamilton during the occupation—because he had observed singing and dancing and signs of a good time.[12] Indeed, there was much singing and dancing, probably, as one student said, "to relieve the tension."

Grier and Cobbs discuss the conflict regarding aggressive assertiveness in blacks:

The black mother . . . must produce and shape and mold a unique type of man. She must intuitively cut off and blunt his masculine assertiveness and aggression lest these put the boy's life in jeopardy.

During slavery the danger was real. . . . The feelings of anger and frustration which channeled themselves into aggression had to be thwarted. If they were not, the boy would have little or no use as a slave and would be slain. . . . Even today the black man cannot become too aggressive without hazard to himself. . . .

What at first seemed a random pattern of mothering has gradually assumed a definite and deliberate, if unconscious, method of preparing a black boy for his subordinate place in the world.[13]

Erikson comments similarly on the subject of assertion in blacks:

Given American Negro history, . . . "instinctive sense" may have told the majority of Negro mothers to keep their children, and especially the gifted and the questioning ones, away from futile and dangerous competition—that is, for survival's sake to keep them in their place even if that place is defined by an indifferent and hateful "compact majority."[14]

Others have discussed this issue,[15] but none has put it more simply and poignantly than an old woman quoted by Robert

[12] Personal communication to the author.

[13] W. H. Grier and P. M. Cobbs, *Black Rage* (New York: Basic Books, 1968), pp. 62–63.

[14] E. H. Erikson, "The Concept of Identity in Race Relations," in T. Parsons and K. Clark (eds.), *The Negro American* (Boston: Beacon Press, 1965), p. 236.

[15] See, for example, A. Kardiner and L. Ovesey, *The Mark of Oppression: Explorations in the Personality of the American Negro* (New York: World Publishing Company), 1951.

Coles in his study of the children who were first integrated into the New Orleans school system. He quotes the grandmother of one of the little girls as follows:

They can scream at our Sally, but she know why, and she's not surprised. She knows that even when they stop screaming, she'll have whispers, and after that stares. It'll be with her for life. . . . We tell our children that, so by the time they have children, they'll know how to prepare them. . . . It takes a lot of preparing before you can let a child loose in a white world.[16]

These passages underscore how black men have been trained over generations not to make demands or assertions that will provoke the white, for the consequences can be deadly. Since World War II, there has been a progressive acceptance of black assertiveness in athletics, outside boxing, so long as the athlete did not get "out of hand" by advocating "black power." In the last few years, the Martin Luther King model of protest has moved to a more militant stance. But even with the current mode of protest, there is the psychological residue of the past—the fears and fantasies and haunting anxieties about what "the Man's" retribution will be. Such conscious and unconscious themes can hardly be eradicated by changes in the attitudes of a new generation. Remember, all the students in Hamilton Hall were born in 1951 or earlier. Blacks particularly understand the rhythm of an oppressive society—that repression begets protest, which engenders more harsh repression, which begets more militant protest, leading to even more repression, and so on. The relationship of the Black Panthers and police across the country demonstrates this.

As repressive tactics toward black protesters diminish, the black will cease to identify with his white aggressor, turning his rage back on himself and thus perpetuating a devalued self-concept. Rather, this rage will turn toward the aggressor—the "white." All "white men" have become a symbolic receptacle for black rage, as all black-skinned persons have been a symbolic receptacle for the white man's projection of what is unacceptable and frightening in himself; individual differences tend to get

[16] R. Coles, *Children of Crisis: A Study of Courage and Fear* (Boston: Atlantic Little Brown, 1967), p. 337.

subordinated. This long-standing theme of the consequences of aggression in white America, which endures in the black psyche, accounts not only for the high level of anxiety in the buildings but also, I suspect, for the fact that many black students remained outside of Hamilton—offering perfectly viable political and moral explanations, but deeply motivated by fear of the consequences of rebellion.

For all these reasons, the level of anxiety the black students experienced was far higher than in the white buildings. Concurrent with this fear (and related to it) was a great sense of brotherhood and expression of one's humanity as a result of sharing danger with peers committed to the same moral goal—of putting oneself on the line for a moral principle rather than personal gain.

A student said:

I am glad I did it. I had always wondered if the opportunity came up —would I? I was proud of myself after. There was a feeling of commitment, a feeling toward each other. We were closer. We came through together. We shared this.

Another said:

I felt important—having done something. I was guilty before, never having stuck my neck out. There's a symbolic meaning to being arrested and going to jail, of having made this sacrifice and mastered fears. It was important to be arrested. It's an institutional ritual. Arrest means being the end of being a "student."

He went on to tell of the bond he now felt with the black Southern civil rights workers of a few years ago, a movement he felt too frightened to join.

Another said:

I proved I had "balls." I had a need to commit myself and prove to myself how far I could go. I wanted to do this, but not irrationally, just to test my courage. I feel more mature and honest with myself. Now I'm glad I'm at Columbia. I realize it's where I should be. Before, I didn't think I could talk with people, except a few. Now with black students we can be at times really different and at times really the same, but be close.

Another said:

There was an openness and mutual concern in Hamilton, a great feeling of unity, of mutual strength. . . . Everyone was willing to pitch in and help.

A student whose background and previous schooling was more typical of the white radicals saw the experience as follows:

For some people, it was the first experience of only seeing "black," of not shielding part of their personality for white observation. It was a new experience in openness. White society expects you to act in certain ways, and if you don't, you are looked down upon. You never feel at home. You feel as if you're in a plastic shell. In Hamilton Hall, we shed the shell and people said what they wanted. People came alive. We felt freer and more human. Everyone was a "sister" or "brother." I really felt there was a humanity and brotherhood toward each other. There was a sense of dignity that gave me pride. For the first time, I was definitely proud of my people for the courage my people were showing.

He added:

When I came out of a week in Hamilton Hall, I had "culture shock." It was strange to talk with whites.

Another student echoed these feelings.

There was a lot of community spirit. I got to know a lot of black students I hadn't known before. It became a black community. It was a really good thing to be part of a black community. Our being there had a meaning. We all understood why we were there.

Another student, who had much more than average experience in the white upper-middle-class world, said:

It changed me a lot. My former white friends seem empty and dead, and black people seem more alive. People notice now that I'm more outspoken. Before, I would think of ghetto blacks as "my kind, but not my type." Now I just think "my kind." It was the best experience of my life.

Thus, the accounts of the experience by the students who spoke with me stressed an underlying anxiety, coupled with a sense of community and brotherhood and commitment that was never before realized in so fulfilling a way. For the first time, they left the arena of private grumbling and embryonic political gestures and felt the exhilaration of their potency as a group, as a black group—a group that could obtain ends, create fear in "the Man," and strengthen their internal bonds. This was, however, at the expense of setting up a bitter cleavage between those of the black student body who were in Hamilton and those who stayed out. This rancor lasted well into the summer.

A black student estimated that twenty-five or thirty students left the building during the six-day occupation. The reasons for leaving were primarily intolerable anxiety, disagreement with the leadership's unwillingness to compromise on the six demands,[17] or disagreement with the power and mode of operating of the four-man Steering Committee.

One of the more curious phenomena in the rebellion was the attitude of the black students in Hamilton Hall toward the white student radicals. The white students were surprised, bewildered, hurt, and then a little resentful when they realized that the black students did not consider them "brothers" in a joint venture. To the contrary, virtually all the black students expressed derogatory feelings about the white radicals.

The Student Afro-American Society had not been particularly vocal on the issue of the gymnasium prior to April 23. The demonstration at the gym construction site, at which a white student was arrested and the fence torn down, was organized by SDS, as were the march from the gym site, the decision to have a student sit-in in Hamilton, and the decision to hold Dean Coleman hostage in exchange for the arrested student.

The use of the gym as an issue by the whites evoked virtually universal resentment among the black students. Typical statements were as follows:

SDS, by raising the gym issue, could get blacks to come in with them. But they were really more concerned with the war in Vietnam and IDA.

The "pukes" defended the gym issue for the wrong reason. They said "community." They couldn't possibly know what the community felt.

They could never feel for the gym issue. They can try to understand but never "experience" it. IDA was more important to them.

[17] The six demands are listed on pp. 3–4.

We were much more serious, tense, and angry than the game-playing whites.

A white student can say all he wants against the system. He can always shave his beard and join the system. Black students can't. They want to join the system. Every other group has melted in.

The blacks felt that the use of the gym issue by SDS was to some degree exploitative or manipulative, or represented a half-hearted commitment. Their underlying feeling was that "you can't begin to know what it's like to be black unless you *are* black." Further, if the fight gets tough, and you are white—particularly well-to-do and white—you can get out. The latter point was confirmed for many blacks by the timidity expressed by the whites when the blacks were willing to assume a militant stand during the first night at Hamilton Hall. Thus, Ray Brown, of the Steering Committee, said:

In addition to . . . ideological and strategic differences there was simply the tactical point that the white students were not prepared to barricade the building as of the time that the decision was made by the black students that that would be the best way of continuing the demonstration.[18]

In this connection, Poussaint and Ladner have analyzed the failure of black-white integration in the civil rights movement in the South in 1964 and 1965:

Most black workers complained that in one way or another the white volunteers acted as if they thought themselves superior to Negroes, an attitude indicating white racism. . . . The black workers complained that these white students arrived and in a week or so behaved like "experts" and "authorities" on all matters concerning the Negro and civil rights.

. . . Black workers, frustrated in their attempt to resolve the chaos precipitated by white participation, began to theorize that the movement was not "ready" for white workers. This attitude propelled the drive "to get the white workers out." This drive took many forms but finally culminated in the development of the psycho-socio-political

18 Donadio, *op. cit.,* p. 377.

concept of "black power" which appears to automatically exclude whites from work in the black community.[19]

Thus, white participation was experienced by blacks as an attitude, conscious and unconscious, of paternalistic superiority. This served to perpetuate white-induced feelings of inferiority and dependency among the blacks. The solution to both the external community problems and the problem of black self-image was for the whites to be assigned responsibility for the behavior of whites, and for blacks alone to carry on the needed activities in black communities.

The situation at Columbia paralleled these dynamics. To have the white students put their bodies on the line over the gym issue, despite the fact that it was done to coerce the white power structure, was experienced by the blacks as a direct challenge. It also must have mobilized guilt that, despite their privately expressed discontent, they had not been willing to risk anything personally up to this point to support their beliefs, while the whites were ostensibly willing to do so. It is a truism that "you can't know what it is to be black unless you are black," and if you are white you can always elect to join the establishment, but these appear to me to be irrelevant rationalizations to bolster the damaged collective ego of the blacks for not having taken an active stand on a "black" issue, while whites did. Given this sequence of events and its concomitant psychological impact, many blacks were unconsciously motivated to assume a more militant and separatist posture. On this point, Bill Sales, of the Hamilton Hall Steering Committee, said:

White students were asked to leave Hamilton Hall because black students wanted to hold at least one building to focus the protest on community-wide issues: in other words, to forge an identification between what black students were doing in Hamilton Hall and what the community was doing in Harlem in relation to Columbia University's racism.[20]

I would suggest that there is no conflict between the sociopolitical

[19] A. F. Poussaint and J. Ladner, "Black Power: A Failure of Racial Integration—Within the Civil Rights Movement," *Archives of General Psychiatry*, vol. 18 (1968), p. 385.

[20] Donadio, *op. cit.*, p. 377.

explanation given by Sales and some of the less conscious forces that motivate men to arrive at consistent and viable policies that command attention.

Finally, the political and social homogeneity of these black students allowed for clarity and unity of purpose politically and for fraternalism socially. As a minority subculture, they had a past history together on campus and would share a future. These bonds made for a more "real" present, in a way that had no counterpart for the white students. They also made the transition easier after leaving the building and obviated the need for "reunions" felt by the white students, who had to recapture the moments in the buildings.

It is my impression that, on balance, there was much more exhilaration and there were fewer painful fantasies among the white students. After the bust, the students who had been in Low and Math were left yearning to recapture the feeling tone of their days there. Most of the students in Hamilton declared that, despite the growth and personal affirmation they all felt they gained, they would not want to repeat the experience.

The rebellion at Columbia involved communal living for close to a week in an "occupied" building. In Chapter IX, I will discuss the psychodynamic interaction between the form of stress felt by the student and the type of gratification inherent in his occupation of a building. Our focus will thus shift to the intrapsychic operations of the individual.

VI: The Students and Their Parents

The occupation of the five buildings brought the radical and militant students into confrontation with the Columbia administration, some fellow students, and the police. In addition, the profound discontinuity it caused in their lives forced the striking students into an intense interaction with and evaluation of two of the most important groups in their lives—their parents and their teachers. The students' action elicited vigorous responses from both, which had deeply vested interests in the outcome. Many of the parents saw their children's futures hanging in the balance; for the faculty, the fate of "their" university hung in the balance. Out of this interaction of the interests of "significant others" with their own behavior, the students experienced perceptions and feelings that for many have been of major significance in their development.

There is no need to belabor here the parents' concern for their student children. Seventy-nine per cent of the white striking students and 28 per cent of the striking black students had upper-middle-class, upper-class, or academic parents. This group of parents have been successful socio-economically and consider themselves enlightened on issues touching their children's lives. Virtually all feel that their views should be given serious weight in their children's significant decisions that will affect their careers.

The more "successful" and educated the parents, the more concerned they seemed to be with the substantive issues and "legitimacy" of the tactics of the confrontation. The less successful and educated the parents, the more they focused on the personal consequences for their child. However, I encountered no parents—regardless of background or of whether they supported their child's actions—who were not concerned about the prospect of their child's being arrested and beaten, having his educational plans disrupted, and perhaps his "record" irrevocably blemished for future purposes. From the student's point of view, whether his parents were overtly opposed to their child's going into the building or supported it, their response was always a significant consideration. At Math, the only unquestioned excuse for leaving the building was, "I have to call my parents." For almost all students, the nature of their relationship to their parents was thrust into a clearer awareness, and, in some instances, altered in a manner that was qualitatively new.

The critical factor was not simply the degree of similarity in the political beliefs of parents and children. Obviously, the parents of most of the striking students had not engaged in dissenting political action of this proportion, although I found family lines that went back to such roots as a father who was a "terrorist" in the IRA and an exiled revolutionary grandmother from Russia. I do not have precise data regarding the sociopolitical attitudes of the parents. However, my impression is that they are predominantly liberal and manifestly concerned with the suffering of deprived and oppressed peoples but have never placed themselves "on the line."

My impressions about the families of the white radicals are completely in accord with the more quantitative data obtained at other "elite" universities. Richard Flacks, studying radical activists at the University of Chicago, has inquired into the sociopolitical views of the parents, their child-rearing values, and the value orientation of the activists.[1] He found that the fathers of the activists were significantly more liberal-radical than the fathers of the "non-activist" students. (For instance, 27 per cent of "activists'" fathers approved of bombing North Vietnam versus 80 per cent of "non-activists'" fathers; 57 per cent of the former approved of civil disobedience in civil rights protests versus 23 per cent of the latter.) However, the finding that 27 per cent of the fathers of radicals endorse a "hawk" policy suggests that there is a sizable minority in Flacks' group of students that have a discontinuity in values with parents.

In addition, Flacks found that the activists tended to come from

[1] R. Flacks, "The Liberated Generation: An Exploration of the Roots of Student Protest," *Journal of Social Issues,* vol. 23, no. 3, 1967.

upper-middle-class families that stressed democratic, egalitarian interpersonal relations; permissiveness (that is, nonintervention if the college-age child made a life decision that they disagreed with); and values other than achievement (that is, the intrinsic worth of intellect, aesthetics, and political ideals). Flacks found values in his group that tended to correlate with these parental values. For example: romanticism (esthetic and emotional sensitivity); intellectualism (concern with and high valuation of ideas and intellectual creativities); humanitarianism (concern with the plight of others and desire to help others); and a de-emphasis on moralism and self-control. Here again, these findings certainly correlate with the spirit of the communes, the tone of the rhetoric, and the substantive arguments of most of Columbia's radicals.

The Columbia students, then, were not the "New Left sons of Old Left activists," as the so-called red-diaper theory has it— that is, they were not the children of activist parents trained since infancy to carry on their elders' work. Rather, very few parents have been radical in action. Most of the parents, however, have been successful in the system. With careers and family structure crystallized, they have been little inclined to take stands that expose them to any risk. The concept of their son's assuming significant risk—in such real and symbolic forms as arrests, police violence, and school suspensions—is new and foreign to them.

Most of the striking students emphasized their parents' capacity to allow them to assume the risks that inhered in this kind of moral-political stand, however they disagreed with the goals and tactics. Two contrasting examples illustrate the point.

One sophomore is the son of a high-ranking officer in a corporation that would be included in everyone's list of firms in the "military-industrial complex." The father is a hawk on Vietnam and the son an ardent dove, with the innocence, romanticism, and much of the philosophy of the "flower children." Father and son have had spirited discussions over the father's company's interests in certain controversial parts of the world. When the crisis began, the son entered a building. Regarding his parents' reaction, he said:

On the one hand, they were concerned. You know, jail record. But, on the other, they were really pleased that I was taking a stand. They believe in action when you should, and they're against apathy. My father said, "It's your life. You're an individual, and you have to go your own way." They're really good people. They don't take what I did personally. Their lives are full, and they don't live vicariously off me. They feel confidence in themselves, and they feel confidence in me.

The parent-son relationship emerged from the crisis stronger. When the chips were down, the parents' philosophy that "principle" and "commitment" were paramount, regardless of whether they supported the content, was maintained. The interaction over the son's role in the rebellion only heightened their mutual respect and affection. After the arrest, the father asked the son to help with a speech he had to give to a nonradical group. At the son's suggestion, father playfully incorporated some of the vocabulary of the New Left.

On the other hand, a graduating senior is the son of a highly successful engineer who had risked a promising future by taking a very active and courageous anti–Joseph McCarthy stand in the 1950's while working for the government. To the present he maintains a Marxist view of society, as does the student's mother. Yet, when the crisis began, both parents tried desperately to force the son not to participate in the rebellion. His description of the interaction over his entering a building was:

This week was "revolutionary" in the family. I went home one day. At first they were very glad to see me. But in an hour we were in a deep argument. A real confrontation. It was amazing—they went through the whole routine—crying, cajoling, yelling, threatening. I thought, "Oh no, I'll get depressed." But I felt unaffected, free, exhilarated. I felt I manipulated them, not they me. I explained where they were. And I did this without turning myself off. Father said they wanted to end it. I said, "No, we'll see it through." At the end, they admitted being motivated by their psychological equilibrium rather than my welfare. The upshot was, they didn't want to be anxiety-ridden over me. I told them this was impossible considering the wide range of things that cause them anxiety. I can't run my life to satisfy them.

What is important was not the argument, but the entirely different psychological underlay. I'm not afraid of them any more. I don't feel I have to lead life by managing my psychological state to balance theirs. I terminated the argument respectfully when I wanted. I felt

I had won the World Series. I never felt so calm and capable and able to relate.

This interview took place late in May. Two months later, this student reported that the confrontation with his family had illustrated to him some of the "double-bind," guilt-evoking essence of what their relationship had been. Whereas before, he had felt guilty and depressed after arguing or opposing them, this was no longer so. Further, the parents had recognized much of this situation and were trying to control their contribution to it, with the result that his visits home had become more comfortable and pleasurable for all concerned. In short, he felt that the strength of his conviction about his decision to enter a building enabled him to take a stand against his parents, which forced all that he described regarding the more basic family interaction to the surface.

Parenthetically, when this young man was in the building, although he took issue with the leadership on certain tactics and positions, his conviction about the "rightness" of his being in the building was very firm. Nonetheless, he experienced considerable depression until, on one occasion out of the building, he had a flood of memories that seemed to be related. They referred to a period when he was about five years old, when there was considerable strife at home, particularly involving a grandmother who was being forced to leave the household. He recalled staying up all night once because, after overhearing some threats of violence, he was afraid that he'd be killed if he fell asleep. With this recollection, coupled with his ability to relate it to his current situation, his depression and fear in the building largely abated. One can speculate that his presence in the building stirred up feelings that resonated with his fears of being murdered in a turbulent household, at night, at the height of his Oedipal period. I do not have enough material to formulate the specific dynamic interrelationships, but this student's reactions are a good example of how such responses are determined both by here-and-now considerations, dangers, and gratifications and by personal historical events and family relationships that, although repressed and unconscious, can profoundly influence the reaction in the present situation.

When major differences did exist between parents and son, and the son relinquished his position in favor of the parents, he did so because of either persuasion or coercion. Although students sometimes spent long hours discussing the situation with their parents, all the students I talked to felt better informed about the specific issues and quite capable of making their own decisions. However, many, although not changed in their view of the correctness of the radical critique and tactics, deferred to their parents' wishes that they remain inactive. These were usually students who had not achieved sufficient differentiation or confidence in their own autonomy to defy their parents' dictates and act without parental or authority support.

The ultimate coercion was the threat to cut off financial support if the son actually participated in the strike.[2] I know of one student who nevertheless entered a building and in fact lost financial support from his parents.

One student who found himself in such a bind was a son of an alumnus who had worked his way through Columbia, where he had become a major campus figure. Then, while maintaining his Columbia contacts and being very active in the alumni group, he became successful in the world of affairs. Upon the occupation of the buildings, the father threatened to cut off support if the son acted out his wish to enter a building. The son acceded, and said:

I was always aware that my parents were not hip to where I was. This intensified the awareness, but I got some understanding of why that was. I could see plainly, Father having been poor and kicked around when he was young and then having "made it." Now he didn't want to be separated from the university he felt he owed everything to. I saw no reason to split, since I always went my own way with my father.

The student appeared to be quite comfortable with this resolution, feeling that he had not "submitted" to his father. He was able to use the mechanisms of denial and rationalization most effectively. Despite his clear submission in this instance, he was able to maintain the illusion ("since I always went my own way")

---

[2] In a parallel manner, the Board of Directors of the 25,000-member College Alumni Association, in the midst of the occupation, explicitly threatened the administration with loss of "support" (that is, financial contributions) if the administration did not follow their hard-line directives for dealing with the "anarchy and mob rule" on campus.

that he had not yielded. He had had a stormy adolescence and suspected that he was at Columbia only because of his father's good name. The college provided one stable and constant framework of his labile life. At this point, he had doubts that he had the resources to make it through Columbia without father's support. So, although markedly ambivalent toward both Columbia and his father, he did not have the psychological capacity to act on his own convictions but, nonetheless, could maintain the illusion of being sovereign. Because he had been more attracted to involvement in "inner experience" (that is, through drugs) than to social action, the thought ("the building occupation is right") was "sufficient," and the act of actually going into the building was relatively incidental. We may further speculate that, with his ambivalence toward authority and the institution, there was also a strong motivation to stay out, but that he delegated that component of his decision externally, to his father. If father were not accessible, he might well have found some other external rationale for staying out, while maintaining the fiction that he really was a full-fledged rebel.

What seemed most common, however, was the experience on the part of white radical students of taking a stand without their liberal parents' clear sanction. By persisting, the students reported a sense of freedom in asserting their own convictions. One leader of the strike related that, when his parents implored him to compromise and withdraw from an active role, he refused without the conscious sense of guilt he usually experienced when opposing them. He took this freedom from guilt as confirmation of his acts and of the deeper motivation behind them.

The information I obtained from the black students regarding their interaction with their parents and their family histories was much more limited than from the white students. Black students were generally reticent in discussing the value systems and dynamic interplay within the family. A few simply refused to talk of their families. Almost all were guarded about expressing resentful or negative feelings toward their parents. This manner of presenting their families probably reflects the repeated experience of finding that whites have condescending judgments to make about the nature of the black family, based on white, middle-class norms, and have little understanding of the strengths and virtues of the black-family variations from these norms. The black student then feels called on to defend his family with elements of both shame and resentment toward the white.

In any event, to the extent that they spoke to this issue, all the black students described a parental attitude of concern for the risks but confidence that the son was in a good position to make the right decision and the assurance that the parents would back him whatever he decided. This attitude seemed independent of the parents' educational or economic background, as well as of whether the student was or was not among those who occupied Hamilton.

As one student said:

They were upset about the arrest. Not angry, upset. I feel closer to my family. They want me to do what I want to do and they will stand by.

Another said:

My parents responded with concern about my education and the consequences. Their first response was, "My God, get out!" Then I explained. I told them the whole point in being parents, "You have to have faith in me." After I explained, they were more sympathetic. They are black parents who want me to get the same education as whites and then really be in a position to help.

Another student who was also inside Hamilton Hall said:

They felt whatever I did was O.K. They said, "We don't know the situation. You do."

The students who remained outside gave similar pictures. A Barnard student described her parents as saying:

"We are glad you're not in, but if you want to go in, we'll support you."

Another student, whose parents were both college graduates, said:

They wanted to see what my position was. They didn't force me. They just wanted to see that I had a logical position for what I did.

There are major differences between the black-family experience and the white-middle-class model. The variations in types of interaction seemed greater for white students and their parents. Many of the black parents, although frightened, were apparently gratified that their sons were able to protest against the racism the parents had been subjected to but, having spent their youth in a more repressive time, could not take a stand against. It is almost as if their sons recognized this and felt some compassion for their parents. They did not see themselves as repudiating parental values in this struggle but rather as fighting where their parents could not.

There were several themes over which white students and their parents differed. Most of the "liberal" parents prescribed gradualism in contrast to the relatively uncompromising confrontation pursued by the strikers. The disagreement was not over goals and ideals, but over tactics and timing. The explanation for this generational difference is complex—related to the interaction between historical events, with their emotional climate and symbolic impact, and the psychological development of the individuals of any generation. The formative psychosocial years for the parents were qualitatively different from the comparable epoch in their sons' lives. As a result, they were out of phase with the tempo of their radical sons' desperate demand for change *now* and their deep cynicism that those in power had any intention of voluntarily giving relief to the economically exploited, the politically disenfranchised, and the socially and psychologically oppressed.

In addition, most liberal parents tended to question the wisdom of their sons' taking the risks involved in confrontation politics— being arrested, injured, or suspended (and thus becoming eligible for immediate draft). Quite apart from the practical disadvantages of having a criminal record, the idea of being arrested has very primitive associations of guilt and badness. An older student described saying goodbye to his three-year-old son before entering a building:

My son was upset. He said, "Daddy, don't get arrested. You're not a bad guy." I explained to him that I wasn't a bad guy.

(It is largely because of the universality and unconscious meaning of this symbol that a book such as Kafka's *The Trial* remains a compelling and timeless classic.) To the extent that parents are unconsciously fused with their children—that is, assign portions of their own unconscious to their children and have unconscious fantasies of immortality via the lives of the children—the arrest represents a symbolic indictment of them—not for sins they are conscious of, but for the repressed sins of their unconscious. The child's arrest is affirmation of their failure. The arrest is fused with the beating, and the parent-child linkage is similar to that as over the arrest. In addition, so much of early parenting involves protecting the child against pain and hurt that to stand helplessly by as the child is beaten is a source of great agony—an agony of helplessness. The sources of the anxiety may be multiple. For some parents who are highly ambivalent toward their sons, particularly at this age, the anxiety relates to the police, who are vicariously acting out the parents' own anger and destructive impulses toward the child. We are all horrified at the direct expression by others of destructive impulses that we keep in a state of repression in ourselves.

Finally, the prospect of suspension is so opposed to the traditions of most of these parents, who have used university education to catapult them into the affluence of their current lives, that it also evokes resistance. All parents have fantasies about the way in which their child's life will unfold. The scenario is written by them, usually based on their values, wishes, and interests, and does not necessarily represent a realistic projection from the child's constellation of personality characteristics, interests, and capacities. The greater the disparity between the parent's fantasy and the son's actual behavior, the greater the narcissistic frustration to the parent. For virtually all of these parents, a successful academic career is a central pillar in their fantasy construct for their child. Thus, the possibility of suspension is deeply disturbing to them.

Perhaps most simply, for some parents, the children's commitment to activism in the pursuit of a better world carries with it the haunting possibility that the parents will in the end be forced to experience the grief of the parents of James Chaney, Andrew Goodman, and Michael Schwerner, the young civil rights workers who were murdered in Mississippi. This was the fear expressed to me by the parents of several radicals.

In the end, the son's capacity to empathize with his parents' concerns and the parents' capacity to express them freely, but as sympathetic partisans, could lead to what one senior described as "the best and most open times we ever had." This kind of response was probably forthcoming only from students who had already been able to negotiate a clear differentiation of themselves from their parents and felt a significant degree of autonomy. It also required parents who had achieved sufficient autonomy to allow their sons to do what they felt they had to do, without feeling their own "identity" compromised.

It was my general observation that in the family interactions in which parents could express their concern but recognize their son's right to make his own decisions, the radical son tended to be characterized by "postconventional, principled morality"[3] and to be relatively idealistic[4] in their sociopolitical philosophy. Also, it was my clinical impression that these students had relatively good ego integration.[5]

In contrast, when there was a clear "discontinuity" in the moral or political values of family and student son, and/or where the parents opposed to the end the son's participation, the students politically tended toward nihilism and had poorer ego integration than the group with "continuity" in values and mutual respect, without attempts at coercion, for each other's position.

If the son's sociopolitical ethic is opposed to the parents', apart from other factors in the society that catalyze the development of higher moral reasoning, the likelihood is great that this represents, or at least encompasses, either a failure of identification, particularly with the same-sex parent, or an elaboration of a theme of rebellion against the parents. In such cases, there is greater probability that the radicalism will be rigid and inflexibly practiced. Also, since the radicalism is more fused with rebellion

[3] As defined and discussed in Chapter IV, page 89.

[4] In Chapter IX, I shall present a schematic continuum of radical behavior, from "idealistic" to "nihilistic."

[5] I am using this term to condense the primary aspects of adaptation that clinicians consider in making a judgment about the psychiatric status of an individual. It includes such factors as capacity to perceive reality and react appropriately, to form loving relationships, to experience pleasure, to adapt to changing situations, to express a wide range of appropriate affect, and so on.

qua rebellion, there will be a greater need to act with compensatory "absolutism" or covert self-destructiveness.

I think that these impressions fit the more theoretical psychoanalytic framework proposed by Seymour Lustman, who distinguishes between "symptoms" and "character traits." Whereas "character traits" are more or less adaptive and consistently related to reality, "symptoms" are geared to inner reality only and are poorly adaptive. Whether a sector of behavior represents a character trait or a symptom relates to the congruence of that behavior with the conscious and unconscious needs and wishes of the parents. Lustman says:

If the structural development of the child—molding and being molded by the parental relationships—produces behavior which is consonant with the unconscious needs of the parents, the likelihood of a character trait is enhanced. The internalization of such aspects of the love object have greater likelihood of becoming integrated, without tension, in the developing ego core. On the other hand, when behavior is an alien to the superego demands of the parent, the likelihood is greater for crystallization as superego elements with corresponding tension and the possibility of symptom formation. This is particularly so if a parental superego conflict is internalized.[6]

Thus, in those students who experienced continuity with the parents' political-moral values and attitudes toward action, the child's behavior would tend to have a quality of flexibility and adaptiveness, because it would not be so dominated by unconscious forces. One implication is that the student would feel less need to undo the gains of or get himself punished for his political efforts, because the behavior would not be so ridden with guilt produced by a harsh superego. On the other hand, when discontinuity characterized the relationship of the parent-child values and attitudes, the political action would tend not to be fulfilling of any core ego-ideal. Rather, it would represent a more compulsive, joyless, defensive operation, more likely to be doomed in the end.

The continuity of social and political values between parents

[6] S. L. Lustman, "Defense, Symptom and Character," in *The Psychoanalytic Study of the Child,* vol. 17 (New York: International Universities Press, 1962), pp. 236–37.

and radical sons is a more complex issue than it appears to be. While it is true that many of the white radical students have heard liberal-humanitarian values expressed at home, it was generally in an atmosphere of inconsistency between ideology and actual life style.[7] They have listened to civil rights rhetoric while at the same time observing the social and economic exploitation of the family's black maid. Many of the white students feel that their parents had the choice of fighting for social justice but "copped out," taking the safer and more remunerative path of life. They are angry at their parents for "leaving to them" the fight against the war in Vietnam and injustices in the ghettos at home. In this connection, I recall an incident in the spring of 1966, during the course of therapy with a student who later became an active radical at Columbia. The student saw me at a peace demonstration. In the following session, he became tearful for the first time, after talking about our meeting there. The feelings that had been evoked related to his disappointment and anger at his father's unwillingness to take a politically active stand, in contrast to the "idealized" image that I seemed to present by virtue of my participation. Keniston noted the ambivalence of the radicals in his study toward their fathers, based in part on their view of their fathers' unwillingness to act on their perceptions of the world.[8]

My impression at Columbia is that the sons are critical of their mothers on the same basis but believe that it is more the role of the male to be a political activist and risk-taker—a concept that the women's liberation movement has set out to overturn. Also, the father's activities have usually been the instrument of the family's socio-economic success, so he is seen as being the more significant "cop-out."

Derber and Flacks, on the basis of interviewing University of Chicago students and their parents, have identified a "variant" in the spectrum of family constellations of white radical students, which, they believe—by virtue of its child-rearing emphasis on autonomy, authentic behavior, ethical humanism, plus the value of

[7] See S. M. Lipset, "The Socialism of Fools: The Left, the Jews, and Israel," *Encounter,* vol. 33, no. 6 (1969), pp. 24–35.

[8] K. Keniston, *Young Radicals: Notes on Committed Youth* (New York, Harcourt, Brace & World, 1968).

activity devoted to eliminating inhumane conditions—explicitly socializes the children for radical social action.[9]

The issue of continuity and discontinuity of values between parents and activist students has been the subject of an illuminating study by Jeanne Block.[10] She studied participants in the 1964 Free Speech Movement sit-in at Berkeley. Those subjects who "rejected" parental political values and denied the influence of their parents on their own personality and value orientation she called the "discontinuity group." The "continuity group" was characterized as accepting parental sociopolitical values and believing that their parents exerted positive influence on their development and values. As part of her study, she had the students describe themselves. Her findings are summarized in Table 10.

TABLE 10

SELF-DESCRIPTION

Continuity Group		Discontinuity Group	
Male	Female	Male	Female
Conventional	Vitality	Amusing	Doubting
Responsible	Confidence	Creative	Shy
Masculine	Responsible		Self-denying
Orderly	Independent		Rebellious
Practical	Assertive		Stubborn
	Talkative		Needs approval
	Perceptive		Worrying
	Informed		

Block then had her subjects give their *ideal* self-description, summarized in Table 11.

One of the noteworthy findings is that the men in the discontinuity group express ideals that are consonant with the "hippie" ethic, while the women place a premium on "keeping cool,"

[9] C. Derber and R. Flacks, "An Exploration of the Value System of Radical Student Activists," paper presented at American Sociological Association meetings, San Francisco, California, Aug. 28, 1967.

[10] J. Block, "Rebellion Re-examined: The Role of Identification and Alienation," presented to the Foundations Fund for Research in Psychiatry Conference on "Adaptation to Change," Puerto Rico, 1968.

TABLE 11

IDEAL SELF-DESCRIPTION

Continuity Group		Discontinuity Group	
Male	*Female*	*Male*	*Female*
Foresight	Logical	Loving	Adventurous
Self-controlled	Considerate	Authentic	Aloof
Critical	Foresight	Creative	Uninvolved
Argumentative		Artistic	Calm
		Playful	Reserved
			Free

paradoxically expressing values of noncommitment despite having been participants in this act of "commitment."

One of the most important aspects of Block's work is the demonstration of heterogeneity within the radical movement. These differences are not random but relatable to the students' personal past, particularly the nature of the parents' values and the parent-child interaction, as Block goes on to show. She describes the child-rearing philosophies and practices in the families of the continuity and discontinuity groups. Table 12 summarizes the differences:

TABLE 12

CHILD-REARING PHILOSOPHY AND PRACTICE

Continuous	Discontinuous
Encourage $\begin{cases} \text{reflection} \\ \text{curiosity} \\ \text{questioning} \end{cases}$	Emphasize $\begin{cases} \text{appearances} \\ \text{conforming to others'} \\ \text{expectations} \end{cases}$
Emphasize $\begin{cases} \text{individual thought} \\ \text{individuation} \end{cases}$	Attempt to circumscribe $\begin{cases} \text{thinking} \\ \text{reactions} \\ \text{behavior} \end{cases}$
Misbehavior *not* ignored—discussed with child (i.e., response "rational," not "punitive")	Misbehavior treated by punishment
Family conflicts acknowledged and negotiated	Socialization by prohibition
Discuss contemporary political-social issues with children	

The differences in values, self-description, and family climate between Block's two groups suggest that there is one group of radicals that has been reared in a communication system involving mutual respect and who possess values compatible with idealism and commitment. They can sustain frustration and seem equipped to adapt to the contradictions, uncertainties, and injustices in today's world by reasoning, flexibility, and willingness to act as agents of change. Another group has been raised in a system of rigid controls and psychological manipulation for the fulfillment of the parents' needs, not the child's. Block concludes that "rebelliousness" is more characteristic of this group, but they are also likely to move back and forth between organized social protest and more alienated patterns of youthful experimentation with their inner world—that is, drugs. Their capacity for delayed gratification is likely to be impaired, and, hence, so is their capacity to work in a long-term programmatic endeavor to obtain benefits for others.

This description of the discontinuity group corresponds to the conceptualization of the relationship between aspects of child-rearing and family dynamics, on the one hand, and student radicalism, on the other, by Bruno Bettelheim, Director of the Orthogenic School at the University of Chicago. He correlates the activities of student radicals with what he calls the "being-permissive-if-it-kills-me" syndrome in parents, particularly mothers.[11] Bettelheim feels that these students were indulged as infants and young children, not out of any sensitivity to the child's needs, but compulsively, in order to make the mother feel good about herself.

Bettelheim, who clearly does not feel kindly disposed to campus radicals, says: "When I see some of these way-out students, unwashed and unkempt—though of course nothing I say here is true of all of them—I cannot help thinking: 'There goes another youngster who, as an infant, was practically scrubbed out of existence by his parents in the name of loving care.' " He goes on to suggest that emotional duplicity on the part of the parents—the manifest show of concern coupled with neglect of the real

[11] B. Bettelheim, "Children Must Learn To Fear," *New York Times Magazine*, April 13, 1969, pp. 125–45.

emotional welfare of the child—is largely behind the students' resentment of professors who place research before teaching.

Bettelheim's conception is one of students searching for issues that correspond symbolically to their early traumata, in a model that stresses the students' pathology, not society's. But whether or not one is sympathetic to Bettelheim's politics, it must be acknowledged that he describes an entity that does exist and a family experience that alerts the adolescent to hypocrisy but usually turns out distrustful, nihilistic radicals.

In her studies of the moral style of student protesters,[12] Haan obtained self-descriptions of the family backgrounds of her subjects. Although the data are somewhat scant, the "individually principled" [13] students seem to have been permitted to be "importantly affected by their own life experience in their own time and place." The parents are not viewed as "permissive" but, rather, as insisting on their own rights while also respecting the needs of the children. The formal power of the parents to "give and take away" is not emphasized. But there is a focus on the responsibilities of each family member as well as definition of individuation.

In summarizing the data on "instrumental relativists," [14] Haan states that the parents of these students did not seem to encourage the development of a sense of responsibility and autonomy. The males were alternately pressured, neglected, and indulged. The females appeared to still be quite dependent on their immature mothers. In a description similar to Bettelheim's, Haan suggests that the instrumental-relativist students were indulged for their mother's narcissistic needs. This indulgence, motivated by parental convenience and self-interest, leads to unpredictability and lack of clarification of rights and responsibilities and, hence, is a less than optimal basis for moral development.

Haan's data, like Block's, are entirely in accord with the pat-

[12] See Chapter IV, pp. 85–89.

[13] The "individually principled" individual acts and is governed not only by social rules but by principles of a consistent and universal ethical system.

[14] The "instrumental relativist" individual acts in the service of satisfying his own immediate needs and impulses without any reference to a consistent social code or ethical system.

tern I observed at Columbia of people united under a common cause of radical endeavor, who initially espouse the same ideals and principles, but who differ vastly in psychodynamics as well as level of cognitive and ethical development. After the initial phase of radicalism, I dare say that the instrumental relativist and the individual-principled activist will try to steer the movement in very different directions. The instrumental relativists will move in "nihilistic" directions and be motivated in political decision primarily in terms of gratification of their personal needs. In contrast, individual-principled radicals will maintain the "idealistic" qualities of the radical movement and will subordinate their own needs in the struggle to achieve humanitarian change.

All this can be translated into the general thesis that the more mutuality exists between parent and son, the greater the son's freedom from guilt and the less inflexible his need to rebel or disrupt current authority.

These are general trends, and there are exceptions—nonradical students whose family histories suggest that they "should" be; students who are rigid and nihilistic but whose family climate appears to be "continuous" and healthy; students who are quite "idealistic" and healthy, although their relation to their families is filled with friction and discontinuity. This is all to say that knowledge of the values of the family, the child-rearing practices, and even the moral reasoning and values of the student in the present, while strongly suggestive, is not sufficient to allow any certainty in predicting whether the student will be radical and, if so, the nature of his radicalism. There is no reason to think that this is less true of black students, although virtually no research data exist on the question. The relationship of the student to his parents' value system is a major factor, but it stands in a dynamic balance with the character structure of the student, his psychodynamics, and the external sociopolitical situation in determining the ideology and commitment of the student.

VII: The Students and the Faculty

The students' reaction to the faculty, like their response to the university,[1] is a composite of rational, objective appraisal and distortion based on needs and wishes that are transferences from attitudes, perceptions, and experiences with parents and parent surrogates in the earlier years of life. That parent and teacher tend to be cognitively fused is well illustrated in the following description by a student:

My parents were terrified but knew I was right. They always knew I was right but thought I couldn't win. This fear—this mother's fear that she's going to lose you. This overprotectiveness I just couldn't take. Every time mother saw me, she'd practically break down. It just made me angry. My mother has always succeeded in the past, not always, but practically destroying me, not destroying me, but preventing me from sort of freeing myself. The thing is I knew they knew I was right. She'd say something like, "I know you're right, but you can't get away with it." This sort of fear. This is what made me angry. It's a typical syndrome because the faculty was the same way. You know, the junior faculty and some of the intermediate faculty. Someone like Professor ———— who kept professing himself a radical and said, "I'm with you. I support you all the way, but Goddammit—this isn't what he said, but practically the

[1] The idea of the fusion of university and faculty was also expressed in the commencement address by Professor of American History Richard Hofstadter, who spoke to the graduates in place of President Kirk. Hofstadter said: "[I]t seems to me entirely appropriate, and also symbolic, that on this unusual occasion a member of the faculty should have been asked to speak. Trustees, administrators, and students tend to agree that in ultimate reality the members of the faculty are the university, and we of the faculty have not been disposed to deny it." This view would undoubtedly be challenged by large numbers of students, who feel that *they* are the university. For the radicals, the concept of "free university" would break down such group distinctions in favor of a "one-person-one vote" principle.

sense of it—"You can't get away with it. Don't you realize you can't win? You can't do it."

I mean, this is sort of the same line. And it's more maddening because it's your friends who are your most dangerous enemies in a case like this. They can demoralize you tremendously. I pointed it out to them, but they'd say, "Yeah, I know you're right. But still." Like she [Mother] was afraid I'd get killed.

In this statement the student focuses on the point in the spectrum of faculty responses that most nearly corresponds to his parents' reaction. The statements attributed to mother and teacher are identical ("You can't get away with it"). He is not unaware of the total range of faculty behavior, but what emotionally engages his concern is what meshes with his set of expectations and familiar familial experiences.

Similar in principle was the response of the striker mentioned in Chapter VI, who said of his relationship with his parents that this period, despite differences, was "the best and most open time we ever had." He had been very close to one professor during his four years at Columbia and considered him his mentor. The student and his professor, a liberal who was highly sympathetic to the strikers, argued vigorously over tactics. The student said later:

Now we can disagree. He had felt before that I was too dependent on him. I could tell him to go to hell and emerge now with a different and stronger friendship.

Here again, the attitudes and relationships to faculty members that engage the student's primary attention were almost superimposable with what transpired with his parents.

Obviously, the responses to parent and to favored faculty person did not move in tandem for all students, because not all faculty acted in the crisis in the same way as parents. One student described his parents as "supportive, but the more I became violent the more I seemed a 'red fascist' in their eyes . . . but they were sympathetic." Then, speaking of his relationship to a professor whose protégé he had been for several years, he said:

One of the most terrifying things to see was professors we loved in the faculty cordon [2]—Professor ———. I realized how sentimental I had been. I was one of the few who felt betrayed. Most people expected it. I was very angry and slurred Professor ——— openly. He was shaken. We keep a hot line now.

For this student, the "faculty" was one individual, and the disparity between the student's relationship to his parents, whom he saw as, in the main, supportive, and his relationship to his mentor, whom the student saw as nonsupportive because he stood with the faculty cordon, reflects a realistic perception of the difference between the two. If not for this reality, according to my hypothesis, he would have focused his greatest attention on the far-left liberals on the faculty, those corresponding to his parents in their sympathy with his goals.

The parentification of faculty is further evidenced in this statement by a student:

If people [faculty] didn't come inside buildings, they would get us killed. Rather than risk tenure, they were willing to let their loved children get killed.

It is tempting to talk of "the faculty" as though it was a homogeneous unit, and, indeed, many authors, as well as students, have done so. The Columbia faculty did not, however, have the unitary position one sees publicly put forth by trustees, the top university administration, or the Strike Steering Committee, despite differences expressed in private. English Professor Eric Bentley made the following categorization of the faculty:

Getting down to cases, the Columbia faculty divided three ways, the three *political* ways: conservative, radical, and center. "Conservative" in this context meant seeing the issue as one of discipline. For the conservatives the question always was, "Shouldn't people like Kirk discipline people like Rudd?" and it was a rhetorical question: The answer could only be yes. "Radical," of course, meant the opposite: "Rudd must be right: Kirk must be wrong." And center meant—as center usually means in revolutionary situations—"We're all terribly nervous and hope there won't be violence." That was how I saw our

[2] He is referring to the Ad Hoc Faculty Group members who stood among the hedges under President Kirk's window to prevent clashes between members of the Majority Coalition blockade and the occupiers of Low Library. Many of the radicals perceived this behavior as tacit sanctioning of the blockade.

faculty divide, and the division was definite enough and unchanging enough for one to see fairly early that there could be no such thing as faculty unity, let alone faculty action.[3]

When radical or militant students spoke of "the faculty" as a generic class, their concept and feeling related almost exclusively to the "liberal" group, those whom Bentley calls "the center." The conservatives, except for a few who served as advisers to the Majority Coalition, were relatively little in evidence on campus during the sit-in. The "radicals" weren't radical themselves; that is to say, they were not willing to abandon their formal roles in the existing university machinery to "force" the university to meet the radicals' demands, although they were strong champions of the student radicals. They were, with a few exceptions, drawn from the younger, junior, nontenured faculty. They numbered between sixty-five and one hundred. Despite their passionate caucuses, they were essentially ineffectual as a political force.

The concept "faculty" eventually became embodied in the members of the Ad Hoc Faculty Group, who were mainly the liberal-center group from the faculty of the college. This self-appointed committee attempted to play the role of mediator in the conflict. It was listened to but never formally recognized or granted arbitrating power by either of the contending forces. I would agree with the assessment of the Group's effectiveness given by sociology professor Immanuel Wallerstein, who served on the Steering Committee of the Ad Hoc Group:

If you are asking me whether the chances were ever particularly high that faculty mediation would have succeeded, I would say, in retrospect, no. That is to say, for various reasons the positions of the Administration and of the Strike Steering Committee, as well as that of the black students in Hamilton Hall, were relatively intransigent on certain fundamental issues. That became quite clear to the Ad Hoc Faculty Group and we stated it publicly. It was very hard to compromise on those issues.

But in retrospect I also think that the whole situation would have been far worse had there not been an attempt at mediation. The attempt at mediation—even though it failed—is one of the things that kept the university from collapsing even more than it did.[4]

[3] S. Donadio, "Columbia: Seven Interviews," *Partisan Review*, vol. 35, no. 3 (1968), pp. 367–68.
[4] *Ibid.*, p. 355.

Although there was no indication that the administration expected the accumulated wisdom of this faculty body to be the instrument of solution, almost everyone else did, and, in the end, most of the students, whatever their position, felt that the faculty had failed their cause. Thus, many professors who were sympathetic to the strike and critical of the administration agreed with anthropology professor Marvin Harris, who stated that:

In the present crisis this enlightened faculty has given little evidence that it comprehends how loudly dignified silence speaks for the *status quo*. Most astonishing is the failure of the liberal Columbia establishment . . . collectively to take a principled and unambiguous position on a single important issue in the current dispute.[5]

In contrast, government professor Zbigniew Brzezinski, who was sympathetic to the administration and critical of the strikers, wrote of the "legitimist reformers and intellectuals" of the faculty:

In a revolutionary situation, their desire for power yet their inability to side with one or the other side prompt intellectuals to adopt a third posture, namely that of interposing themselves between the revolutionary and antirevolutionary forces. . . . [I]n the process of interposing themselves, they are inclined to apply most of the pressure against the established authority, with which they have many links, rather than equally against established authorities and the revolutionary forces on behalf of reformist appeals. In effect, irrespective of their subjective interests, the legitimist reformers and intellectuals in a revolutionary situation objectively become the tools of the revolutionary forces, thus contributing to further aggravation of the revolutionary situation and radicalizing the overall condition.[6]

These statements illustrate the prevailing feeling among representatives of various faculty and student factions that the faculty, as an active party in the struggle, was not simply ineffectual and disappointing, but somehow abetted the "other" side. Probably, the trustees and administration were not disappointed or surprised; they, after all, had never delegated any power of binding arbitration to the faculty or asked for any votes of confidence in controversial administrative actions, such as calling in the police.

[5] M. Harris, "Big Bust on Morningside Heights," *The Nation*, June 10, 1968, p. 757.

[6] Z. Brzezinski, "Revolution and Counterrevolution (But Not Necessarily About Columbia)," *The New Republic*, June 1, 1968, p. 24.

The students' initial expectations regarding the faculty were expressed by a freshman who spent his time during the crisis walking around campus and listening to the campus radio station. This opinion was widely prevalent among the entire undergraduate body, except for hard-core radicals. He said:

I thought the faculty would do the trick. I really had great faith that they had rapport with both sides. I guess they didn't. They're still smart guys, and I still like and respect the faculty. I would have gone along with anything they said. When it looked like a union between students and faculty, it was heart-warming.

A great concern throughout the conflict was that, if fighting broke out between student factions, irreparable damage would be done to the college community. There were numerous instances when clashes were about to take place between middle and conservative students, on one side, and strikers, on the other. With rare exceptions, when a faculty member (identified by a white armband made of handkerchiefs or torn rags) interceded, the moderate or conservative student listened respectfully and followed the directive of the teacher. At a moment when the outbreak of fighting seemed imminent, tall, thin, bespectacled Professor Belknap could say, in his scholarly voice:

I am Robert Belknap of the Russian Department, chairman of freshman humanities. You've read those books by Plato and Aristotle and Thucydides. You know that violence is no good.[7]

And the clash was averted.

The radicals, by contrast, took a cavalier and sometimes frankly contemptuous attitude toward faculty, particularly toward the liberals who counseled compromise. When Professor Alan Westin, Chairman of the Ad Hoc Faculty Group, stated that he believed negotiations had been progressing well, a spokesman for the Strike Steering Committee responded publicly that the talks had all been "bullshit." Most of the faculty responded to this denigration of their efforts with hurt and outrage.

This is conveyed in the following presentation of the faculty's "hedge-ledge" role by a student who occupied President Kirk's office:

[7] Reported in F. W. Dupee, "The Uprising at Columbia," *New York Review of Books,* Sept. 26, 1968, p. 34.

Act I—The Ad Hoc Faculty Sandwich Decision. It is very late at night, virtually early in the morning. The Ad Hoc Faculty Group has been meeting through the night. They are in their second hour of debate on what to do about the sandwiches.

The jocks have surrounded Low Library. Outside the jocks stand angry pukes who want to get food to the protesters inside. White-armbanded Ad Hoc Fac. stand tensely between the jocks and the building, unsure what to do, waiting for the Sandwich Decision.

Back at the meeting, rapprochment has been reached between dissident factions. Votes have been taken. The chairman reads the committee's decision: If the sandwich-carrier tries to cross the hedge, he may be stopped by the jocks.

But if he should reach the ledge, he may no longer be stopped by the jocks.

THE HEDGE IS THE JOCKS', THE LEDGE IS THE PUKES'.
Curtain
End Act I [8]

It was the hope of many strikers that they would not merely arouse Columbia's faculty from its apathy but also radicalize it. This intense wish distorted their perceptions so that they felt the faculty was moving in the direction of recommending amnesty while they were in the buildings. One striker said to a faculty member, early in the sit-in:

Look, you agree with us about the gym and IDA. You've been hiding and did nothing about it. We tried to do something with this so-called due process, and couldn't. Now everything is polarized. The sides are clear, so how can you help but join us? Also, since you know we're right and there was no other way, how can you not give us amnesty?

This argument strongly parallels the wish that is universal among adolescents, to have their parents become convinced of, and then endorse, their new-found wisdom, be it about politics, drugs, sexual mores, or other nontraditional attitudes and practices.

But students are naïve in their hopes for rapid transformation of either established faculty or parents. Despite the fact that a large segment of the faculty was in total agreement with the strikers on the substantive grievances of the gym, the university's general real-

[8] J. S. Kunen, *The Strawberry Statement: Notes of a College Revolutionary* (New York: Random House, 1969), pp. 118–19.

estate policy, its ties with the Defense Department, and the inability of faculty and students to influence policy-making at Columbia, "radicalism" is fundamentally unappealing to most faculty people. The personality and temperament that are generally necessary to obtain the credentials to become a faculty member are those of the intellectual who is more interested in study and inquiry than activism. Most faculty are more comfortable with the concept of the university as an open forum for exchange of thought than with the idea of the university as an arena for political action and confrontation.[9] Most prefer the view of the campus as a sanctuary from a sick society, rather than as a microcosm of the society, as the radical does. It is seen as a place in which the free and creative intellect can formulate social solutions and which therefore must be preserved, not obstructed and closed down. For most faculty, to close a university by unrelenting confrontation is the first stage of anarchy and the destruction of humanistic order.[10]

In the end, the faculty are employees of the university and, among other things, have a specific economic vested interest in the outcome of conflict. No more university, no more job. For teachers with families and little or no independent incomes, there is realistic economic anxiety. This is very different from the response of the bright, economically advantaged radical student who is not dependent on the university for his survival. As one striker said, meaning it less literally than in the spirit of his freedom of options: "So what if we're kicked out of Columbia. We'll just all transfer to Harvard." Although the faculty can perhaps earn more elsewhere and faculty mobility is high among prestigious institu-

[9] Twenty-four hours after the occupation of Hamilton Hall, the college faculty voted to express itself in a resolution that began, "A university exists as a community dedicated to rational discourse, and to the use of communication and persuasion as a means of furthering discourse."

[10] This view of the university has been succinctly articulated by the political philosopher Barrington Moore, Jr. (in "On Rational Inquiry in Universities Today," *New York Review of Books*, April 23, 1970, pp. 30, 34.) "The liberal commitment to intellectual freedom is a commitment to a process, not a specific set of beliefs. . . . Any future society that does not preserve and extend certain traditional liberal values, such as the right to criticize prevailing beliefs and corresponding rights giving protection against arbitrary abuse of authority, will not be a fit society for human habitation."

tions, on balance, to leave Columbia would almost always be experienced as a move down.

This vested interest in the maintenance of a viable institution provides potent psychological motivation for reform as opposed to "destruction and rebirth." Very few faculty are in a position to embark on an adventure of dissent that could so displease the departmental chairman, the administration, and the trustees as to jeopardize their jobs or, if tenured, to pose obstacles to advancement, access to grants, and the other rewards of academia.

The radical students' highly unrealistic expectations of radicalizing the faculty stemmed from their failure to extend the economic principles of their neo-Marxian analysis to the behavior of those from whom they had a strong need for personal affirmation as well as political collaboration. One young, nontenured faculty member who did become "radicalized" and began working with the radical students gave the following explanation of his actions:

I felt impotent. I wrote letters about the gym. I argued on ethical, moral, and aesthetic grounds. . . . As a student I was very comfortable at the university. I was very studious but didn't experience much life. This year my students really woke me up. I'm indebted to them, so indebted that I wanted to work for them.

This teacher revealed an unusual fluidity and potential for radical action, because of several aspects of the structure of his life: He had another profession in which he was skilled and could earn a living, and which he enjoyed; and he was unmarried and liked to travel extensively. Therefore, although he enjoyed teaching at Columbia, he did not feel tied to the university and had relatively little to lose, compared to most of his colleagues, if he incurred disfavor from senior people there. This is akin to how many of the white students felt about their "dependence" on Columbia.

Many faculty members, although not similarly radicalized, had become politicized with regard to university affairs as a direct result of their contact with the students and their empathy for the students' anguish over the effects of the war on their lives.[11]

[11] Professor Dupee wrote: "It is true that my habitual detachment from campus politics had recently broken down as I saw the students growing more and more desperate under the pressures of the War." (Dupee, *op. cit.*, p. 20.)

It is generally true that radicals leave active movement-work before age thirty. The subsistence wage in radical organizing work and the geographic mobility are difficult to integrate with family life. Often, in the past, the aging radicals have entered academic life and become "supporters" of and commentators on the New Left, rather than "activists." This trend may be offset in the future by the emergence of communes of political activists.

Quite apart from political theory and the career and economic consequences of radical action, that part of the New Left critique that is expressed by the radical "life style"—for instance, hirsutism, manner of dress, public use of obscene words—is generally alien to faculty members over thirty. The uninitiated are usually quite startled at their first New Left meeting to hear the easy flow and easy acceptance of words regarded as obscene in the bourgeois world. Professor Sidney Hook stated that at Columbia, "The language and behavior of the gutter have invaded the academy." [12] Professor Dupee said, "Compared to the radicals of the '30's, so stodgy and uninventive, these youths seemed to unite the politics of a guerrilla chieftain with the aesthetic flair of a costumer and an interior decorator." [13] Two of my left-liberal colleagues from the Medical School, fifty blocks away, who had not been on the Morningside Heights campus in years, visited it during the crisis and later described their shock in observing groups of radicals. At first, they were sure that the radicals all should be in the Psychiatric Unit of Columbia-Presbyterian Medical Center. Only gradually, as they talked with the students, did they realize that they were reasonably intelligent, sensitive, and apparently "normal."

In addition, adults have a very conflicted response to what appears to be freedom of impulse on the part of youth. Many faculty are unconsciously drawn to the campus because of a strong residual tie to the undergraduate period of their own youth. Year after year, they share with each new class in the young student's quest for knowledge and experience and his painful search for personal identity. But they feel quite ambivalent about the students' experimentation or activism, which connote potential "loss of control,"

[12] S. Hook, "Symbolic Truth," *Psychiatry and Social Science Review*, vol. 2, no. 7 (1968), p. 22.
[13] Dupee, *op. cit.*, p. 23.

because they can stir up in the adults conflicts from an earlier period of life that were neither expressed and worked through nor comfortably put to rest. There is both a vicarious attraction to and a fear of the sexuality, sensuality, and open rebellion against authority of the new youth "counter-culture." The extraordinarily punitive attitude of adult society toward users of marijuana reflects the need to repress politically a form of behavior that threatens to unleash previously repressed individual impulses.

I have explored in rather cursory manner some of the general factors influencing the faculty position vis-à-vis the rebelling students, in the hope that it will place the "disenchantment" of the students in sharper focus. The students' expectations proved to be unreasonable, reflecting poor judgment growing out of a psychologically conflicted relationship with faculty. The striking students, frequently expressed scorn for the faculty, especially for the outspoken liberals, with whom in previous years they had felt close kinship regarding antiwar activities. A student from Fayerweather described a meeting on the third day of the strike between a group of these liberal professors and the strikers.

Professor ———— made a big pitch. First he begged, then threatened, then said, "We wash our hands." . . . After that, the people in Fayerweather really turned on the faculty. The liberal had "blown his cool," and we were angry at the cajoling, then intimidation.

At this meeting at Fayerweather, as with their parents, what the students wanted was affirmation of their right to do what they deemed necessary in the situation. What they asked of the faculty was impossible, for the reasons we have mentioned: Unlike parents, the faculty comprised a primary constituency in the community, with their own self-interest and sociopolitical philosophies, advocating their own formulas for solution, and only incidentally concerned at such a time with meeting the psychological needs of this group of students.

A student from one of the buildings said:

In retrospect, I feel they [the faculty liberals] sold us out. During it, I felt warmly about the Ad Hoc Committee.

Another said:

I used to think, "They are the professors, they know better." It was hard for a lot of people to see them as just another power group.

A Barnard student said:

Amnesty was such a central issue. The faculty didn't see that you don't accept punishment from authority you don't recognize. They couldn't reject the structure. They wanted us to accept our punishment bravely. They were afraid themselves, and sold us out.

A young graduate student said:

At first I thought their intent nice. They cared. Then I thought them disgusting. Professor ——— was crying. He said, "Can't we do anything to get you out of the building?" God, it was absurd.

A student who was not arrested but was radicalized by the police action said:

The faculty were in the mediating position. They were kind of petty and naïve. A lot of things that happened revealed what happens with people in academia; they're not used to living in life. This was real—social, political, economic. When it got down to this, a lot were pretty silly. A lot seemed to come out of their shell and said, "My God, what's happening?" and did kind of well.

A "loss of innocence" was often described:

We lost both respect and fear of the faculty. They are no longer demigods that know more and are more capable. Rather less so. Next semester, the distance between faculty and me will be much less.

At the conclusion of the crisis in the spring, one had to search far to find a radical student who would publicly express doubts about his perception of the crisis and the tactics finally employed. In this position, calm contemplation of the multiple sides of questions by their intellectual mentors was intolerable. It is not that faculty behaved in an unanticipated way but that the students, having had unrealistic expectations of faculty support, felt betrayed by a hoped-for ally, who could have made the political victory far greater and the psychological experience less conflicted. There was a loss of innocence, a casting away of a residuum of childhood—a time when parental support can usually be depended upon. Untrained, single-minded, and uncertain, the young radicals and militants were writing a scenario on their own before a basically hostile audience.

With the passage of time, the strange and grudging symbiosis between the institutional liberal reformers and the student radicals and revolutionaries has become clearer. The liberal faculty, although far from endorsing the demands and tactics of these students, provide a protective shield against swift or total repression by the administration, so that the activist student elements remain a viable campus force. On the other hand, the activist students create enough disequilibrium on campus to require that changes be effected in order to maintain the university as a functioning community. The changes are in the direction of "reforms" that the faculty liberals had previously proposed but without success. Given the sociopolitical realities of the contemporary university situation, each group needs the other, although neither willingly acknowledges this fact.

VIII: The Students and the Police

For most students, the emotional pinnacle of the crisis was the police action in the early morning hours of April 30. Between 2 and 4 A.M., nearly one thousand policemen cleared the buildings of about a thousand people and cleared the campus and the steps of buildings of about a thousand more. The summoning of police by the administration represented a break in the tradition that the university is a sanctuary from police intervention. This view of the campus has been very important in that it has greatly strengthened the *in loco parentis* aura; all questions of unacceptable conduct became matters to be settled "within the family." To abandon this position by inviting the police to deal with an intramural dispute was to abandon a significant aspect of this symbolic relationship of students, administration, and faculty.

That the administration might call in the police was always recognized as a possibility. On the third night of the occupation of the buildings, at 1:30 A.M., Vice-President David Truman grimly announced to the Ad Hoc Faculty Group that President Kirk planned to ask the police to clear the buildings of the trespassing students. This was greeted by outrage on the part of most of the Group. In a dramatic scene, members of the Steering Committee were able to persuade the administration to rescind the request.[1]

For the faculty, calling in the police at that point not only would have meant the probability of violence but also was a narcissistic wound to them, a declaration that their mediating efforts were useless. They were not yet prepared to accept this judgment. From that third night on, however, the prevailing sense was that it was

[1] A full account of these events is given in J. Avorn *et al., Up Against the Ivy Wall* (New York: Atheneum, 1968).

only a matter of time before the police would be summoned.[2] Not only did the summoning of the police mean that the Ad Hoc Faculty Group had failed in its principal goal; it became a signal event about which the Ad Hoc Faculty Group had pledged itself to take an active stand by interposing themselves physically between the police and the buildings.[3] Defending students in buildings, who are there because they have not followed your counsel, with all of the attendant physical risks, is not exactly an attractive prospect to the family man and scholar. Yet, not to be there car-

[2] In this connection, the dilemma of the Cox Commission in making a retrospective judgment about the police action is of interest. The report states: "The risk of violence, even with the best of planning, is an inseparable incident of police action against hundreds of demonstrators. The situation at Columbia on April 29–30 was plainly different from a sit-in demonstration by twenty-five or thirty or even one hundred students. Inside and outside the buildings perhaps 2,000 people were involved. . . . In chaotic conditions, with intense emotions surging through crowds of rival youths, the degree of risk becomes so high that it must be taken into account in any decision to invite police action. The violence and ensuing injuries have had such disastrous effects upon Columbia in intensifying divisions, mutual distrust, and self-supporting cycles of fantasy within insulated factions that one is tempted to conclude that some other course simply had to be found.

"Yet we cannot say that the decision to call in the police was wrong, once the situation on April 29 had been developed. Three courses of action were open, and the Administration had to choose one: (a) to call in the police with all possible safeguards; (b) to grant amnesty, abandon the gymnasium, and concede whatever additional demands were necessary to induce the students to leave voluntarily; or (c) to close the University for an indefinite period, probably until the end of the semester, and hope that order could be maintained despite the rising tensions among groups seeking to isolate or recapture the buildings. To talk of further negotiations or other solutions is to ignore the hard choices the Administration had to make; there was virtually no chance of successful negotiations. Furthermore, the third possibility was scarcely feasible; letting things drag along entailed a high degree of risk of serious violence." *Cox Commission Report, Crisis of Columbia: Report of the Fact-Finding Commission Appointed to Investigate the Disturbances at Columbia University in April and May, 1968* (New York: Random House, 1968), pp. 165–66.

[3] The Charter of the Ad Hoc Faculty Group states: "We, the undersigned members of the Columbia University Faculty and teaching staff make the following proposal to resolve the present crisis: . . . (4) Until this crisis is settled, we will stand before the occupied buildings to prevent forcible entry by police or others." Approximately 150 members of the teaching staff signed this statement, written in the first twenty-four hours of the life of the Ad Hoc Faculty Group.

ried its burden of guilt, because many of the faculty do regard the students as their children, and also shame, for, like many men, many of the faculty confuse physical fear with moral cowardice or lack of masculinity.

The students' reaction to the police action had to do almost entirely with the violence involved rather than with the arrests. According to the *Cox Commission Report,* after the April 30 action, 103 people (77 students, 14 policemen, 8 faculty or staff, and 4 others) received medical attention at the two local hospitals. Many others received medical attention at first-aid stations set up on campus. Presumably the largest group comprised those who were bruised but did not seek formal attention from a physician and are therefore uncounted. The clearing of the blacks from Hamilton Hall was a nonviolent operation. With a few exceptions, all the police violence was directed at white radicals and their sympathizers. Hence, this chapter will pertain almost entirely to the responses of the white students to the police.

The students' reaction to violence depended essentially on three variables: (1) his physical relationship to the violence—that is, whether he was the object of it, a witness to it, or absent from campus; (2) his political and moral attitude toward the objects of the violence—the radicals; and (3) his character structure, regardless of (1) and (2).

Very few white students, in or out of the buildings, had had firsthand experience with police violence. A freshman in a building said:

Physically I was never afraid [beforehand]. Maybe because I never saw a police beating. I thought, "It won't happen to me."

Increasingly, however, violence is becoming a part of the radical's life, and he is therefore forming a better idea of what to expect. Viewing televised shots of violence at demonstrations in the comfort of one's living room never conveys the profound terror of being in the midst of a situation where the ultimate agents of control and order, the police, are themselves performing violence. For some of those who had participated in previous demonstrations where violence had occurred, the reality of what happens was a factor in their position. Thus, one student who sympathized with the building occupation but stayed outside said:

I was at the Hilton [4] and knew what the cops are like. I didn't want to be beaten. That was another reason for not going in the building.

The violence was terrifying to virtually all of the students who were seeing their first example of it. A typical reaction was expressed by a liberal, nonactive senior who was inadvertently caught up in the clearing of the campus:

They kept charging. They kept clubbing. Violent looks on their faces. I thought, "Gee, I want to call the police!" But there they were. I broke down completely. That was frightening. Everything that I had believed in was completely different from what I had seen. I'm now trying to reconcile it, to put something together.

Another student put it simply:

Abstract policy concerning the use of force was reduced to basic reality when I saw friends and professors dripping blood.

In contrast to the firsthand experience with the police action, the issues of the strike were abstractions. Until April 23, most students probably did not know what the initials "IDA" stood for. But witnessing violence for the first time had a profoundly politicizing effect on inactive but "liberal" students.

Responses by students who did not participate in the building occupation included the following remarks:

The police bust represented the climax in my private learning process. What the sight of this brutal occurrence did was to chip away the last remnants of my "it can't happen here" way of thinking. This is a notion that most Americans seem to hold dear. . . . Vicious police brutality is not limited to Hitler's Germany, Stalin's Russia, or even Selma, Alabama. It can happen here, at one of the world's great universities. . . . America is not the Promised Land. Any false sense of security I had about this land evaporated one Tuesday morning when America showed its new face.

That was police brutality in living color. That's what the whole thing was about. I learned about what was going on in the world. . . . It was scary to see police, a police state—what life could be like in a police state.

The impact on all students was profound. Shifts in position

---

[4] At an earlier demonstration protesting a speech by Secretary of State Dean Rusk.

occurred not only in students who were moderates or left of center. One member of the Majority Coalition related:

The arrival of civil forces banished all possible resolutions. I had always respected the police . . . never really liked them but respected what they stood for—law. In this case the police action revolted me; I became a striker.

After the police action, 6,000 students, including a majority of students in Columbia College, supported the strike. Even among those moderates and conservatives who did not shift to a position supporting the strike, the impulse to do so was strong. A senior who had joined the Majority Coalition said:

I could not believe my eyes that night. Blood all over the place, wounded people here and there, police clubbing people indiscriminately. . . . It was that evening alone that swung a great number of students right into the SDS fold. Emotionally, I myself might have followed this course had I not sat down and decided not to let this police action make up my mind about what I thought to be right or wrong.

The shift, or impulse to shift, in position to support the strike and oppose the administration was related to the overwhelming impact of the violence, which had the effect of causing cognitive fusion of police violence and administration. Where one ended and the other began was unclear to the students. For the non-activist witnesses, the violence stirred up primitive anxieties of the latent destructiveness of the good (or, at least, controlled) parent, which could be directed at them should their own rebellious impulses ever get out of hand. For many of these postbust converts, however, the response was short lived; their need for external order and inner repression soon reasserted itself. They could not easily tolerate the sustained expression on campus of disruptive impulses and returned to their previous critique of the tactics of SDS and the SDS leadership for prolonging the struggle and interfering with their free access to the educational process.

Some of these themes, particularly the view of the "unleashed" administration followed by the return to condemnation of the demonstrators, are evident in this statement by a student:

The administration became the sadistic monster which had used violence against innocent people to gain its ends and then congratulated itself on its victory. Kirk and the rest had been forced "up against the wall," and we could finally see the evil within Low Library.

On the Thursday following the bust, the events of the past week began falling into place, and I returned to the sphere of reason. The key to this sudden understanding was the revelation that Grayson Kirk was a man, and since he is a man, I can identify with him and understand him and what the demonstrators had done to him. The implications of "up against the wall, mother-fucker" became crystal clear, and I knew what had happened was completely wrong.

Just as a normally friendly animal will strike with vehemence when cornered and threatened, the administration was forced to hate and strike back irrationally. . . . Since President Kirk is perhaps weaker than most, the method proved extremely effective. Even Vice-President Truman, who was respected and admired, . . . succumbed to this tactic and began behaving irrationally. The demonstrators have a "tiger by the tail," and they may never know it. Through impatience, . . . self-righteousness, and lack of understanding, the demonstrators have condemned themselves to the pursuit of just goals at the cost of unwittingly destroying themselves and their fellow men.

Abrupt introduction to violence on the campus caused many breakdowns in the defensive patterns that students typically use to manage familiar stresses and anxiety. There were short-lived panic states, as reported by a student who had shifted, over the course of the week, from sympathy for the radicals ("They were doing what I didn't have the balls to do") to support of the Majority Coalition ("To my own amazement, I found myself cheering the jocks") with some stops in the middle ("I went to sleep that night [the third night] feeling pretty much out of it and hoping the whole thing would blow over"). He was on campus during the police action and, after describing the violence and his assistance of bleeding students, wrote:

I returned to my room. I looked out the window over to College Walk. I saw cops and paddy wagons and an incredible wave of hate and fear swept over me. "You fucking cops," I screamed out the window. "Up against the wall, mother-fucker!" The window slammed shut. My heart was racing. Someone knocked on the door. I was afraid to let him in.

The event was so sudden, so overwhelming, that for many it was isolated; they reacted almost as to a nightmare—a word which, incidentally, I heard used repeatedly to describe the event.

This dreamlike feeling is conveyed in the following description by an uncommitted liberal student:

At about 6:30 A.M., they allowed us back on campus. . . . The scene was almost surrealistic as I walked across campus in the gray light of that cloudy morning. The campus was virtually empty. There was a slight breeze that blew debris across my path. A squad of motor-cycle policemen passed talking together in low voices. One of them laughed. It was hard for me to believe what I had seen in those five hours. . . . It was for me a sudden and nightmarish thrust back into reality. I felt a youthful futility born out of opposition to an inexorably powerful establishment.

Resolution of the anxiety caused by the violence depended to a large measure on whether the student could, within the structure of his intellectual and political position, identify one side as the "good guys" and the other as the "bad guys." Thus, a student who was vigorously opposed to SDS said:

I opposed the police violence, but, unlike others, I had expected it. I know the feelings of police who have been taunted but cannot take any counteractions.

A junior who was active in the Majority Coalition gave the following description:

When a friend came in at 3 A.M., I quickly dressed and went out to watch the pukes get what I strongly felt they deserved. Boy, was I looking forward to their getting what was coming to them. I knew full well . . . that some people would get hurt in the course of clearing out the buildings. But if you resist arrest, as all the inside demonstrators did,[5] the police are totally justified in using all necessary force. I saw much of the brutality, and I don't deny its existence, but in just about all the instances I saw this brutality was somewhat justified. . . . When he [the demonstrator] goes limp, proceeds to kick you in the chest and groin, and gives you as hard a time as he can, then I don't call the use of the billy brutal.

Of the immediate postbust period he said:

My reaction to all the furor was an even stronger feeling of support for the administration. They were right in what they did. I agree with their behavior, even though I think it should have been done sooner.

[5] This, of course, was not the case.

Thus, for those conservative students who were not burdened with ambivalence in their feelings toward the radicals, the police action was explicable and justifiable, and did not cause inner turmoil, as it evoked in the more middle-ground and liberal students. This illustrates, once again, that the ability to identify clearly with one position against another provides a stable base for adapting to events. Students in whom this was not present were left confused by the police action and unable to mobilize themselves in any satisfactory direction, if only for a brief period:

After the bust I was a very confused young man. I felt that the university was through. I felt I could never respect the police. I felt the demonstrators had caused this destruction, but I also felt the administration, above all, was ineffective in trying to settle this crisis. To sum it all up, I felt absolutely defeated and disillusioned.

The response of the students in the building, the cause and the object of the police action, was very different from that of the students inadvertently caught up in the clearing of campus or those who simply observed the activity. From the moment they entered the buildings, the radical students were concerned about the consequences of the inevitable police action. "Defense Committees" were formed in the buildings, and there were endless discussions about what tactics to use when the police came.

The progressive radicalization and unification of those in the buildings served to alleviate much anxiety regarding the police. Every evening there were rumors of bust that night. Anxiety would run high, and preparations would begin. The pattern, however, changed over the week. A girl in the Math building said:

At first I didn't know what mace was. Why am I putting vaseline on my face? Physically I was really scared! I felt betrayed. I wasn't sure why I was putting myself up for this. That didn't come until later—a real political sureness. So I had nothing to bolster this real physical fear. Then it became boring.

Many had grave doubts mingled with curiosity as to how they would respond when the police came. How much punishment or pain one can tolerate is an almost universal concern. The anxiety was experienced by many as a puberty rite. A student, discussing this aspect, said:

I never knew if in the real situation I could go through with it. That was the real exhilaration. In the crisis, by God, we did it. We really proved ourselves.

Many males felt that to stand up against the police was a proof of their masculinity. A senior said:

The thing about this was that all of us were proving that we have balls—the strikers, the jocks, the police, and the administration.

A student from Fayerweather said, "To be busted is to have balls —to come out on top." Another student described his "super-masculine feeling afterwards." Some students who sympathized with those in the buildings but chose not to join them emerged with doubts that their motivation for staying out was anything other than fear of the police. To test this, they sought arrest at later stages of the crisis. One such student was arrested at a later demonstration at a university-owned apartment house. He said: "I thought I wasn't a coward and had convictions, but needed to make sure, by the arrest."

What was experienced, perceived, and felt by the students during the arresting process is eloquently communicated by the following account, by a Barnard student who was in Math:

THE BUST

"We waited two hours for the cops to come, crouched on the floor of Prof. ———'s office on the fifth floor of the Math building. We joked, played cards, did card tricks, arranged a barricade, and clutched plastic bags to put over our heads for tear gas. Looking out the window, we saw cops with pale blue helmets lined up at the side of the building. Out the other window, lots of people are walking by in support of us. We make the victory sign to each other, they wave. G. leans out the window. S. holds her tensely by the ankles. We barricade about two or so; the cops come and knock politely on the door about three or three-thirty. 'You can't come in, I'm not dressed,' I whimper. 'Nobody home,' says somebody, 'Dyuh, cheez it, it's the cops.' Suddenly two of the longer-haired boys in the room look very young; they seem scared. We put banana peels on the floor for the cops. They keep coming.

back and knocking politely on the door. We all have to go to the bathroom. The boy with a moustache puts a stethoscope in Prof. ————'s desk as a parting gift. Finally the cops start banging on the door. They bang so hard everything shakes; it hurts your ears and I'm a little scared. They're saying things to us like, 'Come out and we'll make it easy for you,' but only half-heartedly and we really can't hear them. And we have no intention of coming out anyhow. Word by word, starting from the end, we erase 'Up Against the Wall, Mother-Fuckers' from the blackboard because we're afraid of the cops beating us.

"They bang and bang but the door is thick and our barricade good: a big heavy desk (six feet long at least) wedged against the wall with lots of chairs and bookfilled cartons. Then they start hitting the door with an axe. 'Should we take down the barricade?' For the first time R. seems a little scared and his eyes move fast. Two hands raised for, six opposed, so we sit still and wait. I am very surprised that some of the boys vote to take down the barricade. Everyone else is *not* braver than I am after all. The axe keeps hitting for a long time; I was thinking I should be scared, although it is funny and dramatic at the same time. Finally the wood breaks a little and two prongs of a crowbar creep through the door edge. Then there's a hole in the middle of the door and they keep hitting at it and the wood starts shattering and big splinters come flying and you're scared of it hitting you in the eye because it flies fast, and you are glad there is finally something to be realistically scared of, the splinters. I hide my face behind my bookbag and feel a little afraid because I'll be the first one they see when the door opens. The hole is getting bigger. Then a hand can get through. The first thing we see is a white-gloved hand, edged with dirt around the fingers, on a police-blue sleeve. It comes through and tries the door handle. The hole gets bigger and a little red-faced policeman jumps heroically through. 'You're in there all alone, boy,' another cop yells like a football coach, and a little red-faced cop hops about pulling heroically at the desk. 'It's this big desk geez *I* can't get it,' he shouts and runs around huffing and sweating while we sit against the wall watching with calm interest. He throws the cartons off the desk as if he were in a Chicago warehouse in 'The Untouchables' and finally, jumping a lot, he gets the desk pulled away and they've knocked down the door by this time and the police, about six, came charging it. 'All right, get up, let's go. You know you are all under arrest,' their chief says loudly and theatrically, enjoying himself. We stand up to walk and go, except S. He just sits. 'All right, boy,' a big fat red-faced cop with a helmet strapped under his chin and holding a club snarls really loud and jumps over to S. 'You're gonna get up. None of this, godammit. We'll show you who's gonna get up,' and he starts hitting him with the billy stick and kicking him and about four policemen surround him and I don't know what else they did because we had to go out into the hall, but S. got a fractured finger and three stitches in the forehead.

"They made us walk down the hall between two rows of policemen, maybe fifty on each side, a really long line, and the faces of all the cops turned toward each girl to look us over. It was easy for me. But somebody told me the guys got clubbed or at least prodded as they walked down between the lines. I saw them throw S. up against the wall and the fat cop said gruffly, 'Yeh, now, stand up like you shoulda done back there in the first place, now you see how to act.' They were frisking the guys who leaned on the wall, on their arms stretched out above their heads, and they prodded them in the groin. Then they got us down the steps and separated the girls. We went into the 'living room,' where the other girls were sitting in a circle on the floor singing freedom songs: 'Liberation, Liberation,' and 'We Shall Overcome.' They greeted us with 'Hello, sisters.' The cops took us out then. They always called us broads.

"We marched across Low Plaza, which was bright from CBS newsreel lights. 'What do you think of this, Miss?' a reporter asked one of the girls. 'I don't know, go away,' she said. There were ugly-looking plainclothesmen who you would have thought were ditch-diggers standing on a grass plot opposite, laughing raucously and shouting 'The Marines' Hymn' at us, out of tune. We climbed into the paddy wagon, which was all dark and closed in, with one tiny window up front into the cab. And no john.

"We all make the V for victory sign as the newsreel lights light up the wagon for a few seconds. We shouted 'Up Against the Wall Mother-Fuckers' as they closed the paddy wagon doors and drove away down College Walk.

"I don't feel like talking in the paddy wagon. It's dark and as we hurtle down Broadway the girls by the window say there are hundreds of kids on the street running after us. We cheer. I can never tell where we are; I see only broken-up neon lights, purple and green and red, through the small jalousie windows in back. After what seems a half-hour someone shouts out, 'We're at 106th Street,' but it seems to me that we are going around in circles in the center of some strange city, not New York. The ride is endless. It is as if we're all going to summer camp together; girls ask each other what it's going to be like. 'They let you take one if you haven't taken one tonight and then they take your pills away from you,' one of the girls told us. They passed around a box of cookies, and everybody puffed on one cigarette. G. taped up her film and they told her to make sure to declare it unexposed or else the police would 'accidentally' expose it. I felt I should ask her how she was, be a friend to her, but I really just wanted to be quiet. We could hear the policemen talking through the window of the cab. They had bad grammar. They stopped for coffee and doughnuts and asked how many we were. I thought they were going to get us all doughnuts. They didn't. Then all the way to the station they kept complaining about the sugar on their uniforms. I was glad I was going to jail because my parents had a close friend whose daughter had gone to jail in Mississippi. The jail was filthy dark and deep . . . some of the policewomen prodded the girls' breasts and genitals. I picked a nicer one to search me. She was delighted to have to search my bookbag. You had to pull down your pants to prove you were a female. The cell was dirty and you couldn't stretch your legs except by standing, which you were much too tired to do. Some girls slept on the floor, their legs bent. The black girls came in last and sat separately from us. Girls talked to one another quietly: we argued whether to answer the parole officers' questions before seeing a lawyer. At seven they brought our 'feeding,' sour, inedible baloney sandwiches and too-sweet, undrinkable coffee. Finally about nine o'clock I found a space under a bench where I could stretch out halfway to sleep, but girls kept stepping on me. At eleven a blue-eyed, long-side-burned, handsome arresting officer from the Bronx came and took us up to the court. After the arraignment we rode home on the BMT and I kept wondering why people didn't look at us with more interest."

This young lady mastered her anxiety largely by giving herself the task of intellectually recording and remembering every detail of the event. In so doing she maintained a real sense of control and never felt herself a passive victim. Other students remembered little obsessive, wishful thoughts that would pop into mind as the police moved in. For example, one would look at a policeman and say to herself, "Oh, he's nice—he won't hurt me." A junior in a building said that he kept recalling the words of Mayor Lindsay: "Children will not be killed in this city."

The response of many students, particularly the males, was to isolate the affects of fear and anxiety. Students, so to speak, "watched" themselves in the process, feeling numb, losing their sense of time. One student said: "I would be lying if I said I felt anything. I was just protecting myself. I wasn't aware of others in the room."

Thus, those students with solid obsessional defenses of intellectualization, denial, and isolation were able to go through the experience with seeming "cool." This character structure was not universal, however, and many students experienced transient panic. All buildings reported students screaming and crying—and this was not confined to females. A male said, "I cried during the beating. I knew the cops were enraged because I cried and was weak. It brought out more sadism." Another said simply, "I was scared shitless when they came in."

Almost all described a blend of euphoria and fatigue in the paddy wagons and on being released after booking at the police station. A male freshman said, "In the paddy wagon we were exhilarated. I had the feeling we just started to fight." The euphoria partly represented relief at surviving this ordeal, which, for all students, at some level represented a threat to their lives—a situation in which they were helpless and at the mercy of an armed foe who was in total control of how far the violence would go.

Almost every student who was in a building reported nightmares about the police action in the week following. There was little variation. Some examples, from different students, are as follows:

Kids being beaten. Girls are screaming. It's the worst thing I've ever heard. I woke up in a cold sweat.

I was being beaten by the police.

Police were coming after me for all the money I owe for parking tickets.

Strange scenes of darkness and spotlights glistening off helmets.

I got shot by a cop, or someone did.

To infer the unconscious meaning from manifest content of dreams without the dreamer's associations and substantial knowledge about the past and current themes in his life is always a problematic undertaking. But, at the most parsimonious level, one can conclude that these nightmares reflected the dreamers' attempts to master the residual anxiety from this psychologically traumatic event.

Does the manifest dream material clarify the issue of whether or not the students felt unconscious guilt for their action? That is, is the painful content of the nightmare a way of satisfying their superego's demand for punishment? Given my thesis that aspects of the radicals' behavior reflected their guilt, it would be tempting to reach this conclusion regarding the dream material. However, the material is not sufficient either to validate or invalidate such a conclusion. At the time of the interviews, I did not consider this a major line of inquiry and hence did not pursue the students' associations to their dreams.

Some of my therapist colleagues told me of student-patients in and out of the buildings who, in their dreams, fantasies, behavior, and mood, conveyed that they viewed the encounter with police unconsciously in Oedipal terms, associating the police violence with retaliation of the vengeful father for the transgression of rebellion and usurpation of authority. One student, for example, kept running back and forth during the police rushes on campus, always remaining just beyond the reach of the police, in a euphoric state. When he got to his room he masturbated immediately, as did a number of other students I heard about. This act was a way of reassuring themselves unconsciously about their genital intactness and thereby attenuating anxiety related to mutilation or castration.

Prior to April 30, small groups of police officers were generally present on campus and were rather casually accepted by the radicals as part of the scene. Most of the direct contact was in the form of students trying to engage the policemen in dialogue, in an attempt to convince them what a good thing the rebellion was, not only for Columbia, but for the working class, which they believed the police represented. More than that, however, the police represented the potential agent of the punitive authority. To gain them as allies, then, would decrease the anxiety surrounding the prospect of the inevitable confrontation. During the occupation, most observers felt that there was little overt provocation of the police. Yet on April 30, before the police engaged the building occupiers, there was violence to the students and faculty who were on the steps of the buildings, passively protesting their entry. Apparently, inherent in the act of occupying buildings and in the identity of radical Columbia students are factors that are provocative to a policeman. The breaking of rules means repudiation of the central ethic on which their whole identity as policemen rests. Further, Columbia represents an elitist institution; to see students who had been accepted in this privileged milieu so contemptuous of what they could never have must have engendered rage.

Following the April 30 bust, the police became, for many students, the enemy in their own right. During the month of May, they were subjected to frequent verbal abuse in the vicinity of the campus. When they massed outside the university's gates, on May 22, a few objects were hurled along with epithets from behind the barricaded gates.

An interesting fact emerged from the confrontation of police and student rebels: The white radicals on the campus were virtually incapable of acts of violence against individuals. Despite their rhetoric of violence and obscenity, assaultive violence was rare. Many psychoanalytic critics of campus activists have said that the pacifism of the antiwar and civil rights movements is a reaction-formation against the activists' unconscious impulses toward aggression. This may be partly true, but, rather than being an indictment, it illustrates how functional and humanitarian personality defenses exist in some individuals to accommodate more primal impulses that are universal. The aggressive use of obscenity thus serves to sublimate more overtly aggressive impulses that are rarely acted upon.

There is no question but that some of the more sophisticated of the radicals sought a confrontation with the police as a means of exposing the violence of the establishment, thereby discrediting the university administration and mobilizing support from liberal and moderate quarters. For the larger number, violence was not an objective to be engineered by purposive planning; yet the confrontation served them well as an integrative event, solidifying their conviction of the justice of their cause. It also helped to expiate the guilt they felt for the successful disruption of the administration and the college, and, I think, for unconscious sins unrelated to the rebellion at Columbia. One could detect a disappointment, a sense of "incomplete" experience, in those who escaped abusive behavior from the police.

Thus, for the white students, the reaction to the police behavior as a personal as well as politicizing event was contingent upon the student's political identifications, personal experience of violence at the time, and his character structure and psychodynamic currents.

As we have seen, there had been great anticipatory anxiety among the students in Hamilton, followed by relief after the non-violent bust there. Had the police included the blacks in their display of violence, I think that the effect would have been to more firmly unite the black students in militancy. For those who were in Hamilton and had some misgivings about the use of militant tactics, guilt would have been expiated and their view of the brutality of the system would have been dramatically reconfirmed. But, further, great guilt would also have been mobilized in many of the blacks who chose to stay out, ultimately making them more militant. When felony charges were being pressed against a member of the Hamilton Steering Committee for his alleged behavior in an on-campus fracas with police on May 22, the entire black student body seemed to be united in demanding that the university use its influence to obtain dismissal of the charges.

I mentioned earlier that the white radicals were generally astonished by the resentment that most of the blacks felt for them. This carried over to the black students' reaction to the police violence.

Whereas the white college community and the media were

shocked and outraged by the police violence in clearing the white buildings, no black student I talked with shared this feeling of indignation. One student said:

My head tells me that I should be outraged and sympathetic to the kids who were beaten, but I know that in my heart I am glad it happened to them. All of our lives we've been beaten in the ghettos. You never heard about it in the *New York Times* and on TV. It happens once to white kids and all the media, all of the city, are shocked, like they just discovered it.

Other students echoed this feeling. It is clear that the era of the early 1960's, with its spirit of "Black and White Together, We Shall Overcome," had ended. Some blacks expressed some sadness at this: One said:

At first I was glad. I thought it was nice to have SAS and SDS together. But I didn't think it could last.

Another said:

I would have liked to see black and white students together, to see how that could have worked out.

As black students move toward separatism, with its concomitant psychological liberation, the resentment that has so long been dormant is becoming manifest. The feelings they had toward the beating of white students by the police was one small reflection of this. A significant part of our future social and political destiny will be determined by the directions and forms in which this emerging rage is channeled.

IX: Individual Factors in Radical Activism

Every Columbia student who occupied a building reached April 23 with his own history of life experience and character structure. Some aspects of developmental history were common to all students; some only to blacks or to whites; and much was unique to the individual. In attempting to understand student behavior during the rebellion, I have come to view the political beliefs and actions of each student as the outcome of three individual and two socio-political-historical factors.

The individual factors include the following:

1. *Individual character*—the student's ego-organization and psychological adaptation, which is the outcome of the parent-child interaction
2. *Value orientation*—deriving largely from the individual's family and social origins
3. *Responses to the nature of the radical action*—the affect of the occupation of buildings on the individual's psychodynamic constellation of needs, impulses, and defense mechanisms

The socio-political-historical factors include the following:

1. *The external sociopolitical situation*—particularly the capacity of the university and the larger society to change in order to meet the needs and pleas of students (among others)
2. *The psychohistorical context*—the manifest experiences and symbolic historical themes that have been shared by a generation and that profoundly affect their political philosophy, life style, and psychological integration.

166

In this chapter, we shall consider the individual factors affecting the student's political commitment. In Chapters X and XI, we shall discuss the socio-political-historical influences.

Individual Character

We have noted earlier that the psychoanalyst's trained tendency to conceptualize all aspects of behavior in terms of the psychodynamic and unconscious motivational factors in the individual can be highly instructive but can also lead to the confusion of psychodynamics with psychopathology. Because psychoanalysis developed out of Freud's study of the maladaptive behavior of disturbed people and has continued to be primarily a therapeutic science, we tend to view all socially deviant behavior from a psychopathological frame of reference. On this point, Robert Michels notes:

In any area of human behavior, pathology lies, not in conflict, but in the maladaptive patterns of conflict resolution. One does not understand someone simply by discovering that he has an Oedipal complex. The diagnosis and treatment of social problems involves a consideration of society's institutionalized modes of dealing with universal conflict.[1]

In a similar vein, Howard Zinn has written:

Psychological explanations of protest are comforting to those of us who don't want our little worlds upset, because they emphasize the irrationality of the protester rather than the irrationality of that which produces protests.[2]

The "act" of rebellion at Columbia attracted students widely varying in motivation and strength of psychological integration. Erikson has provided a developmental orientation that helps us to explain and analyze these differences. He speaks of certain characteristics, the outcome of various developmental epochs, as the "rudiments of virtue developed in childhood." His essay on "Human Strength and the Cycle of Generations" opens by saying,

[1] R. Michels, "Pseudo-analyzing the Student Rebels," *Psychiatry and Social Science Review,* vol. 3, no. 5 (1969), p. 5.
[2] H. Zinn, "Young Demons," *The New Republic,* May 31, 1969, p. 27.

The psychoanalyst has good reason to show restraint in speaking about human virtue. For in doing so lightly he could be suspected of ignoring the evidential burden of his daily observations which acquaint him with the furrowed ground from which our virtues proudly spring. And he may be accused of abandoning the direction of Freudian thought in which conscious values can find responsible re-evaluation only when the appreciation of the unconscious and of the irrational forces in man is firmly established.

Yet the very development of psychoanalytic thought, and its preoccupation with "ego strength," suggests that human strength be reconsidered, not in the sense of nobility and rectitude as cultivated by moralities, but in the sense of inherent strength.[3]

We know that the behavior of all men is influenced by internal psychological conflict and unconscious motives. However, our concern with "human strength" leads us to become interested in the distinctive intrapsychic organization of a few men that enables them to effect changes in their community by giving them the capacity to perceive external conditions and communal needs rationally and to integrate these perceptions with adaptive, original forms of action that also happen to fulfill their own unconscious aims.

Each student has passed through a series of developmental epochs and crises in which the outcome was the basis for later character traits, either "virtuous" or "nonvirtuous." I have conceptualized five of these epochs and their polar personality outcomes in connection with various types of radicalism or militancy. (See diagram on page 169.) In considering these types of action, it is useful to conceptualize radical and militant students on a continuum from "idealistic" to "nihilistic" radicalism. This conceptualization is equally applicable to white and black students.

At the "idealistic" pole, the student will:

1. emphasize programs with "realistic" and negotiable goals
2. not pursue violence and disruptive tactics as sources of psychological gratification
3. have the capacity to empathize with the oppressed and powerless

[3] E. Erikson, *Insight and Responsibility* (New York: Norton, 1964), p. 111.

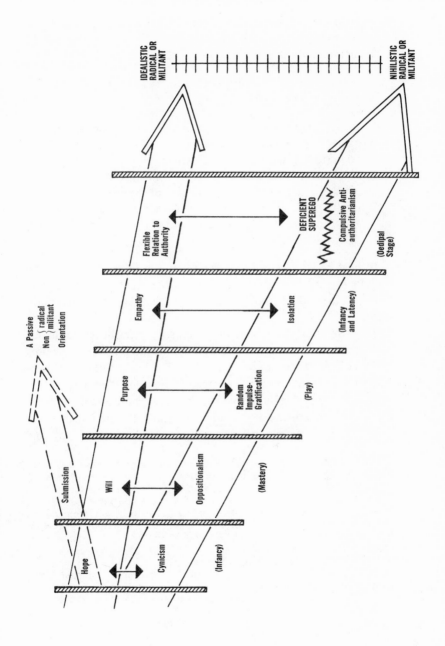

4. have sources of pleasure and relatedness apart from political activity
5. maintain a humanistic credo and follow it in his daily life

In contrast, at the "nihilistic" pole the student will:

1. offer no programs for constructive change
2. focus his planning on violence and disruption as ends in themselves, and as sources of pleasure if achieved
3. relate to and use people as pawns in a political struggle
4. be obsessed with issues of politics and race to the exclusion of other relationships, interests, and pleasures
5. totally mask dreams of what might be with rage at what is and deny anything positive in order to maintain an essentially paranoid view.[4]

It must be emphasized that these are two polar extremes; most individuals fall between them and, further, continuously shift in position, depending on both external events and inner readjustment.

The commitment of the more "idealistic" radicals and militants involved such character traits as hope, will, purpose, empathy, and a flexible relationship to authority. The more "nihilistic" radicals and militants were characterized by such "nonvirtues" as cynicism, oppositionalism, random impulse-gratification, isolation, and a deficient superego or compulsive anti-authoritarianism.

Just as most people fall between the poles of "idealism" and

---

[4] Lewis Feuer, in his Oedipal-theory-oriented interpretation of student movements, defines nihilism in generational terms: "It asserts that whatever our fathers taught us is wrong. Nihilism is thus the pure form of the aggressive component in younger generational revolutionary ideology: it states that the values, philosophies, attitudes transmitted to us, foundations of our cultural heritage, are basically at fault. . . . The purport of nihilism is to negate this whole heritage in fundamental ways. . . . Nihilism is characterized by a psychology of compulsive negation; it is a generational 'no,' the cultural equivalent of the primal parricide." In L. Feuer, *The Conflict of Generations: The Character and Significance of Student Movements* (New York: Basic Books, 1969), p. 514.

For Feuer, all explanations of student movements lead to this theme—"the cultural equivalent of primal parricide." He disregards both other manifestations of nihilism and other causal factors.

"nihilism" so the pure form of virtue or nonvirtue is rarely, if ever, the outcome of a stage. Here, too, varying mixtures exist.

HOPE-CYNICISM

Hope is an indispensable quality of the idealist. Without the conviction that there is a real possibility of reward—that is, a better society that will yield gratification and higher fulfillment to himself and others—commitment to activism is not possible for the idealist.

Where the reality is unalterable and relief is unavailable, passive acceptance of the dreaded fate almost always ensues. Thus Jews in concentration camps, slaves in the old South, and dying patients, aware of the hopelessness of their condition, have tended to resort to the mechanism of "denial" regarding some of the consequences of their state and develop a psychological orientation of passive acceptance, which attenuates the unbearable anxiety. The suppression of hope also prevents rebellion, which accounts, as Hannah Arendt has pointed out,[5] for the absence of rebellious or revolutionary movements in political states that are effectively repressive.

Erikson defines hope as "the enduring belief in the attainability of fervent wishes, in spite of the dark urges and rages which mark the beginning of existence." [6] It is the outgrowth of a positive encounter with "trustworthy maternal persons" during infancy, persons who responded to the baby's need for "intake" and "contact" with warm and calming envelopment. This expectation is then verified by continuous experiences in the preverbal era of development.

No data are available on the kind of mothering the students in this study were given as infants. Even in the best of clinical circumstances, the answer to this kind of question can only be inferred, since few people remember their infancy. We usually infer the quality of the mother-child relationship by extrapolation from much later epochs of development, in the belief (sometimes mistaken) that the relationship has historical consistency. In this study, there is the further problem that much of my conceptual

[5] H. Arendt, *On Violence* (New York: Harcourt, Brace & World, 1969).
[6] Erikson, *op. cit.*, p. 118.

thinking developed after the data had been collected. My conclusions are based on the accumulation of trends in the data, but the quality of mothering was not the subject of specific inquiry with most of the students I talked to.

Despite these limitations, on the basis of my clinical impressions of the Columbia students interviewed, as well as other activists and idealists I have seen over the past four years, I concluded that *most* of these young people had predominantly positive kinds of care from their mothers and mother-surrogates during infancy.

For some activists I have seen, the component of free-floating rage leads to a destructive orientation toward the university in political confrontation. It is as if they were saying, "The structure of the university is such that it can never be changed into a positive institution." This is accommodated by the radical postulate that the university, like all establishment institutions, prepares people for and perpetuates the evils of the society.[7] A student of this type told me, in discussing plans for class disruptions at Columbia, that whatever violence he committed against the university or its faculty was "less than the violence that the university and professors do to the students here." A mimeographed explanation for the disruption, in the fall of 1968, of a class conducted by history professor James Shenton, one of the most popular faculty members and a "left-liberal" in politics, stated:

We aim to criticize our insane, repressive and inhumane society. Within our society the University serves as an "Officers' Candidate School," socializing tomorrow's leaders. . . . It is precisely because he [Shenton] is a "good teacher" and a "nice fellow" that he is dangerous.[8]

The statement goes on to argue that Shenton's professed radicalism "conceals the reality of his role. He accepts a position within

---

[7] It is interesting that Herbert Marcuse, the principal theoretical mentor of the radical student movement, exempts the universities from the main thrust of his critique of American society. As recently as October, 1968, Professor Marcuse stated, "One must distinguish among American universities. The large universities are always sanctuaries for free thought and a rather solid education." In "Marcuse Defines His New Left," *New York Times Magazine,* October 27, 1968.

[8] "A Response to Questions About Classroom Intervention" (mimeographed statement).

the existing hierarchy. He lives the status of 'professor' and thereby perpetuates the inferior status of the student."

Thus, the substantive issues of the moment become simply transient battlegrounds for the continuous war. The rage is focused on the university because of the intimacy of the relationship of student and university. In the end, then, these students suffer from "nonhope," a state of despair that has yielded to cynicism.

Their cynicism is reflected in their lack of concern for the personal consequences of their action. Education is irrelevant because it leads to "mind-fucking" and not to new personal possibilities. Students of this orientation, although present among the ranks of campus activists, have generally tended to be part of the drug subculture on campuses.[9] Cynicism involves the expectation of the worst of human conduct or motives, and the conviction that *all* behavior is motivated by self-interest. It becomes at points inextricably bound with paranoid perception. The body of people to be trusted becomes increasingly limited, even within the movement, leading to acrimonious internecine struggles, always suffused with suspicion of the other's personal motives.

Cynicism is the adaptive outcome of experiences with mothering persons in which the infant has been exploited by the adult for her narcissistic gratification while his needs and demands were disregarded. The result is an enduring sense of futility; the individual believes that he can never obtain nurturance and comfort by the usual communicative means. This quality prevailed in the behavior of the following student, as reported by a colleague:

———— was a very bright young woman whose past history included minor delinquent activities, a period of immersion in the drug subgroup on campus, undue risk-taking in mountain climbing, during which she had many brushes with death, and the conviction that she was ugly and unlovable. She suffered from pervasive despair and

[9] I have described this group and their dynamics, particularly the dynamics of "boredom," more fully in "Drug Use: Symptom, Disease or Adolescent Experimentation—The Task of Therapy," *Journal of American College Health Association,* vol. 16, no. 1 (1967), pp. 25–29. They characteristically isolate themselves in the campus "head" subculture, are obsessed with the mystique of the drug experience, feel no sense of mutuality with the vast majority of fellow students, faculty, and administration, and have no sense of themselves in any integrated time continuum of their past, present, and future.

cynicism associated with the belief that education, political action, and intimate relationships would lead to nothing for her. She had not the slightest idea of what she ultimately would do vocationally. This state of being was in part determined by an infancy of rigidly scheduled feeding, "crying it out," and little . . . concern on the part of her attractive, emotionally labile, and detached mother. With therapeutic help, she was able to overcome much of her alienated pattern of existence and function far more effectively in school and in relationships. However, the core of cynicism remained. Her re- action to the rebellion was to participate actively with a temporary "high" from the communal experience, but also with a belief in the immutable evil of the university. Her sense of futility allowed her to join in an effort (averted, as it happened) to engage in wanton destruction of university property. Her initial response to the police action was to decide to leave the United States and join a small commune. This transient decision, like the destructive effort (which occurred after the second massive police action), was a reaction to the enormous stress of the campus conflict. But she remained doubtful that any good would come of the rebellion.

The overwhelming majority of the striking students emerged after the arrest with profound contempt for the administrators, trustees, and the nature of authority as exercised at Columbia, but also with the hope and the conviction that things would change and that they would be there to taste the fruits of their efforts. I have not heard of a single arrested student who planned to trans- fer to another university, regardless of how strong his grievance against Columbia.[10] In fact, I encountered several instances of students who before the rebellion had planned to transfer or to take a leave of absence, but decided to remain at Columbia follow- ing the events of the spring.

An interesting example of "overhope" based on a narcissisti- cally inflated self-image was provided by an honor student who was arrested in a sit-in on May 23. Despite Dean Coleman's ex- plicit announcement that any student arrested for trespassing that night would be suspended, he was convinced that he would not be so dealt with, reasoning that his outstanding and unblemished record not only would spare him punishment but would impress

[10] An almost universal finding in the alienated and despairing student is the impulse to move on—to another school, to a commune, to Europe, or just to keep traveling. Whatever the change, there is no hope for relief of psychic discomfort in that situation, and the search continues.

the administration with the fact that people of high caliber were included among the protesters, and therefore might serve to change policy. This young man's unrealistic evaluation of the consequences of his actions reflected the climate of his childhood as the indulged only son—"the prince"—whose needs were usually catered to and who was rarely disciplined because of his facility in talking his way out of a jam.

Thus, we see that hope or cynicism were present in differing degrees in students who were active in the rebellion, affecting the nature of the action and the quality of the psychological experience. But hope is not sufficient to produce the idealist-activist. Hope can be part of an orientation of passive expectation, submission to the omnipotence of authority, which is viewed as benevolent; thus it can produce an unwarranted optimism that negates the need for struggle.

WILL-OPPOSITIONALISM

In late infancy, the child renounces to a significant degree the narcissistic view of his own omnipotence and delegates controls to the parent figures. Out of the conflicts of this stage, the balance between self-will and submission to the will of others emerges. As Erikson says:

> To *will* does not mean to be willful, but rather to gain gradually the power of increased judgment and decision in the application of drive. Man must learn to will what can be, to renounce as not worth willing what cannot be, and to believe he willed what is inevitable.[11]

Inasmuch as one of the main foci of this stage is control over the excretory function, the outcome of the struggle over inner and outer control can lead to a sense of defeat, which engenders shame and doubt as to whether one ever really willed what one did or really did what one willed.

The idealistic radicals had will in the sense of the capacity to take organized, effective action in a direction consistent with their convictions. They could not only initiate and sustain the action but could harness it. They had also to carry out this action against the inner deterrents of guilt, shame, and uncertainty. Their guilt

[11] Erikson, *op. cit.,* p. 118.

was considerable in relation to the consequences of the rebellion—dislocating the lives of fellow students, effectively questioning the legitimacy of authorities, and in most cases disagreeing on tactics with ("disobeying") parents and faculty. The shame was less salient, but for many it involved association with more militant and "hippie" types than they cared to identify with. It also involved doing something illegal, which in principle was counter to their traditional upbringing. The uncertainty was betrayed by the continuous meetings, by the early suspicions, particularly in Fayerweather and Hamilton, that they were being manipulated by the strike leadership, and by the students' absolutism in discussions with liberal faculty.

An unsuccessful outcome of this interaction over the child's relinquishing total control over eliminative functions, locomotion, exploration, and other "controversial" activities can be such character traits as "submissiveness" and "oppositionalism."

Submissiveness, which involves selective exclusion of an awareness of aspects of a situation that would generate a loss of faith in the capacity of the current authority to govern wisely, is a trait that leads one to attribute undeserved omniscience to authority. It is obviously not a trait that would propel a student into rebellion.

In contrast, oppositional behavior may indeed impel one into the role of rebel. Whereas a submissive person can rise moderately far (but not to the top) in the establishment, severe oppositionalism produces symptoms that almost always preclude getting into or staying at a good school or a good job. The cluster of associated behaviors, such as extreme work and study procrastination, messy exams and term papers, argumentative classroom behavior, and a tendency toward antisocial acting out, generally produces poor grades and negative reference letters. The unbounded anger of people with this trait makes them unappealing. If, by chance, they do gain admission to a good university, they frequently force their way out before obtaining a degree, usually then becoming more paranoid by adulthood.

There were a few such people among the rebel students, but they generally are found in fringe nonstudent radical groups. One such youngster who occupied the building was so far behind in his work that he knew academic suspension was inevitable. His behavior was motivated more by amorphous rage toward the university than by any political ethic. His family history was marked by an extraordinarily possessive, overcontrolling mother. In desperation, he had made a number of manifest suicidal gestures during late adolescence, accompanied by fantasies of his death, representing the ultimate defeat and frustration of his mother.

PURPOSE—RANDOM IMPULSE-GRATIFICATION

Out of the child's preschool play, with family guidance, the child learns to delineate the boundaries between play and realistic, purposeful behavior.

Erikson defines "purpose" as "the courage to envisage and pursue valued goals uninhibited by the defeat of infantile fantasies, by guilt, and by the foiling fear of punishment." [12] This formulation captures the essence of the experience for most of the "overnight" radicals at Columbia. The "valued goal" they pursued was the restructuring of an institution that in their view had aligned itself with a barbarous war and unjustly exploited powerless neighbors. Since excavation of the gym site had already begun, they pursued a tactic that was harshly realistic and in the end largely successful.[13] "Guilt" was present, as we have noted, and influenced certain aspects of their behavior and tactics, but it did not deter involvement. Finally, with regard to "the foiling fear of punishment," the prospects of arrest, beatings, university discipline—possibly suspension or expulsion—and varying degrees of parent disapproval did not dissuade them.

If the child is not able to negotiate this transition from private fantasy-dominated play to a consensually validated purposeful orientation, he will be left with a propensity to seek random impulse-gratification. It is this tendency that makes the extreme anarchic wing of radicalism attractive to some students. In these

[12] *Ibid.*, p. 122.
[13] The success of the rebellion was grudgingly admitted by many anti-radical liberals. For example, Columbia sociologist Amitai Etzioni concluded: "It is a sad fact that the current New Left confrontations may have been the only means of bringing about the reforms necessary for liberal processes to work effectively at many of our major universities." In "Challenge to Liberalism," *Psychiatry and Social Science Review,* vol. 2, no. 7 (1968), p. 12.

groups, with the emphasis on "doing your own thing" and using "shocking" personal style as a tool to expose the absurdity of the social order,[14] there is rarely a viable political program.[15] Programs bring order, whereas anarchy brings the external world into harmony with the internal chaos. One student told me: "As long as I can keep focused on how screwed up the world is, I don't have to think about how screwed up I am." Another student described his exhilaration at impulsively pulling out his penis and urinating on the steps of the Pentagon during the antiwar demonstration of 1967. The act was highly symbolic for him (and for the many there who applauded him)—a denial of his impotence against this "impenetrable" governmental fortress. The exhibitionistic pleasure belied his fear of castration by the government troops for his defiance. But, in the end, it was no more than a private gratification of an overdetermined impulse; such acts are more expressive than functional as system-movers. The student-initiated rebellion in France in the spring of 1968, followed a quasi-official policy of "spontaneity" rather than any programmatic attempt to restructure French society. Although large cadres of students could accommodate to the relative state of anarchy, the workers did not, and the lack of coherent program of change contributed heavily to the failure of the rebellion.[16]

[14] A few, under the banner of their moral crusade, gave me the feeling, expressed by Columbia sociologist Sigmund Diamond, that "Violence of language is not an expression of exuberance [or] of . . . hostility alone; it is the portent of the violent deeds to come." (S. Diamond, "Language and Politics: An Afterward," *Political Science Quarterly*, vol. 84. no. 2, 1959, p. 382.) But, then, this is what revolutions are. And those of us who abhor violence are repelled. The pacifist sympathizer with revolutionary causes is, in the end, alienated from both sides.

[15] Paul Goodman points out that *"Anarchism* is not anarchy. It is against existing social and political systems, but it proposes to replace them with some form of ordered, *decentralized, individualistic community cooperation."* ("The Black Flag of Anarchism," *New York Times Magazine,* July 14, 1968, p. 20.) Goodman's social vision stands in contrast to Jerry Rubin's prescription for anarchy, which alternates between spontaneous provocative political psychodrama and mass "freak-outs." See Rubin, *Do It! Scenarios of the Revolution* (New York: Simon & Schuster, 1970).

[16] In an interview with Jean-Paul Sartre, Daniel Cohn-Bendit said, "Our movement's strength is precisely that it is based on an 'uncontrollable spontaneity.' [To create political awareness] we must avoid building

EMPATHY-ISOLATION

"Empathy" can be defined as the capacity to participate sub-jectively in the affective or cognitive experience of another, with awareness of the separateness of the self and the other. This is the positive outcome of the child's identification with a mother who understands and attends to his preverbal needs. The trait itself, however, does not emerge, as Piaget has demonstrated,[17] until the seventh year of life, when the child has the cognitive ability to abstract the experience of another as a separate entity. Lacking this mutual accommodation of mother and infant, the child develops the quality of "isolation," which usually means that he can intelligently formulate the experience of another but without any affective component.

A simple contrast of empathy and isolation is illustrated in two student responses. One described his reaction to the entrance of the police into a building he was occupying:

I looked around and saw that the girls looked very scared. A few were crying quietly. I felt suddenly sorry for them and very scared for myself. I took Linda and held her very tightly to comfort and protect her.

In the same circumstances, another student said:

The police broke in and started beating up people. I didn't feel scared or anything—just numb. I thought that I should protect my head and kept thinking that I should have worn my motorcycle helmet.

The polarity of empathy-isolation is complex because many of the healthiest, most idealistic radicals often have the subjective sense of isolation even though nothing in their lives resembles the manifest pattern generally ascribed to schizoid individuals. That

---

an organization immediately, or defining a program; that would inevitably paralyze us." (H. Bourges, ed., *The French Student Revolt: The Leaders Speak*, New York: Hill and Wang, 1968, pp. 78–79.) For an incisive dis-cussion of Cohn-Bendit's political philosophy and its consequences, see Raymond Aron, *The Elusive Revolution: Anatomy of a Student Revolt* (New York: Praeger, 1969).

[17] J. Piaget, *Moral Judgment of the Child* (Glencoe, Ill.: Free Press, 1948—originally published 1932).

is, these students have passionate romances, intense friendships, soul meets soul under the spell of pot now and then, they "dig" good guitar and good rock. They laugh, cry, and protest. Yet they complain of the frequent, intermittent, subjective pain of isolation. In contrast, many students who neither are activists nor feel particularly alienated do not report a sense of isolation, although their peak intimacies seem less intense than those of the "isolated" activists. I suggest that for many of the "isolates" the early years of life were characterized not by inadequate warmth, intuition, and care on the part of the mother, but rather by inconsistency, with wide fluctuations. They have experienced higher levels of "feeling" and "communion" with mother, but these levels were inconsistently maintained, so that there always remains an expectation that the blissful peak should be and can be recaptured. This leaves them always searching, with a vague sense of deprivation, as if they were operating out of the memories of the peak pleasures possible in life. Many of the upper-middle-class parents of these students characteristically move in and out of their own isolation, intellectuality, and busy lives to give intense concern and love on occasion, only to pull back.

In general, families that are warm, humanistic, and respectful of their children create an "ego-ideal" for the children, not only of what families should be like, but of what all social groups, the university as well as the larger society, should be like. Students from such families are often disenchanted in encounters with social units outside the family. This creates the tragic paradox of individuals reared in a "good family" who are sentenced to lives of alienation from a society in which the values and models for behavior learned from their families are not realized. When these students become radicalized, the issues and values that had separated them from society reach clear articulation, and, as they are committed to an ideology that permits actualization of the family ethic, their existence becomes far more tolerable.

To recapitulate, many radicals have had early mothering of such quality as to endow them with the potential for empathy, but also of such unevenness as to give them a sense of deprivation and a psychological rhythm of peak relatedness alternating with isolation. The isolation is the reflection of unacceptable rage at the withdrawal of the parent.[18] It is this combination of emphathy and a sense of deprivation—both personal past and social present —that contributes to their deep concern for truly oppressed and deprived people.

Where an individual has constant and pervasive isolation of affect, it is often in the service of repressing from awareness the destructive fantasies and profound amorphous rage that is usually near the surface. Such people will seek to place themselves in external situations or to manipulate situations, so as to justify the expression of the rage. Thus some of the Columbia students would provoke a policeman until he finally used excessive violence on them. Then they had the justification for their pre-existing anger.

French sociologist Raymond Aron discusses this point:

Symbolic illegality—the interruption of classes and the occupation of buildings—has the function of *provocation* . . . inspired by two different states of mind, although the two are usually combined. Either provocation as conceived and desired by the leaders is a means of bringing about a confrontation, or provocation becomes an end in itself. The demonstrators want to live the experience of the demonstration.[19]

The dilemma of the young person who needs to rely heavily on isolation to prevent the eruption of anxiety associated with his unacceptable impulses and affect is that there coexists a yearning for relief of the isolation and a desire for intense feeling. This is often sought from safer (that is, more distant) sources of arousal, ranging from movies or books to being "around" people without any real intimacy, to participating in "happenings" or passion-

[18] This parallels the observation in Spitz's classic study of anaclitic depression. Spitz observed that when infants were separated from their mothers after receiving warm and consistent maternal care, they experienced severe anaclitic depression. Infants who had not received the tender care of their own mothers, but had been in foundling homes from birth, did not experience depression. The implication is that in the former group "the loss of a loving relationship" caused the depression. In R. Spitz, "Hospitalism: An Inquiry into the Genesis of Psychiatric Condition in Early Childhood," in *The Psychoanalytic Study of the Child*, vol. 1 (New York: International University Press, 1945).

[19] R. Aron, "Student Rebellion: Vision of the Future or Echo from the Past?" *Political Science Quarterly*, no. 2, 1969, p. 292.

filled group confrontations. "Compromise," "mediation," "peaceful coexistence" connote forms of social interaction or resolution that are unconsciously repudiated, because they will diminish the external excitement that masks an inner void. Nonetheless, many isolated students can feel personally involved and empathic with remote oppressed individuals. The Vietnamese peasant, the Chicano grapepicker, or the ghetto black can, for some, be invested with feeling because they are symbols that the student need not confront in a direct interpersonal relationship. This in itself can be socially useful, regardless of the "authenticity" or psychodynamic function of the feelings, but it can also be destructive, when the unconscious need for confrontation dominates its rational political function and the oppressed peoples are therefore used as pawns in an attempt to achieve psychological relief from isolation.

RELATION TO AUTHORITY

The Oedipal conflict, its resolution and its enduring unconscious influence on behavior, is the central developmental concept in the psychoanalytic theory of neurosis. Freud described the process whereby the male child crystallizes his masculine sexual identification, his respect for authority (traditionally male in our culture), and his conscience (superego).[20] In simplified form, the child, having enjoyed the pleasures of autogenital stimulation, reaches a stage when the quest for genital sexual pleasure becomes associated with satisfaction from another person—an "object"—and he develops a genitally eroticized attachment to his mother. He recognizes his father as the rival for his mother's affection and the possessor of mother in bed. This rivalry evokes deep resentment and "murderous" wishes toward the father. However, he fears the father's retaliation for his amorous desires for the mother and for his anger at the father, a fear concretely symbolized

[20] S. Freud, *Complete Introductory Lectures on Psycho-Analysis* (1916-17); in *Collected Papers*, vol. XVI (London: Hogarth Press, 1963). Later (in *New Introductory Lectures on Psycho-Analysis*, 1933), he postulated the comparable development of the reversed-gender identity and superego for the female child, in which the process operates in an essentially parallel way.

by castration. Under this threat, he renounces (represses) his sexual desire for the mother and his anger at his father and resolves his inner conflict by progressive identification with the father, the male authority. This experience produces the foundation for conscience, an emotionally authentic sense of right and wrong, and moral responsibility—that is, "superego." The Oedipal conflict is at its height between the ages of four and seven. Commenting on the role of this life crisis in transforming the child into a social being, Freud wrote:

From this time onwards, the human individual has to devote himself to the great task of detaching himself from his parents, and not until that task is achieved can he cease to be a child and become a member of the social community. . . . These tasks are set to everyone; and it is remarkable how seldom they are dealt with in an ideal manner— that is, one which is correct both psychologically and socially.[21]

In the literature on student radicalism, the Oedipal conflict has at times been given the central role as an explanation of the movement.[22] Interestingly, the authors who invoke the Oedipal-rebellion theory are decidedly disapproving of student radicals and, in some cases (for example, Feuer), are clearly resentful of all that seems youthful and free.[23]

The outcome of the Oedipal stage can leave contrasting characterologic traits that will influence the nature of the radical or militant commitment. This scheme is modified by such factors as the mother's role in this stage of her son's life—for example, her seductiveness, her attitude toward the father's authority—and the role of other siblings who may share in the struggle or of older siblings, who may serve as authority surrogates. It must be emphasized that, even in a patriarchal society, children's attitudes toward authority vary with the degree and quality of authority actually exercised by individual mothers. In many black families, for example, the authority of the mother is a more dominant theme than in many white families. Similarly, in the "separated"

[21]*Complete Introductory Lectures . . . , op. cit.,* p. 337.

[22] See Feuer, *op. cit.;* also B. Rubenstein and M. Levitt, "The Student Revolt: Totem and Taboo Revisited," paper presented at the American Psychoanalytic Association Meetings, New York City, December 16, 1969.

[23] As Robert Michels said in his review of Feuer's book "To put it simply, Feuer just seems to hate kids." (Michels, *op. cit.,* p. 3.)

household, where children remain with mother, obviously the mother exercises greater authority than the father. Also, in many families, the mother is assigned far more authority in the rearing of the daughter than of the son.

If the relationship of the parents is one of mutual satisfaction and support, with sexual gratification for both, the likelihood of covert sexual demands on the part of the mother toward the son, as well as resentment on the part of the father for the warmth and attention the son appropriately receives from the mother, will be minimized. The father will not feel his masculinity or primacy with his wife endangered and will therefore not feel impelled to exert his supremacy over his son by harsh, inconsistent, or unreasonable authority and control. His affection for his son will be relatively unambivalent, and he will not be apprehensive about interdicting unacceptable behaviors and encouraging acceptable alternatives in the service of growth. In short, he will provide rational and appropriate controls, free of punitive attitudes and unconscious "murderous" wishes toward his son. Out of this family climate, castration fears or, in more general terms, fear of attack, harm, or malevolence in the hands of a resentful, punitive father will not predominate. The son will learn to trust and respect and identify with the father's authority. He will not harbor repressed rage toward the father. He will develop a flexible relationship to authority, based on the freedom to perceive accurately the true nature—the motivations as well as the effects—of authority as exercised in the institutions that affect his life. Hence, when authority is exercised justly and wisely and is deserving of respect, it is respected. When authority is exercised arbitrarily and exploitatively, it is repudiated. Both attitude and action are determined by the evaluation of the rationality, competence, and moral legitimacy of the authority. This is not to say that residues of the Oedipal conflict do not endure and influence behavior, but they need not do so in neurotic and destructive ways.

Students at the idealistic end of the radical spectrum expressed very specific criticism of Columbia's administration and its policies. The students may have been opposed to war or racism generally, but the specific way in which Columbia was governed made that university the object of the protest. In students with a flexible relationship to authority, it is not their psychological organization alone that produces rebellion; the nature of the authority in question is also a critical determinant.

In contrast are two groups of students whose relation with the father during the Oedipal developmental crisis would impel the son in a nihilistic direction as a radical. The first of these pathways is the family situation in which the mother is the source of authority and strength in the household and the father is passive, ineffectual, and frequently absent, delegating what authority exists to the mother. Here, one can infer not only that the mother will influence her son to become passive, ineffectual, and uncertain of his masculinity, because that is the kind of male she is most comfortable with, but also that there will be no positive male model. While the son's self-concept is uncertain regarding his "masculinity," meaning courage and action, there may exist the basis for reckless action, even violence, to deny his inner doubts. This was clearly present in the view of many strikers that the rebellion was a puberty rite, a proof of courage and commitment. Many students echoed the statement: "The thing about this was that all of us were proving that we have balls."

Beyond this, however, where the father abdicates his authority and control during the Oedipal stage, the eroticized interest in the mother does not progress to satisfactory resolution; namely, to an awareness of mother's sexual commitment to someone else, and the necessity to curb, repress, and sublimate impulses on the child's part. Castration anxiety is not mobilized, and this essential step in the formation of superego—a sense of acceptable and unacceptable impulses—is missing. The father remains the hated rivalrous object, and identification with him as "good" authority does not take place. These sons develop the characteristic of deficient superego,[24] which can be observed in many nihilistic radicals. The possibilities for destructiveness are uninhibited by any internally moral ethic. Thus, such acts as the burning of a professor's research notes can be justified by revolutionary rhetoric.

[24] It should be noted in passing that this family constellation may also produce an individual with a highly punitive and rigid superego, for reasons that are beyond the pale of our discussion. See S. Freud, *New Introductory Lectures on Psycho-Analysis* (1933), in *Collected Papers*, vol. XXII (London: Hogarth Press, 1964).

The other pathway of resolving Oedipal conflict that leads to nihilistic radicalism is characterized by compulsive anti-authoritarianism. This orientation can be the legacy of an Oedipal triad in which the father is resentful and jealous of the relationship between his wife and their son. Because of a combination of discord with his wife and his own unresolved Oedipal wishes, the patricidal element of which is projected onto the son, he asserts his dominance over the "usurping" son by the exercise of arbitrary and punitive authority. In many such families, this is coupled with the father's clear preference for warmer relationship with his daughters. The outcome is a son who has had a primal experience with destructive authority. This view of authority will be transferred unconsciously to all authority thereafter and often is quite apparent in conscious attitudes. "Participatory democracy," "anarchism," "student power," and other such concepts have idiosyncratic meaning and appeal to these students. For some, the manifest form of relationship to authority is obsequiousness, but this represents a reaction formation against the unconscious rageful view of authority. In any event, in this group of individuals there will be some who seek the destruction of authority qua authority, regardless of what it stands for. Just as they fight authority at the university, so they will fight their own leaders within the New Left.

For this group, action against authority is accompanied by an unconscious element of guilt, and not only the expectation of but the need for punishment. The successes of the rebellion must be undone, for success in the struggle against authority cannot be tolerated. Most of these students have not done well in school because the classroom has always been, consciously and unconsciously, an arena for struggle against the instructor; doing well therefore means defeating the instructor. To undo or stop short of success is a way of warding off castration anxiety or its adult transformations. In confrontations, this group tends to seek to be arrested, beaten, expelled, and so on, as means of buying off the greater threats of castration or annihilation.

Like other developmental epochs or crises, then, the Oedipal period is a stage that all children must negotiate. Depending on a complex and not yet fully understood interaction of factors, the child will emerge with enduring "virtuous" or "nonvirtuous" characteristics specifically attributable to this stage that will be important components and determinants of his commitment to radicalism.[25]

[25] There have been many previous attempts to explain student activism on the basis of Oedipal conflict, most notably by Lewis Feuer (*op. cit.*). Professor Feuer's fundamental assumption is that the participants in all student movements share the same Oedipal dynamics. Regardless of the time and place, he believes, all student movements are based on conflict between the generations. The generation of sons becomes alienated, unable to identify with and join the generation of fathers. They then are propelled by predominantly unconscious drives to rebel against and destroy the "de-authoritized" father. The unconscious destructive motivation toward the father and father-surrogates is unsuccessfully sublimated in the form of political action. Tactics inevitably become violent in all student movements, and these are not in the service of useful goals but are intended to "satisfy the needs of generational hatred on the latent, unconscious level." In the end, since the student movement is not a reflection of a healthy ego capacity to perceive social reality or injustice, the guilt engendered by this patricidal operation leads the movement to destroy itself. Feuer applies this thesis uniformly to nineteenth- and twentieth-century student movements in Germany, Serbia, Russia, China, Japan, Africa, the United States, and elsewhere and then finds the student movements responsible for such historic events as World Wars I and II, the rise of Hitler, Stalinism, Castroism, and McCarthyism (Joseph), in what Howard Zinn (*op. cit.*) refers to as "Feuer's demonology."

There are several fundamental errors in Feuer's thesis:

1. He makes the student movements a repository for individuals all of whom have the same conflict, and resolve in the same way. Thus he assumes that the course of the Oedipal march is not significantly affected by differences in the child-rearing patterns and family structure of different cultures, among other factors, and that other developmental conflicts are not significant in motivating radicals. Nor is social reality or the nature of a particular university relevant; they only provide the stage on which an unconscious fantasy is compulsively played out.

2. He confuses psychodynamics and psychopathology. For Feuer, the discovery of unconscious factors is sufficient basis for the diagnosis of psychopathology. He does not take into account any of the ego processes that, in the end, determine whether widely held unconscious impulses are resolved in individually and socially adaptive or maladaptive behavior. (See Michels, *op. cit.*, for an extended discussion of this point.)

3. He offers no explanation for the noninvolvement in student protest of nonactivist students with the same psychodynamics as activists.

4. He makes no attempt to reconcile his thesis and profile of student activists with the very different conclusions of other observers.

5. He offers no adequate explanation for the presence of females in contemporary student movements.

An example of the several variants of Feuer's approach is a recent paper

I have presented in schematic form a model suggesting how the resolution of a series of normal developmental stages can leave character traits that can influence where on the spectrum from "idealistic" to "nihilistic" radicalism a student will fall. All people go through these epochs and develop traits somewhere on the continuum from "virtuous" to "nonvirtuous" for each stage. Yet, clearly, not all become radicals. These characteristics therefore must be understood in conjunction with other essential components, to which we now turn.

Value Orientation

The ideological content of the student's sociopolitical commitment is shaped by a set of values assimilated from his family. In a heterogeneous society such as ours, the variety of approved social and political values and of family interest in political action is enormous.

It is our liberal reflex to accept as "moral" and "good" those values that stress equality, justice, and conscience, which are the heart of radical ideology. As values, they provide a conception of what is desirable and then influence the selection from available

---

by two psychoanalysts, Rubenstein and Levitt (*op. cit.*). They concluded (without citing any data) that most contemporary activists come from child-centered, "progressive" families, characterized by weak and passive fathers, incapable of administering firm discipline, and dominant mothers. According to these authors, the radicals have never resolved their Oedipal conflicts and castration anxiety and have failed in superego development. Thus, they are attracted to what Rubenstein and Levitt see as an essentially immoral, destructive movement, because of their need to deal with castration fear through revolutionary activity and identification with such men of action as Che Guevera. They go so far as to link criticism of college administrators to the "murder of the primal father." These authors, too, offer a simple, uniform explanation for most (at least not all) participants in what they see as "acting out" psychopathology, based on Oedipal dynamics. They suggest no explanation of why, at specific moments in history, at particular universities, groups so different in family dynamics and child-rearing patterns as black students and white students engage in similar radical political action.

In summary, the fault of works such as Feuer's and the Rubenstein and Levitt formulation is not that they mistake the universality and later influence of Oedipal dynamics but that they misuse the concept as the explanation for "psychopathological" social-group behavior.

means and ends of action.[26] The values constitute the standard by which alternatives for action are evaluated. Certain clusters of interrelated values become organized into a cohesive "value orientation," which then functions as a generalized conception that influences not only the individual's relation to other individuals but also his relation to the institutions that affect groups of men—his sociopolitical value orientation.

In discussing the role of values in governing an individual student's political behavior, a typology proposed by M. Brewster Smith is useful. Smith distinguishes between two modes of integrating values into the developing personality: "superego-requiredness" and "self-requiredness." [27] Superego-requiredness applies to values that are so internalized that they are inflexibly held and indiscriminately acted upon and operate from the hidden reservoir of the unconscious. Paradoxically, the student can be tyrannically driven by his "noble" values to find "causes" in order to discharge his unconscious directives. For such a person, *not* to pursue protest activity results in a welling up of tension and guilt.

In contrast, the values and attitudes characterized by "self-requiredness" may be the same as the superego-required values, but they are subordinated to conscious executive control by the individual. They are integrated into the person's concept of himself, but with more conscious formation. Hence, they are applied flexibly, in appropriate situations. In the face of external realities, they can be modified and implemented innovatively and constructively.

Whether the value orientation is in the service of the superego or the self is determined largely by the manner by which the values were transmitted, rather than by the nature and meaning of the values per se. Values that are imposed arbitrarily, without reasons that "make sense" to the developing child, that are

[26] This definition of values is taken from Clyde Kluckhohn's basic contribution to this subject. C. Kluckhohn, "Values and Value Orientations in the Theory of Action," in T. Parsons and E. A. Shils, eds., *Toward a General Theory of Action* (Cambridge, Mass.: Harvard University Press, 1951), pp. 388–433.

[27] M. B. Smith, "Personal Values in the Study of Lives," in R. W. White, ed., *The Study of Lives* (New York: Atherton Press, 1963).

adopted by the child primarily out of fear of the parent, will be internalized as superego-required. In contrast, self-required values are assimilated by the child with a sense of participation in their formulation. Perhaps, therefore, as Michels has suggested, the child-rearing of many activists has been characterized not simply by their having learned specific formulas of "why" and "how" but also by learning the meaning of the concepts "why" and "how." [28] In such children, the concept of "self" is continuously evolving—synthesizing internal drives and external realities and teachings. A part of this dynamism is the progressive modification and application of the values derived from the parents or from school, church, and other carriers of the culture.

I would postulate a correlation between "idealistic" radicalism and self-required values and another between "nihilistic" radicalism and superego-required values, although the values themselves may be the identical humanistic, egalitarian ones.

In our discussion of "continuity" and "discontinuity" in values between parents and activist children (Chapter VI), we pointed out the correlation between "idealistic" radicalism and value "continuity" and between "nihilistic" radicalism and "discontinuity." In the students whose moral-political values and attitudes toward action were continuous with their parents, the students' behavior tended to be "egosyntonic," fulfilling an ego-ideal, and hence more flexible and adaptive, accompanied by less need to undo the political gains or to get themselves punished for their "rebellious" views and acts. In contrast, the likelihood is great that the existence of "discontinuity" represented either a failure of identification, particularly with the same-sex parent, or an elaboration of a theme of rebellion against the parent. In such cases, the probability that the radicalism would be rigid and compulsively and inflexibly practiced is greater, and it is more likely to be self-destructive.

In sum, although the political values and principles of the radical and militant students represent the most humanistic ideals of Western sociopolitical philosophy, the individuals attracted to

[28] R. Michels, "Student Dissent and Adult Response," presented to the Michigan Society of Psychiatry and Neurology, Oct. 2, 1969, Detroit, Michigan.

the movement do not necessarily express in their political behavior the humanism that is the substance of their ideology. The developmental process by which the values were acquired and the consequent role they play in the individual's psychodynamic organization can significantly modify his political activism. Further, values constitute only one of a number of areas that influence the political thought and action of students.

The Nature of the Radical Action

The final class of internal factors that determine participation in a specific radical or militant action is the individual student's response to the form of action, growing out of the interaction between the stress he experiences, the gratification inherent in the action, and the individual psychodynamic constellation of impulses, needs, and defense mechanisms.

The concept of anxiety is germane here, inasmuch as the quality of the experience of the Columbia communal action—indeed, of participation at all—depended in part on the amount of anxiety the student felt. A major shift in emphasis in psychoanalytic thinking over the past four decades has been to understand man's adaptation, not simply as the defensive resolution of internal mental conflicts but also as the achievement of a functional equilibrium between the "conflict-free ego" of the individual [29] and his environment. "Conflict-free ego" refers to ego or personality faculties that operate "realistically," in response to external stimuli, free of significant influence from intrapsychic conflict. For example, if a speeding car is heading toward a person, his conflict-free response includes realistic perception of the oncoming car, comprehension of the danger, the "decision" to step aside, and the motoric execution of this decision. With the growing tendency to include man as responsive to his environment and his culture in the concept of adaptation, "anxiety" has continued to play a central role in determining behavior.[30]

[29] H. Hartmann, *Ego Psychology and the Problem of Adaptation*, (New York: International Universities Press, 1958; originally published in 1939).
[30] This shift in thought about adaptation followed Freud's major theoretical revision in this concept of anxiety, as presented in *Inhibitions, Symptoms, and Anxiety*, 1926. His original formulation (*Introductory*

Every radical action has elements that are experienced in common by all participants. But these "actual" elements contain many possible conscious and unconscious meanings for the people exposed to them. For example, if tear gas is to be used, all will share the response of fear and avoidance behavior. But, beyond that, being tear-gassed has private symbolic meanings that vary from person to person.

Thus, in a simple way, whether one is drawn to or repelled by a particular activity, whether one enjoys or does not enjoy his participation, depends on the final personal balance of pleasure *versus* pain; of fulfillment of needs and acceptable gratification of impulses *versus* anxiety and fear in that situation.

Why was the week of radical action and communal living so profound an experience for those who participated? In broad terms, because it involved unusually high degrees of pleasure as well as counterbalancing anxiety and fear. The "pleasures" were manifold:

1. It actualized an ego-ideal for a significant faction of youth—"selfless commitment to a humane ideal."

2. It gratified in institutionalized form both hostile unconscious Oedipal wishes, by displacing them to a "bad" authority surrogate, and hostile rivalrous impulses toward siblings, displaced to politically opposing fellow students.

3. It commanded expressed approval from an important faction of the "good" authority surrogates—the faculty.

4. The commune became the "world" (particularly where exit and re-entry were restricted), and every fellow-communard became endowed ("cathected," in psychoanalytic terms) with more

---

Lectures on Psychoanalysis, 1915–16) was that anxiety represented a manifestation of libidinal impulses that were repressed and not expressed as symptoms. Being barred from manifest expression, the energy from the repressed impulse was transformed into anxiety. In his 1926 revision, Freud reached the position that anxiety was not caused by repression. Rather, repression and the other mechanisms of defense came into being as a result of the potential presence of anxiety. Defenses were now viewed as being in the service of (1) reducing anxiety that originated from the threat of the emergence in thought or action of unacceptable impulses from within; and (2) the awareness of threatening stimuli from the external environment.

feeling and importance than is ordinarily possible in life outside the communes, with its much more diffused social intercourse.

5. The intensity of the crisis and the form of the commitment allowed the release of "passion." [31] This made for a pleasurable sense of internal psychological organization—a unity of thought, feeling, and action.

These pleasures were opposed by fear and anxiety deriving from several sources:

1. There was fear related to the accurate perception and comprehension of the possible consequences of the radical action and the probable response of those who were being confronted. The fear centered about possible personal consequences leading to "foreclosure of career," including suspension or expulsion and a record of being arrested, and also the prospect of police beatings and parental disapproval. Fear also centered on nonpersonal secondary effects, such as conservative backlash leading to repressive legislation, the election of conservative candidates, or igniting the neighboring community into uncontrolled rioting.

2. There was anxiety of intrapsychic origin resulting from the conflict between superego and the gratification of unconscious negative Oedipal impulses, sibling-rivalrous impulses, and generalized aggressive and sadistic impulses.

3. For some, there was anxiety related to the interpersonal aspects of the communal-living situation, including the arousal of impulses due to the continuous bodily proximity to fellow communards and the heightened emotional atmosphere in the commune.

4. For some, there was anxiety related to having to place trust in their leaders, who might "use" or dupe them.

"COMMITMENT TO AN IDEAL"

"Commitment to an ideal" has become an increasingly significant component of youth's "ego-ideal"—that concept of oneself that a person tries to actualize in the conduct of his life.

---

[31] The use of the term "passion" in this context was suggested by Robert Michels.

Such commitment was a major motivating force for many of the participants in the Columbia rebellion.[32] Their idealistic, dedicated quality was demonstrated dramatically by the "clean for Gene" youth campaign in New Hampshire. Otherwise avenues for actualizing their ideal were closed. White students were progressively excluded from any major role in the civil rights movement. And, as we have discussed, channels for effective reform at Columbia also appeared to be nonexistent. In one sudden burst of energy, the campus was polarized into forces for "order and due process" versus those who "took a stand" for an "ideal." As a student said: "I was doing a criminal act for ideas, not for profit. I was going to take a stand and sacrifice something."

Not all who possessed this ego-ideal entered buildings, because of the other factors involved in the decision. But to the extent that "commitment to an ideal" was part of their self-concept, if they did not enter a building, they suffered loss of self-esteem by not measuring up to this internalized standard. This is conveyed in the following undergraduate's statement:

Did I expect the injustices of the world to wait until I descended from my ivory tower and dealt with them in a legitimate way?
Then came slowly the realization that this guilt was mixed with pangs of jealousy. I felt guilty about not being in the buildings. . . . They were doing something worthwhile, something that would make the world a better place to live.

Because of his shame and failure to realize his expectations for himself, he turns on himself self-derisively, thereby expiating some of his guilt:

And where was I when all this was going on, where was this radical among radicals? He was outside the buildings, filling the shoes of a wishy-washy liberal, drowning in the quicksand of his own indecision. Those in buildings were walking on water, and I only moved close enough to watch the splendor from afar.

If this commitment to an ideal is unconflicted, it will usually

[32] Keniston has suggested why this has emerged in the 1960's as a compelling psychological motif for a sizable segment, albeit a minority, of youth, in "You Have to Grow Up in Scarsdale to Know How Bad Things Really Are," *New York Times Magazine,* April 27, 1969. I will discuss the historical evolution of this ego-ideal in Chapter XI.

be found to have continuity and congruence in its content with the ego-ideal of the parents.[33] If continuity exists, the radical action will be egosyntonic—therefore pleasurable and less accompanied by anxiety. As the child moves out of the exclusively parental sphere of influence and comes into contact with teachers, camp counselors, and other models, further identifications can be made, and these new ego-ideals may be internalized in a later stage of development. However, if so, they are more remote from the early ego-core, and the counterforces of anxiety from superego sources will tend to hold sway.

For black people, there have been more direct opportunities for commitment to social action on behalf of ideals of justice and equality in the civil rights movement. There is also among black students considerable unease about pursuing an education to advance their own careers, at an insulated Ivy League campus, without also being a civil rights activist. This "commitment to an ideal" was a pronounced theme, and the enhanced feeling of self-esteem that came from actualizing it is seen in the following two statements by black students from Hamilton:

I was proud of myself after. There was a feeling of commitment.

I felt important—having done something. I was guilty before, never having stuck my neck out.

It should be noted that this need to fulfill a commitment to an ideal is satisfied in rebellions in which the issues involve humanistic principle, with no immediate gain for the individual. In this respect the Columbia rebellion contrasts with college protests concerning liberalization of parietal rules or union strikes for higher wages.

INSTITUTIONALIZED GRATIFICATION OF UNCONSCIOUS IMPULSES

We come back to the controversial question of the role of destructive Oedipal impulses in motivating student rebellions. Because of the students' psychological fluidity at this point in their lives, a profound event of any sort will tap and interact with

---

[33] This concept was elaborated in Chapter VI, in the discussion of Lustman's conceptualization of symptom versus character trait, based on parental affirmation or disapproval of the child's values or behavior.

currents of unconscious thought. Specifically, any rebellion will reach into the unconscious Oedipal arena—of faculty, administrators, and observers as well as students. If one could isolate and weigh differentially the many determinants of radicalism, there would be some students in whom acting out of negative Oedipal wishes would be found to play a major role. That is quite different, however, from saying that no one has fully resolved his Oedipal conflicts and that everyone will therefore derive some direct or vicarious satisfaction of these hidden impulses from rebellious action. To follow the logic of the "Oedipal theory" of student rebellion would lead us to conclude that all who disagree with radical actions do so primarily in defense against their negative Oedipal feelings.

So much for these exercises in psychoanalytic thought. The rebellion, with appreciable peer-group support and participation, varying degrees of parental approval in a sizable percentage of cases, and endorsement by the "big brother" junior faculty, allows for gratification of these universal impulses. The politically sympathetic observer might then say that this radical action represented an excellent sublimation of the unacceptable infantile impulse and satisfaction of it through a higher social aim—that is, giving up self-interest for social interest.

Although we cannot say simply that the rebellion was motivated by sibling rivalry and that the hidden goal was to occupy the buildings (inner space of alma mater, unconsciously the womb) while leaving the hated siblings locked out, sibling rivalry and competition are, nonetheless universal motivational themes and, as such, were served by the action. This could be inferred from the great delight the white radicals took in observing the efforts of the Majority Coalition, whom they derisively termed "jocks," to force them out of the buildings. The theme was also applicable to participants in the Majority Coalition who acknowledged their pleasure in watching the police club radicals. This resonates with the pleasure a child derives from observing his sibling being spanked.

APPROVAL FROM AUTHORITY SURROGATES

We have noted that the radical action commanded approval from an important faction of the "good" authority surrogates—

the faculty. I venture to say that if each student were matched with his favorite and most respected faculty members, the similarity in political orientation would be very high. These faculty are important developmental figures for the students, filling the role of catalyst in the last stages of the process of achieving autonomy of intellectual position.

Faculty were very much on the minds of the white radical students, who devoted much effort and concern in attempts to radicalize the faculty—that is, get them to support the radical action, in particular by voting for amnesty for the radicals—but out of moral-political conviction, not simply expediency. To the extent that a sizable number of junior faculty and some major members of senior faculty supported them, there was an affirmation that made the rebellion egosyntonic for the students and allowed for contact with faculty members of a more emotional, direct, and serious nature than is possible in the usual course of campus life. Although the predominant reaction of radical students to the "mediating" position of the faculty ranged from disenchantment to contempt, the salutory effect of the pro-radical minority was vitally important. It is hard to conceive that such a large-scale rebellion could take place in the face of uniform faculty condemnation. Faculty support for the 1964 FSM protestors at Berkeley and for the 1968 French student rebels was likewise important.

THE COMMUNE AS THE WORLD

The commune became the "world," particularly in Low Library, Mathematics building, and Hamilton Hall. The fellow communards became invested with singular importance and a feeling that remained etched in memory for many as their most glorious experience in relation to other beings.

This marked intensification of affect in group experiences was described and explained by Freud as follows:

A group impresses the individual as being an unlimited power and an insurmountable peril. For the moment it replaces the whole of human society, which is the wielder of authority, whose punishments the individual fears, and for whose sake he has submitted to so many inhibitions. It is clearly perilous for him to put himself in opposition to it, and it will be safer to follow the example of those around him and perhaps even "hunt with the pack." In obedience to the new authority he may put his former "conscience" out of action, and so surrender to the attraction of the increased pleasure that is certainly obtained from the removal of inhibitions.[34]

In this somewhat less than romantic conceptualization, Freud viewed the libidinal attachment to authority figures as being redirected to the "group." Because of the increase in libidinal energy connected to the group, the group "experience" is more profound and memorable.[35]

The experience for each person approached that of every other person in the commune. They were afraid together and elated together, sang together, used coed bathrooms (in one building), ate the same food, and so on. Distinctions among individuals in the commune were blurred; all communards were more or less equally "brother" and "sister." In the process the differences between oneself and others also diminished, allowing for the subjective experience of communion. This communal form of fusion of egos had elements of "regression in the service of the ego" [36]—a characteristic of an earlier child-parent bond, which, in this political situation, provided strength that enabled the commune to function creatively and effectively as a group and, at times, gave an illusory sense of clarity.

Since the "radical action" at Columbia involved communal living, which met many psychological needs, it attracted many students who had been essentially apolitical before April 23. Some of these people came from the campus drug subculture, although very few of the campus "heads" became actively engaged. Others were relative social isolates. After the bust, many of this special

[34] S. Freud, *Group Psychology and the Analysis of the Ego* (1921), in *Collected Works,* vol. XVIII (London: Hogarth Press, 1955), pp. 84–85.

[35] John Spiegel has utilized Freud's "group psychology" to explain, in part, the motivations of occupants of university buildings. (J. Spiegel, "Campus Conflict and Professorial Egos," *Transaction,* vol. 6, Oct., 1969.)

[36] Ernst Kris introduced this term to describe the process by which the ego regulates its own capacity to regress. The organizing functions of the ego include voluntary and temporary withdrawal of cathexis, from one area to another, in order to later regain improved control. E. Kris, *Psychoanalytic Explorations in Art* (New York: International Universities Press, 1952).

group of students again became politically inactive, returning to their previous adaptation when the exhilaration of the commune was no longer there to sustain their political commitment.[37]

The communes present an interesting interaction between psychoanalytic orientation and radical critique. A radical student said to me:

Psychoanalysts see this [the commune] as artificial relief from individual psychopathology. But being an emotional drop-out is a response to the present institutions of the society. With a revolution in consciousness the communal way would become the norm and the kids that you call psychiatrically sick and say use the commune for a "high," for relief from their sickness, wouldn't be so hung-up. The institutions are sick, and these kids just reflect that.

This radical view of adaptation is in harmony with the psychology and social philosophy of the British psychiatrist Ronald Laing, who enjoys widespread popularity among these youth. Laing states, for example "Alienation as our present destiny is achieved only by outrageous violence perpetrated by human beings on human beings." [38]

Behavioral scientists can focus on all the transient ingredients of the crisis commune situation and conclude pejoratively that it is "artificial." But the students' reaction was not an illusion produced by the toxic effects of drugs. It was for many a few moments of the high integration we all search for throughout life. Some take the route of disorganized ego regression—that is, psychosis; others, drugs and alcohol; others, private artistic creativity; others, making money; and some few seek a transcendence of self in the balance of self-interest and ethical brotherhood, fused in action, feeling, and thought, which is what the communes represented for many of these youth.

A young revolutionary, discussing some of the great risks involved in revolutionary commitment, remarked that Che Gue-

[37] Bruno Bettelheim has elaborated this point, but his bias would lead one to believe that the radical movement is little more than a creation to accommodate the therapeutic needs of bands of paranoid leaders and isolated followers. B. Bettelheim, "Obsolete Youth: Toward a Psychograph of Adolescent Rebellion," *Encounter,* vol. 23 (Sept., 1969), pp. 29–42.

[38] R. D. Laing, *The Politics of Experience* (New York: Pantheon, 1967), p. 13.

varra's death at thirty-nine was irrelevant. "In his living years he felt more, achieved more and had more meaning in his life than those of us who are more self-preservative, and slowly live on only to die of hardening of the arteries at age sixty-five."

REALISTIC FEAR AND ANXIETY

Not all the students who were sympathetic to the ideology and tactics of the Columbia radicals and militants joined them in the buildings. For many of these students who remained outside, the potential pleasure and fulfillment of the involvement were opposed, and in the end, outweighed by anxiety and fear derived from several sources.

Virtually all students in the buildings were preoccupied intermittently with the possible consequences of the radical action. This was not neurotic anxiety but the appropriate self-protective signal from conflict-free spheres of ego functioning. All male students had to consider the possibility that participation would result in termination of their college career by suspension or expulsion, which would make them immediately available for the draft, unprotected by student deferment. In addition, there was the risk of arrest, jailing, and a criminal record, which could foreclose a career in law, government, or other occupations requiring security clearance. The disadvantages of having a "criminal record" certainly were a deterrent to many students who would otherwise have entered a building. A Barnard striker described a meeting with one such student during the first hours of the occupation of Hamilton Hall:

In Hamilton Hall, this straight kid came up. He said he didn't want to get arrested because he wanted to go into the Civil Service. We had a really good conversation for ten minutes. I don't know his name and he didn't ask me mine.

The threats to education and future career are significant because it is simply untrue that all the white radicals had renounced bourgeois career goals. And very few, if any, of the black students foresaw a career as "black militant," comparable to the full-time "organizers" in the white New Left.

The anxiety and fear that were specific to the black students in

Hamilton Hall have been discussed in Chapter V, in relation both to realistic factors in their lives and to the deeper, unconscious level of anxiety and fear that has to do with the inhibition of assertion that is part of the childhood training of blacks in white America.

Anxiety of Intrapsychic Origin

We react to everyday experiences not only in terms of their immediate, realistic qualities, but also on the basis of their symbolic linkage to earlier repressed memories and to unconscious enduring themes. For example, when a student allegedly spit in the face of Vice-President David Truman, our response to the incident goes beyond indignation at the manifestation of loss of civility, or compassion for Truman. It interacts in all of us with buried impulses to lash out and humiliate authority, originally in the form of father. Depending on one's own resolution of this conflict, the incident may be vicariously titillating, it may evoke rage and the desire to punish the whole movement (that is, reaction-formation), or it may be seen in relative perspective as a particularly offensive personal-political gesture by an individual.

Regardless of the final balance for each individual at Columbia, there was a component of anxiety for all. For a few, both whites and blacks, this anxiety was of such intensity that psychological disorganization occurred, and they had to leave the building. For others, some of the exhilaration was secondary in the sense that staying in the buildings represented the conquest of more primal superego-generated anxiety, a release from the control of these intrapsychic forces.

For some who were conflicted, parental opposition to their participation served to recharge faltering primary superego dictates. The fact that parents were not always effective in dissuading their sons from participation was in some cases due to the normative maturational process of subordinating the early superego constellation to later modifications based on other people and ideas. It is here that teachers and respected leaders play necessary roles.

ANXIETY IN COMMUNAL LIVING

A major arena of anxiety for some students was related to the interpersonal aspects of the communal-living situation. In the buildings, a large number of males and females lived together in very limited space. Augustus Kinzel [39] has discussed the concept of "body buffer zones," arguing that, in general, the more unbridled a person's aggressive impulses, the more physical distance he must have between himself and others in order not to feel anxious. I think Kinzel's findings can be generalized to individuals with conflicted sexual impulses (for example, homosexual, passive or aggressive heterosexual, and so on). Such students either played supportive roles outside, looked for privacy in the building they were in, or went to Fayerweather, where the policy of free exit and entry was exercised. One such student, who had a history of episodes of depersonalization when too much emotion was aroused in the company of friends, was intellectually committed to the rebellion but unable to endure the emotion-filled life in the commune. He found his niche by joining other supporters in sleeping on the lawn of the campus and conducting candlelight vigils, and doing supporting tasks on the outside. This allowed him to maintain a psychological equilibrium that would not have been possible inside a building.

This model for understanding the forces involved in the decision to enter or avoid a commune and the quality of the personal psychological experience can be extended to participation in other New Left and black-militant movements. At Columbia the life style demanded by the communal nature of the radical action for blacks and whites provided an atmosphere in which the political action carried with it a passionate conviction. In its own right, this dictated to some extent the composition of the radical population, attracting some who were not "political" basically and precluding others, some of whom were arrested in other kinds of radical action. (For example, sixty-four Columbia students, almost none of whom had occupied campus buildings in April, were

---

[39] A. F. Kinzel, "Body Buffer Zone in Violent Prisoners," American Psychiatric Association Meetings, Bal Harbour, Florida, May 8, 1969.

arrested at the May 18 protest at a Columbia-acquired off-campus apartment house.)

Beyond the politics involved, the radical action points out to us qualities of life sought by youth that are rarely present or possible at universities as they are structured today. Radical critique might consider it co-optation to so improve the quality of life at the university that its students are sufficiently pacified to lose sight of the relation of the university to government and to the non-student community and, therefore, do not become radicalized. I think that, if such humanism and sense of community could become a part of campus life, a disequilibrium would be created between the campus base and the society outside that would serve to mobilize a student-radical movement directed at appropriate targets in other sectors of society.

X: Social and Political Realities in Political Activism

In addition to certain elements of the individual's character structure, value system, and response to the nature of the radical action, the activation of radicalism requires a conviction that the existing societal institutions and machinery for change are inadequate to meet the needs and pleas for change of people who are without power, deprived, and oppressed.

If we look beyond the specific issues that are usually enumerated as the external causes of student rebellion, we become aware of a pervasive sense of powerlessness that increasingly is a significant part of our American identity. I am referring to the inability of any individual, or even of individuals banded together, to act in a way that will alter, by constitutionally sanctioned and legal means, those features of the external environment that are regarded as objectionable.

In colonial days, when American society was rural, largely agrarian, and decentralized in governance, a citizen could participate directly in the decisions that affected his life, simply by attending the town meeting. The fact that the production of goods depended on hand tools or muscle power allowed him direct physical control over and connection to the fruits of his labor. Relatively few aspects of life were dictated by forces outside his community.

Over the next two centuries, America evolved from a direct democracy to a representative democracy (at first with total disenfranchisement of certain groups—notably blacks and women). In terms of social structure, a predominantly urban society has emerged, regulated by vast communications networks, huge bureaucratic agencies, and mammoth corporations and conglomerates whose interests link them to an unimaginably powerful military establishment. This evolution in the social order from colonial days to the present has been accompanied by a progressive diminution in personal political power.

As a result, it is not only the social minorities (for instance, blacks, college students, women, homosexuals, intellectuals, prisoners, and others) who feel powerless but the mass of adult male Caucasians as well. In every significant area of our lives, the complexity of organization, rapidity of change, and level of technological sophistication reduce most men to psychological passivity. Some compensate for personal powerlessness by identifying with the destructive might and potential of America. Thus, for example, they support continued fighting in Vietnam, psychologically equating fighting with strength and withdrawal with weakness.

The sense of powerlessness is especially acute for minority groups that have no true representation in decision-making. Is there a more revealing example of the myth of our democracy than the fact that hundreds of thousands of young males, without the power to vote for the officials determining their fate, have been obliged to serve and, in some cases, die in a war that they deplore as barbarous?

It is only in the context of this dilemma of powerlessness that the radical dissent of students has its full meaning. It is only in this context that the importance of the issue of "freedom of speech," usually involved in any campus confrontation, can be comprehended.

In terms of this issue of power, activist students in the main comprise two groups: (1) the economically and socially disenfranchised, who are demanding political power as a means to a larger share of the wealth of industrial society; and (2) those who can or do share in the wealth, but who find the quality of life unsatisfactory in meeting other, more subtle human needs. The latter group seeks "meaning" in life, a climate in which a sense of self can develop that is not dependent on external labels provided for or forced upon the individual in our consumer society. The problem is compounded for youth, who are cultivated as consumers but not utilized as producers or creators. In their rejection of a consumer society and their search for an "existential humanism" for themselves and others, they have become engaged in the "second revolution," [1] members of the "youth counter-culture." [2]

So we are, in broad terms, witnesses to two "revolutions" being staged concurrently on certain college campuses by these two groups—one comprised mainly of blacks, the other mainly of "comfortable" whites. The two revolutions grow out of different definitions of needs, use somewhat different tactics, and certainly pursue different goals. Neither can be comprehended without understanding the nature of the external conditions that frustrate their realization.

To draw an analogy: If someone is malnourished and hungry, it may be because he has a chronic gastrointestinal dysfunction or because nutritious food is unavailable for some reason—for example, because the potential suppliers of the food are either innocently or deliberately holding back potentially available food. Knowing only that a person is hungry tells us nothing about his social condition. We must also know about the nature of the institutions that hold the possibilities for relief. And so with the student. We must know about the psychological and political conditions of the institutions and society that he is protesting against to have a dynamic understanding of the process of protest.

The differences between the black and white student movements can be ascribed in part to the fact that they are regarded and treated differently by the same institutions. There are also certain historical events and forces that have influenced all American student protestors at this time, such as the universal threat of nuclear annihilation and the more personal threat of the draft. And there are local differences, dependent on the socio-economic-political conditions at a particular institution.

If one examines a university where a major student protest has taken place in recent years, the immediate "cause" is likely to be what the students perceived as an encroachment on their freedom of speech. It is in the process of attempting to remedy these restrictions that students become aware of their ineffectuality in making

[1] K. Keniston, "You Have to Grow Up in Scarsdale to Know How Bad Things Really Are," *New York Times Magazine*, April 27, 1969.

[2] T. Roszak, *The Making of a Counterculture* (New York: Doubleday, 1969).

contact with the decision-making apparatus and begin to question whether these traditional "rights" of freedom of speech are meaningful channels for action, in view of the transformation of governing bodies and universities into bureaucracies.[3] In the Columbia rebellion, as we saw in Chapter II: President Kirk's ban on indoor demonstrations, which ran counter to the recommendation of a tripartite committee he himself had appointed, was the original issue. Student challenge to this prohibition evoked disciplinary action. The ensuing spiral of moves and countermoves resulted in the April 23 rebellion.

Similarly, at Berkeley, in 1964, the occupation of a university building by almost 900 students, had to do with a limitation on freedom of speech, as the name of the group (the Free Speech Movement) implies. A brief survey of the recent history of student-administration confrontation at Berkeley will illustrate how the issue of student powerlessness relates to the issue of free speech.

In a traditional sense, freedom of speech certainly existed at Berkeley—teachers could teach what they wished, and meetings were held on campus with invited Communist Party, John Birch Society, and American Nazi Party speakers. The matter at stake was the university's policy that "university facilities may not be used to support or advocate off-campus political or social action" and its attempt to discipline students involved in such action. Under challenge by the students, the policy was modified by the California Board of Regents shortly before the sit-in to grant students the right to use the campus for political activity advocating *"lawful* off-campus action, not . . . *unlawful* off-campus action."* This was on the heels of the 1964 Mississippi Summer Project and at the zenith of the integrated student civil rights movement. Hence those students who were involved in or sensitive to the movement saw the remaining restriction as a barrier to tactics they thought were necessary to realize their goals. The principle was: Should there be any distinction between the political rights that a student had off-campus as a citizen and his rights on-campus as a matriculated student?

As occurred later at Columbia and other colleges affected by

[3] Hannah Arendt has explored this issue in *On Violence* (New York: Harcourt, Brace & World, 1969).

sit-ins, the issue was complicated by disciplinary procedures directed against leaders. Finally, with faculty support, the FSM was able, by confrontation, to force a constitutional solution to a political problem, when the Faculty Academic Senate, by a vote of 824 to 115, adopted a resolution reading, in part:

(2) The time, place, and manner of conducting political activity on campus shall be subject to reasonable regulations to prevent interference with normal functions of the University. . . .

(3) . . . the content of speech or advocacy should not be restricted by the University. Off-campus political activities shall not be subject to University regulations. On-campus advocacy or organization of such activities shall be subject only to such limitations as may be imposed under Section 2.

The implications of the victory were weighty in the lives of the students. It brought the university more into phase with the world outside the university. It also gave "official" sanction to radical social action on the part of students and indirectly acknowledged the fact that conditions in the United States at times require radical action against social and political inequity.

In a parallel way, the first stage of the massive rebellion in France in 1968 was a demonstration and rally protesting police infiltration on campus and the rumored expulsion of Daniel Cohn-Bendit for engaging in a provocative verbal exchange with the Minister of Youth and Sport. This student assembly, held in January, at the University of Nanterre, was in direct violation of the university regulation that no political demonstrations could be held on campus. Local administrators who tried to enforce the regulation were shoved. Police were called, but the students, armed with sticks and stones and bottles, drove them off the campus. The "enragés"[4] of January 26 were successful in provoking police reaction, and the climate was set for the "22 March Movement," which originated at Nanterre and by May had spread throughout France, almost toppling de Gaulle's government.

The inability of students to be heard, even with the right to speak, is a product of the centralized control of the university,

---

[4] The term "enragés" was first used to describe an extreme revolutionary group in 1793. It was adopted by Cohn-Bendit and his original followers at Nanterre in 1968.

either from a location within the university or from a government agency in a different city. In either case, the source of power is often remote and inaccessible to both students and faculty. At Columbia, university governance had evolved slowly since the forty-three-year rule, from 1902 to 1945, of the autocratic Nicholas Murray Butler. With no student government or faculty senate, power was exercised by a few individuals—administrators, trustees, and faculty—who made the important administrative and educational decisions through what Kay Trimberger has described as:

. . . an informal process of behind-the-scenes politics. . . . This system of decision-making meant that little consideration was given to the interests of the University as a whole, or to its general values and goals. . . . Policy was made and carried out by a few persons, unaccountable and often invisible to the University community as a whole.[5]

With this structure, as we stressed in Chapter IV, there was no adequate machinery for modifying university policy regarding community relations, its implication in the conduct of the war in Vietnam, or regulations governing much of student life. Thus the impact of the alleged "strawberry statement" by an administrator.

Associated with this problem of remoteness of control in the university is the fact that in the first six months of 1969, although there were protests at only 10 per cent of American colleges and universities, these institutions included over half of those universities with an enrollment of more than 10,000. Institutions of this size represent only 7 per cent of the colleges in the United States, but 36 per cent of all student protests occurred there.[6] One implication of these statistics is that, in a large institution, the system of remote centralized governance cannot be responsive to the needs of the student body.

The issue of the inaccessibility of power is especially complex in public institutions and in other universities where economic control is exerted by the state or city or by off-campus, noneduca-

---

[5] K. Trimberger, *The Student Rebellion and University Reform: The Politics of Restructuring at Columbia* (unpublished manuscript).

[6] *Student Protests 1969: Summary* (Urban Research Corporation, Chicago: 1970.

tor trustees and alumni. Although Nanterre was new and had a "model" physical plant, it was caught in the rigidity of the French national education system, in which virtually all decision-making power resided in the central Ministry of Education in Paris. Local administrators were expected to implement the policies but could not deviate from the rules that applied uniformly to all twenty-three national universities. Their impotence made them objects of contempt to the students at their universities. The inflexibility of the centralized system, which could respond only to local confrontations involving the breaking of regulations but not to dialogue about the appropriateness of these regulations, bred mounting incidents of confrontation.

Since 1966, a number of California state universities and colleges have experienced virtually continuous low-grade and intermittently violent confrontation. Berkeley and San Francisco State have been the most prominent. Why? Paradoxically, in 1960, the state legislature enacted a "master plan" for higher education that seemed to be a pioneering democratic accomplishment. It set up three levels of higher education—state universities, state colleges, and state junior collges. The system was designed to provide free higher education to all California youth in an institution appropriate to their academic capacity.

Despite its truly admirable intent, the system has been tragically incapable of adapting to the changing needs of the campus populations. Not only has it produced unrest, but the structure of the system has been grossly inadequate to allow for resolution of conflict.

The ultimate power for finance, construction, and administration of the universities resides in a Board of Regents consisting of sixteen appointees of the governor and eight ex-officio members. Of the twenty-four regents, only one is an educator. Similarly, the state college system is subject to the remote governance of a Board of Trustees consisting of sixteen appointees of the governor and five ex-officio members. In each system, communication between the regents and trustees, on the one hand, and the separate schools is channeled and filtered by a managing executive—the chancellor of the state-wide system. This is a crippling limitation on the capacity of the local institutional administration to innovate in education or to negotiate resolutions of conflict.

The continuous confrontations, student strikes, police violence, burning of buildings, arrests, and suspensions at Berkeley during the academic year 1968–69 developed out of a building occupation by students protesting the Board of Regents' attempt to withdraw a course on "Social Analysis," which had previously been approved by the duly authorized body at the Berkeley campus. Attempts by the Faculty Senate, the students, and the Chancellor to use legal avenues of petition and appeal failed to move the Regents. The feeling of the students was eloquently expressed by the editor of the university newspaper and the president of the student body, who went on an eighteen-day fast to:

. . . protest . . . the disenfranchisement and impotence of students in the governance of this University and universities throughout this country. It is an appeal to those in power in the educational and political structure of this state to open the avenues so that students can participate in the governance of their society.[7]

The chain of events proceeded from nonviolent protests by students to the Regents' action to a "State of Emergency" proclamation by Governor Ronald Reagan later in the year, with its overtones of a police state. Were the actions by state political officials necessary responses to the destructiveness of a small group of revolutionaries? It is doubtful. The repressive tactics authorized by the politicians had a profit of their own. On February 28, 1969, the Field Research Corporation announced the results of a survey, which found that 42 per cent of the people thought Reagan was doing a good job as governor at the time, compared to 30 per cent in May, 1968. They concluded: "Reagan's popularity resurgence is due essentially to the public's approval of his handling of widespead student unrest. Rarely has one single issue given a state political leader so much public support for his actions." [8]

Another issue that served as a focus for the familiar Berkeley pattern of escalating confrontation was the proposal by students that a Third World College be established as a division of the university. The goal was to provide the highest quality education while allowing students to retain their cultural identity, so that they might return to their communities to create an atmosphere conducive to political, social, and economic change. But the pro-

[7] *The Daily Californian,* Nov. 13, 1968.
[8] Reported in the *San Francisco Chronicle,* Feb. 28, 1969.

posal contained features, particularly regarding admissions procedures, that were not permissible under the state-wide master plan of 1960, with the result that negotiations at Berkeley itself became meaningless.

Events at Berkeley raised the question of the viability of a political system in which the taxpaying citizens who support an institution can demand, through their elected officials, that their will be heeded, even though the social vision it embodies is not shared by a significant number of the direct participants in that institution. This problem is raised in every area where the issue of public-school decentralization is being fought.

Two political scientists, Sheldon Wolin and John Schaar, have brilliantly analyzed the Berkeley revolt in terms of the irreconcilable conflict between human needs and institutional structure. Since 1965, they write, life at the university:

. . . has been marked by an enervating anxiety and hostility which cannot be dismissed as a "failure in communication." The melancholy truth is that there is little to communicate because there is no widely shared understanding about the meaning and purpose of the institution. Lacking the unifying force which flows spontaneously from common understandings, the system is held together by a bureaucratic organization whose weakness is exposed whenever it is directly challenged. This is partly the result of Berkeley's legacy as a public university.[9]

A new basis of campus confrontation is emerging. The mass of young people express and fulfill needs that are barely comprehensible to any but their own peers. The values of this youth "counterculture" conflict with the values of older generations and those that are given priority by the institutions of the establishment. It is in that context that the extraordinary controversy over the "People's Park" in Berkeley, in the spring of 1969, is important in the study of student-university conflict—because it portends a future confrontation growing out of the incapacity of a large institution to accommodate people with values, life styles, and needs that are outside the traditional arena of political discourse.

[9] S. Wolin and J. Schaar, "Berkeley and the University Revolution," *New York Review of Books*, February 9, 1967, p. 23. See also Wolin and Schaar, "Berkeley and the Fate of the Multiversity," *New York Review of Books*, March 11, 1965, and "Berkeley: The Battle of People's Park," *New York Review of Books*, June 19, 1969.

From May 16 to 22, 1969, Berkeley was the scene of waves of terror (including the fatal shooting of a bystander by police) and militaristic suppression over the issue of a 450- by 270-foot parking lot that had been converted into a grass- and shrub-planted playground-park by an alliance of several hundred Berkeley students, nonstudent hippies, and nonhippie Berkeley residents representing several generations. Again, there was disagreement over what was legal and what was morally "right." The university had clear title to the land, having purchased it in 1968 as a site for future development. In the interim it was used as a dirt parking lot. In April, 1969, the student-citizen alliance started planning and working on more "humanistic" interim use of the land. Then, a week after the area became a People's Park, the university announced its intent to develop it first as an athletic field and eventually to use it for a dormitory. The student-citizens threatened to "hold" the park. Then followed a week of negotiations, committees—essentially no communication and no progress. The university, at that point sealed off the park by erecting an eight-foot steel fence, ostensibly to allow for interference-free testing of the soil and surveying of the lot.

The all too familiar Berkeley "game" was in full operation, each side demanding that the other yield or concede. Here in microcosm was a great symbolic struggle of the times—a conflict between the multiversity that must continuously expand to fulfill its destiny, with the money, the influence in the legislature, a security force, and "understandings" with other police agencies—in short, the "power"—to pursue its legally sanctioned prerogatives; and a band of people, unconvinced of the merits of the "technectronic" society or even of the need for the planned dormitory, who act without benefit of court-sanctioned authority, on the belief that flowers and children's wading pools and other such things are being systematically taken away from them in the new order of social and political priorities. Given the totally different frames of reference and values and purposes of the "people" and the "university" [10] in a political setting like California, violence was inevitable.

[10] The term "university" is used here not in the sense of a community of students, faculty, administrators, and office and maintenance employees, but the policy-makers—the administrators, regents, technical consultants, and so on.

To the question of why, after five years of almost continuous strife and no small amount of experience on the part of the administration in dealing with groups making radical demands, the battle of People's Park could occur, Wolin and Schaar say:

It is significant that the Berkeley administration repeatedly expressed irritation with the failure of the Park people to "organize" a responsible committee" or select "representatives" who might "negotiate." The life-styles and values of the Park people were forever escaping the categories and procedures of those who administer the academic plant.

Likewise, the issue itself: the occupants of the Park wanted to use the land for a variety of projects, strange but deeply natural, which defied customary forms and expectations, where, at worst, the University saw the land as something to be fenced, soil tested and processed through a score of experts and a maze of committees, and finally encased in a tight and tidy form of a rational design. At best, the most imaginative use of the land which the University could contemplate was as a "field-experiment station," where faculty and graduate students could observe their fellow beings coping with their "environment." In brief, the educational bureaucracy, like bureaucracies elsewhere, is experiencing increasing difficulty because human life is manifesting itself in forms which are unrecognizable to the mentality of the technological age.[11]

To summarize, student radicals and militants at all universities act in political ways and express not only inflexible elements determined by their unconscious needs but also flexible elements based on conflict-free, rational evaluation of the sociopolitical situation. In the idealistic radical, the latter are the primary motivators of the manifest form of the political behavior. In the course of understanding the sociopolitical organization of the larger society and particular institutions within the society (such as the university), attitudes are developed that accurately reflect the characteristics of these institutions. Thus constructive institutions tend to engender positive support, and destructive institutions tend to evoke disapproval and opposition.

I do not believe that most of the students who occupied buildings at Columbia in 1968 would have rebelled at whatever college they were attending. The more nihilistic ones might have, out of

---

[11] Wolin and Schaar, "Berkeley: The Battle of People's Park," *op. cit.,* pp. 27–29.

their need to focus on those elements, in any situation, that fit their unconscious need to feel oppressed and to ignore the elements that did not fit their psychologically preordained analysis. For most of the thousand Columbia students who occupied buildings, the action grew out of political and moral judgments based on their understanding of specific activities of the university with regard to the war, the surrounding community, and the students themselves.

To say that the issues in question were "real" is not to deny that they may also have had overdetermined meaning for particular students based on their own family socialization process. A restriction in freedom of expression on campus, for example, may resonate with a childhood experience in which the student's parents limited his freedom to make his needs known. Similarly, "secret" research in the university may have special meaning for a student in terms of his embarrassment as a child over his father's extralegal business operations, or, at a deeper level, over his parents' "secret" life in their bedroom after dark. But that these private associations exist does not nullify the objective fact that university policy and activity impose insignificant hardship on many other lives.

On campuses where students can effect appropriate changes in policy and structure through due process (which usually is possible only in a small, private college), where the interests and identity of the university seem less tied to serving the ends of militaristic and oppressive factions in the society, student rebellion is certainly less common.

To resort to rebellion in the face of extreme deprivation of human rights is accepted as courageous, moral, and even adaptive, as, for example, in Algeria, Hungary, lunch counters in the South, or the Warsaw ghetto. In certain university confrontations the radical and militant students have received wide support on campus. At Berkeley in 1964, the faculty, in a ratio of seven to one, supported the FSM. At Columbia, some 6,000 students supported the strike following the police action. At Cornell, in 1969, 4,000 white students sat-in at the fieldhouse in support of 100 black students who had "occupied" the student union. In France, in 1968, the support the students received from millions in the country is modern legend. In all these instances, support of this magnitude was forthcoming because the issues of discord were seen as "real" and important. At institutions where protests occur over issues that are not viewed as significant or symbolizing major trends of oppression or "immorality" in the university, support for disruption is negligible, even where the student bodies are highly similar in composition. In these cases, the result of the confrontation is not the radicalization of others but, rather, isolation and repression of the radical element by the majority of the campus community.

Thus, to "know" a radical, one must also "know" the state of the external conditions in which and against which he rebels. The political scientist Christian Bay, following in the existential tradition of Albert Camus,[12] views the relationship of the rebel and society as follows:

Every new human being is potentially a liberal animal and a rebel; yet every social organization he will be up against, from the family to the state, is likely to seek to "socialize" him into a conveniently pliant conformist.[13]

Yet most of the radical and militant youth I talked with hold to the possibility that men may ultimately forge social structures and institutions that can enhance their humanity and freedom by channeling energies in directions and forms that serve our highest communal aspirations.

A young revolutionary said to me:

We may not offer programs just yet. But we do offer now the dreams of human possibilities.

[12] In *The Rebel* (New York: Vintage, 1958), Camus wrote, "I rebel—therefore we exist."

[13] C. Bay, "Political and Apolitical Students: Facts in Search of Theory," *Journal of Social Issues,* vol. 23, no. 3 (1967), p. 90.

XI: The Psychohistorical Context

Thus far, I have stressed the fact that no one pathway was traveled by all the communards. To comprehend the events at Columbia in the spring of 1968, if only from the limited perspective of some of the actors, it is necessary to understand the students' lives in a psychohistorical context. Why did the rebellion take place then—"then" being spring, 1968, a point in the time cycle of history, and also a stage in the individual actor's life cycle—"youth"? What manifest experiences and symbolic themes did these youthful activists share that profoundly affected, not only their political philosophy and life style, but also aspects of their psychological integration—and how were their experiences and themes different from those shared by young men and women in the past?

History and psychoanalysis both have the goal of enabling us to understand human behavior in terms of the past. Twentieth-century historians in the main have undertaken their reconstruction within the framework of social, political, and economic theory, largely ignoring that aspect of human behavior that is the manifestation of unconscious conflicts and repressed impulses. On the other hand, students of psychodynamics generally focus on the single individual,[1] treating the economic, political, and social forces in which the individual swirls as confusing extra dimensions that are better assigned to other disciplines—thus preserving the elegance of the psychoanalytic model. The effect of this emphasis has sometimes been to give a false impression of timelessness to the organization and operation of man's psyche and to

---

[1] A notable exception is Freud's classic psychohistorical model, presented in *Totem and Taboo* (1912–13), the account of the "great event with which culture began." By Freud's own admission, this is "psychomythology," a concept of universal psychological potential. (In *Collected Papers,* vol. XIII [London: Hogarth Press, 1953].)

suggest that the unique qualities of the great men studied were a fortunate by-product of their unusual neuroses.

Erik Erikson is one of the few psychoanalysts who has successfully crossed this interdisciplinary barrier. In his studies of exceptional men in history,[2] he has stressed the need to understand in detail, not only the "stage of life" in which the leader acted, but also the relation of his life cycle to the "history" of his community.

The psychohistorical question is not only how such men come to experience the inescapability of an existential curse, but how it comes about that they have the pertinacity and the giftedness to re-enact it in a medium communicable to their fellow men and meaningful to their stage of history. The emphasis here is on the word *re-enactment,* which in such cases goes far beyond the dictates of a mere "repetition compulsion," such as characterizes the unfreedom of symptoms and irrational acts. For the mark of a creative re-enactment of a curse is that the joint experience of it all becomes a liberating event for each member of an awe-stricken audience. Some dim awareness of this must be the reason that the wielders of power in different periods of history appreciate and support the efforts of creative men to re-enact the universal conflicts of mankind in the garb of the historical day, as the great dramatists have done. . . . In all re-enactment, however, it is the transformation of an infantile curse into an adult need that makes the man.[3]

Thus, Erikson creates the "approach" of psychohistory, specifying the complementarity of the inner dynamics and social conditions that makes history appear to repeat itself and yet ever progress.

Robert Jay Lifton has significantly broadened the psychohistorical approach from Erikson's emphasis on the exceptional man to include the psychological themes shared by all individuals in a given time. Lifton is concerned with the process by which *all* men and women of the same epoch achieve their sense of "self"—an identity that is continuously changing in response to the symbolic meaning of historical forces and events to which they are collectively exposed. His concepts and his application of them to vari-

[2] See E. H. Erikson, *Young Man Luther: A Study in Psychoanalysis and History* (New York: Norton, 1958); "On the Nature of Psycho-Historical Evidence: In Search of Gandhi," *International Journal of Psychiatry,* vol. 7, no. 7 (1969), pp. 451–76; *Gandhi's Truth: On the Origins of Militant Non-Violence* (New York: Norton, 1969).

[3] Erikson, "On the Nature of Psycho-historical Evidence," *op. cit.,* p. 473.

ous groups, notably the survivors of Hiroshima,[4] provide new insights into a national character change and emerging subcultures. The work of Robert Coles [5] and Kenneth Keniston [6] represent outstanding applications of this orientation to social groups. Recently, Joel Kovel has pioneered in the application of the psychohistorical method to a form of social pathology that is shared by virtually everyone in our culture.[7] Within the framework of rather orthodox psychoanalytic theory, he articulates the psychodynamic meaning and economic function of the organized system of shared symbols that comprises "culture" and that in our society allows for the perpetuation of white racism.

In this chapter, I will attempt to relate the Columbia rebellion to the shared meaning and collective impact on the students of certain recent historical events and to discuss some of the historical forces and themes that have made these youth different from previous generations in ways that predispose significant numbers of them, both black and white, to embrace the ideology and tactics of radical movements. The developmental phase during which particular events were experienced and integrated, I believe, is a major determinant of the manner in which the symbolic theme is later expressed in behavior. In this venture I am far more certain about the legitimacy of and, indeed, need for this approach than I am of the correctness and adequacy of my conclusions.

In addressing the problem of *who* was radicalized, the psychohistorical orientation leads us to ask also how, by what psychological process, events in the world during the students' lifetime—events shared by all of us [8]—made them willing to engage in this

---

[4] R. J. Lifton, *Death in Life: Survivors of Hiroshima* (New York: Random House, 1968). See also *History and Human Survival: Essays on the Young and Old, Survivors and the Dead, Peace and War, and on Contemporary Psychohistory* (New York: Random House, 1970).

[5] R. Coles, *Children of Crisis: A Study of Courage and Fear* (Boston: Little, Brown, 1964).

[6] K. Keniston, *The Uncommitted: Alienated Youth in American Society* (New York: Harcourt, Brace & World, 1965); *Young Radicals: Notes on Committed Youth* (New York, Harcourt, Brace & World, 1968).

[7] J. Kovel, *White Racism: A Psychohistory* (New York: Pantheon, 1970).

[8] I stress "all of us" although many of us defend ourselves against the painful awareness of unpleasant reality by attempting to purge those who threaten our denial. Thus, student activists, as well as other members of

social action. The influence of certain world events is readily apparent. A climate of optimism prevailed in the period prior to the rebellion. The elevated hopes for peace in Vietnam inspired by the Tet offensive, McCarthy's victory in New Hampshire, and President Johnson's announcement of retirement, and the hopes for acceleration of civil rights legislation as a reaction to the assassination of Martin Luther King potentiated the activation of large numbers in the Columbia student body.[9]

We suggested earlier that unless "hope" is present—both in the psychological capacity and in its actualized form—constructive political action is unlikely. But abandonment of the liberal-reform position for a radical stance also requires sharp disillusionment, even despair, based on negative appraisal of the possibilities for peaceful change within "the system." The assassination of Dr. King was another confirmation of the futility of nonviolent civil disobedience. The politically naïve expectation that his death would be compensated by a new dawn of racial justice was largely a psychological defense to mute and deny the grief and loss, for the creation of lasting change by martyrdom is a road to immortality. While there were elements of this kind of hopefulness among the students, the overwhelming feeling they reported was grief, despair, and rage, exacerbated by the fact that the actual trigger man was still at large. Hence the vengeful feelings of King's followers had no focus in an identifiable person. They nonetheless sought outlet, and the object became the amorphous "system" that produced the murder. The militant action at Columbia, one of the two major issues of which was racism, not only accommodated the rage but

---

today's youth counterculture, tend to be viewed by established elders through a filter of the assimilated values of their own lives. By damning these young demons, the elders attempt to suppress the anxiety and anger that is generated in them by youth's rejection of what they have settled for and who they have become in the process. But, as Keniston has said, "What is articulate and visible in these young men and women is also in all men and women. The difference is only a difference in awareness, not in kind: history is the fabric we are all made of." In K. Keniston, *Young Radicals, op. cit.,* p. 259.

[9] Immanuel Wallerstein has noted that these factors are determinants of the number of people radicalized. See his discussion of my paper on "Radical and Militant Youth: A Study of Columbia Undergraduates," *The Psychoanalytic Forum,* forthcoming.

was impelled by it. For many students the action was a defense against the anxiety produced by identification with King, the passive victim. To be active affords at least the illusion that one is controlling one's fate.

For black students particularly, the identification with King was profound. During their preadolescent and midadolescent years, many of them consciously and unconsciously internalized King as their leader and model. Therefore, a part of them was murdered with him. Freud, in his classic elaboration of the dynamics of mourning, explains grief as emanating from "an identification of the ego with the abandoned object." [10] The manifest self-reproaches in grief are unconsciously directed against the abandoning person, who is an internalized part of the "self." Immediately following King's death, we saw black rage turned on itself in the burning of black communities in many cities. A much more successful technique for discharging grief and assuaging self-reproach and guilt is to continue the work of the lost one. In the case of the blacks at Columbia, King's assassination was one force activating them. In this instance, a recent historical event affected many psyches in a similar way. The affected individuals, in a collective adaptive behavior, moved toward resolution of their inner psychological conflict, and in a way that also constructively altered history. I do not contend that the black students' action was "caused" by King's murder or motivated by the need to resolve the inner conflict generated by the murder. The murder should be viewed, rather, as one of a complex constellation of factors, both inner dynamics and historical forces, that determined the action.

The students' radical action, in turn, affected the life of the university. Although we do not have an epigenetic model for institutions, I think that we can conceive in these terms of the institution that is the object of radical thrust. The 214-year-old Columbia, whose structure was once appropriate to the times, had become rigid and anachronistic, unable to "comprehend" contemporary needs and stresses, and "angry" at those who insisted it do so. The thirty-one-member Board of Trustees, averaging in age over sixty, filled its own vacancies and, in thus perpetuating

[10] S. Freud, "Mourning and Melancholia" (1917), *Collected Papers,* vol. XIV (London: Hogarth Press, 1957).

itself in monolithic form, bred ever narrowing vision. The President, Grayson Kirk, reflected this structure.[11] Columbia was a prisoner of unmodified codes of its own youth, in another era. To survive, it needed to renew itself with the strength and vision of its young.

Whether Columbia has truly been renewed as a result of the events of 1968 remains to be seen. My doubts about the outcome, as I said earlier, are related to the changing nature of large universities and the consequent decreasing ability of students to influence the life cycle and destiny of their institution.

Students are not only students at their university but concurrently citizens of their nation. And societies and nations also have life cycles that affect and are affected by the psyches of each generation of youth. Martin Wangh has observed, for example, that wars profoundly shape the psyches of the young in ways we little understand, and that the young who are thus altered later dictate the direction of their nation's political destiny.[12] Wangh utilizes Freud's concept of "repetition compulsion"[13] in proposing a psychological explanation of why nations make wars. Throughout life, Freud said, one tries to master the residual anxiety connected with unresolved conflicts and traumatic experiences from early childhood, major aspects of which have become repressed, by placing oneself in a symbolic replication of the original conflict or situation. What was passively experienced as a child becomes the source of a compulsion to repeat and actively master. And thus in all compulsions—in fact, in all behavior driven by unconscious forces having little to do with the here-and-now—reality

---

[11] A revealing joke, popular before the rebellion (illuminating because, like much humor, it is a way of permitting unacceptable impulses to slip through the usual repressive guards) went: "Two senior faculty members are crossing South Field. They see a disturbance. One shakes his head sadly and says to the other, 'This never would have happened if Grayson Kirk was alive.' The joke provides, for teller and listener, safe expression of the destructive wish in response to anger at Kirk's anachronistic style and ineffectuality in dealing with the contemporary scene.

[12] M. Wangh, "Further Reflections on the Psychogenetic Factors in War and Civil Upheaval," presentation to Chicago Psychoanalytic Society, Feb. 21, 1969.

[13] S. Freud, "Beyond the Pleasure Principle" (1920), *Collected Papers*, vol. XVIII (London: Hogarth Press, 1955).

is ignored. Consequences are disregarded as men pursue their buried past into the future.

Wangh cogently argues that in wartime the sons of soldiers, traumatized by the early absence of their warring fathers and un-shielded by their mothers from the wartime anxiety, develop the compulsion to live up to the idealized image of father-as-soldier and thus "need" to become soldiers themselves. War provides the psychological climate in which as adults they can master the child-hood traumatic experience.

The problem is even more complex in that in war there are winners and losers, and the image of "victorious" soldier father significantly differs from that of "defeated" soldier father as an introject and formative factor for the son. In Germany, the effects of losing World War I, coupled with economic collapse twelve years later, were devastating for the generation that became the exterminators of 6 million Jews.[14] In a parallel manner, the more overt manifestations of racism that are normative for much of the South may be casually related, along with economic and other explanations, to the reparative psychological needs of the Southern male, beaten and humiliated in Civil War and, until recently, po-litically impotent against the Northern-liberal Congressional coali-tion.[15]

Psychohistorical formulations like Wangh's clarify the ways in which the history of nations shapes the psyches of their citizens. These collective psyches, thus affected, act in predictable and cyclically repetitive ways, thereby determining the further course of history.

Our examples of these concepts have stressed the effect of

[14] This psychohistorical relationship is the subject of Martin Wangh, "Na-tional Socialism and the Genocide of Jews: A Psychoanalytic Study of a Historical Event," *International Journal of Psychoanalysis*, vol. 45, no. 2–3, 1964. Erik Erikson has also discussed psychohistorical factors involved in the ascendancy of Hitler in *Childhood and Society* (New York: Norton, 1950). The unwillingness of American leaders to accept "defeat" in Viet-nam and withdraw stems more from their reluctance to accept the collective psychological consequences of defeat than from repugnance toward the political consequences.

[15] For discussions of racism in America stressing the psychohistorical approach, see: Kovel, *op. cit.*, and H. Butts, "White Racism: Its Origins, Institutions, and Implications for Professional Practice in Mental Health," *International Journal of Psychiatry*, vol. 8, no. 6, 1969.

trauma on the young child's mind. However, we must consider how these profound events were perceived and integrated not only at the stage of life when they occurred but also at the stage of life when the individual takes the action for which the seeds had been planted years earlier. The stage of life in which the actor acts has characteristics that are molded by the psychobiological potential for that age. The radicals and militants at Columbia, for example, were acting in a stage of life that Keniston has termed "youth," in a refinement of Erikson's more general discussion of late-adolescent identity formation.[16] This emergent period between adolescence and adulthood is a time when social role and the individual's relationship to the structures of the established society are focal concerns. The task in these years, as we have noted, is to establish an integrated sense of self that includes both autonomy from and positive interaction with the institutions of society. But to speak of institutions in America is a complex matter. Ideologically, there are many Americas, and conflict among them is traditional. In childhood, these conflicting currents deeply imprint themselves on the developing psychic structure, but the child's overt concern and ability to comprehend do not extend beyond egocentric life space of self, family, and a few playmates. In adolescence, the cognitive sphere expands, and, in conscious, articulated ways, he increasingly defines himself and others in terms of the existing and competing ideologies in the environment. His psychosocial identity, however, remains yet to be actualized, for the possibilities for individual paths of deviate development are severely limited. The prevailing philosophy is, "During your teens, equip yourself with the tools of the culture, and then, when you are old enough (that is, experienced enough), you can make your own choices."

With the increasing politicization of high school students, the idea of postponing independent decision is losing strength.[17] Yet very few high school students have developed enough distance from parents to embark actively on an autonomous life course. More common are rebellions into "negative" identities (for ex-

---

[16] K. Keniston, *Young Radicals, op. cit.;* E. Erikson, *Identity: Youth and Crisis* (New York: Norton, 1968).

[17] A sense of the high school politicization process may be obtained from John Birmingham, ed., *Our Time Is Now: Notes from the High School Underground* (New York: Praeger, 1970).

ample, "head," delinquent, drop-out) that allow them to deny consciously their tie to parents while simultaneously preserving the more unconscious hostile-dependent bond. The result is that parents are usually activated into frantic, often punitive efforts to "save" their youngsters. In the healthy adolescent, along with ventures in intimacy and experimentation in activities and life styles, there is high concern for issues of ethics, intellect, sometimes religion, and the meaning of life.[18] This work of adolescence is the foundation for reasoned and rational evaluation before embracing or repudiating the competing institutions the society offers.

"Choice," which implies a considerable degree of intellectual and emotional "freedom," requires not only freedom from domination by unconscious conflicts persevering from earlier epochs but a latitude provided by the culture. The psychosocial stage of youth, midway between adolescence and the fixed adult roles of spouse, parent, and worker, is a phase of "disengagement," a moment between the past and future when many have the clearest vision of what men actually are, not what they say they are. This vision is made possible for increasing numbers in our population by the achievements of the industrial age.

Among the fruits of industrialization is the liberation of large numbers of people from the need to labor. Fewer and fewer adolescent children are required to work in order that the family may survive economically. This liberation, coupled with the increasing need for specialized training to organize and operate the production apparatus of the society, has sent markedly increasing numbers of Americans to the universities. From 1957 to 1967, university enrollments increased from 2.2 million to 5.1 million. It is projected that, by 1975, some 7 million will be in university attendance. At present, about one out of every four males and females between eighteen and twenty-four is matriculated at a university, and approximately one out of four graduates goes on to graduate school.[19]

[18] Anna Freud has made the point that these philosophical concerns are a normative part of adolescent development, in the service of mastering the upsurge of instinctual drives. In *The Ego and the Mechanisms of Defense* (New York: International Universities Press, 1946).

[19] L. A. Mayer, "Young America: By the Numbers," *Fortune,* vol. 79, no. 1 (1969).

For all these students—despite their diversity in regional, racial, religious, and economic backgrounds, in career goals, and in a host of other areas—the university provides a psychosocial "island" in development. Away from the family of their past and not into the family of their future, they stand "disengaged" but intellectually and biologically mature. In the university milieu they are exposed to the "subversive function" of the university —to expose, interrelate, and ultimately question the foundations of the society. This function is probably represented more dramatically in the large university than in small liberal-arts colleges, because it coexists with the large university's function as society's "service station"—supplier of technical knowledge, trainer of technicians and technocrats, and architect of the designs of the dominant powers in the society. With the freedom to "see social reality" that they can have in this stage of life, increasing numbers of them accurately perceive the sociopolitical order and penetrate the rhetoric that masks the real values of the system.

The disengagement of young students is not a new phenomenon. But there are more of them now, and they are more likely to cry out that the "emperor is naked" than the apolitical students of the silent 1950's. Not only did the students of the 1950's not cry out or act; they did not, and could not, perceive what "was" as against what "could" or "should" be. They were, among other factors, so successfully indoctrinated to be vigilant against the threat of Russian communism that they were cognitively incapacitated to see the dangers within the country.

As a group, then, our present youth have become active critics of our social order, active catalysts of progressive change. They, in turn, act on and alter history. Thus, when the final chronicle of the United States' policy in Vietnam is written, it will certainly assign a major role in influencing the de-escalation of the war and the end of Lyndon Johnson's political career to the activism and opposition of youth. Similarly, the history of the civil rights gains cannot be separated from the history of student activism. And the universities that have provided the physical base for this stage are now themselves being altered by the insistence of these same young men and women.

To come back to the question of why youth are "active" now,

there are two levels of historical causality. First are the more obvious contemporary precipitants, those overt crises that threaten to tear apart the fabric of our society—the moral horror, cost of life, and sacrifice of social programs because of the war. And it is the young who fight and die in wars.

The other contemporary theme is the awakening to the inhumanity of racism. Participation in civil rights activities, ghetto tutoring, and even the media have demonstrated to many of these students the quality of life of the poor black with an impact that the older generation could more easily ignore. Hope has turned to despondency, then to bitterness, with awareness of the meager achievements of the civil rights movement. Massive urban rioting, looting, and violence have shown the resistance of those who no longer will remain subordinated. In fact, given their impotence in the established political process, large numbers of white youth as well as blacks generally consider urban violence highly adaptive. A group of eleven prominent black psychiatrists stated, in the wake of the assassination of Dr. King, "To burn and destroy are forms of release of rage and frustration when people don't know where to turn." [20]

Liberated by advances in technology, transportation, and communications, youth at the same time question the assumptions of the society that is responsible for war and racism. Knowing that there can now be "enough" for everyone, they question why the distribution of material necessities and comforts is so unequal. In this respect, what we are witnessing is not a revolt of the oppressed against their rulers but a repudiation by the peripheral members of a class of the central values of that class. Many of them feel superfluous in terms of the economic direction of the society. Unable to find places in the technological structure that conform to the values they have been taught, they sense their presence in the universities as a "holding operation," with little purpose except, perhaps, to prepare them to teach courses even less relevant to the direction in which the society is moving than the courses now being taught.

In this connection, Keniston lists the goals of this "second revolution," the revolution for personal fulfillment:

[20] Quoted in Butts, *op. cit.*

1. Repudiation of economic quantity and materialism as ends in themselves—concepts of quality ascendant
2. Revolt against the "technologization of man"; against uniformity, equalization, and standardization—technology itself is accepted so long as it allows for individuality and diversity.
3. Opposition to rigidity in both institutional and individual behavior
4. Revolt against centralized power with a concomitant demand for participation in decision-making [21]

The white participants in this "second revolution" are by and large children of economically privileged families. They are probably the first generation since the Industrial Revolution to live in a style that expresses social impulses in a manner that challenges traditional behavioral codes of repression and restraint. Herbert Marcuse, who has provided the principal theoretical justification for the American student radical movement, has articulated the concept of "surplus repression" to clarify the relationship between this new life style and the historical and political situation.[22] While defending all the basic tenets of Freud's theory, Marcuse argues that the current repression of sexual impulses, sensuality, and aestheticism far exceeds what is necessary to maintain a humane society. He concurs with Freud's view that repression of nongenital sexuality has been necessary to maximize man's capacity to "work," and that work has been a historic necessity for survival because of the fact of "scarcity." But, he contends, scarcity is the consequence of a specific social organization imposed on the masses—first by violence, then by the more rational utilization of power—in the service of "domination" by the ruling class.

Marcuse's belief that the technical achievements of postindustrial society would do away with scarcity, and therefore with the rationality of domination,[23] has not been substantiated. Rather, technology has created counterfeit needs, for electronic gadgets,

[21] Summarized from K. Keniston, "You Have to Grow Up in Scarsdale to Know How Bad Things Really Are," *New York Times Magazine,* April 27, 1969.

[22] H. Marcuse, *Eros and Civilization: A Philosophical Inquiry into Freud* (Boston: Beacon Press, 1955).

[23] This is the central thesis of H. Marcuse, *One-Dimensional Man* (Boston: Beacon Press, 1964).

large automobiles, and machines of destruction. Instead of liberating libido, technology has supported the irrational and repressive organization of contemporary life. The distribution of power and, therefore, the locus of domination is more hidden but unchanged.

The youth of whom we are speaking not only reject the ethic of the reigning technobureaucracy, with its alienation of the individual from the product of his labor but, in their life style, openly express previously forbidden bodily pleasures and impulse-gratification. The shift from the use of alcohol to the widespread use of marijuana is very much related to this trend. The appeal of marijuana stems from its effect in eroticizing the skin and taste buds and heightening narcissistic pleasure in one's own thoughts and perceptions. The nature of this response challenges the whole ethic that pleasure should be renounced except as it is prescribed by a profitable network of manufacturers of leisure-time products —the "entertainment" industry, distillers, and tobacco-growers. The inevitable outgrowth of this challenge is the extraordinarily punitive legal consequences of possessing the drug, established and maintained by those who hold power in the system. Related to this is the political usefulness of the laws for "busting" politically dissenting youth.

The enduring attraction of Norman O. Brown's quite apolitical book *Life Against Death* for students in the university subculture stems not from his brilliant and complex critique of Freud's theory of instincts but, rather, from the prescription for "the way out" that grows out of his inquiry. Brown, in a Dionysian plea, calls for abolition of repression and, in traditional Christian language, for the resurrection of the body:

The resurrection of the body is a social project facing mankind as a whole, and it will become a practical political problem when the statesmen of the world are called upon to deliver happiness instead of power, when political economy becomes a science of use-values instead of exchange-values—a science of enjoyment instead of a science of accumulation. . . . Contemporary social theory (again we must honor Veblen as an exception) has been completely taken in by the inhuman abstractions of the path of sublimation and has no contact with concrete human beings, with their concrete bodies, their concrete though repressed desires, and their concrete neuroses.[24]

[24] N. O. Brown, *Life Against Death: The Psychoanalytical Meaning of History* (Middletown, Conn.: Wesleyan University Press, 1959), pp. 317–18.

The lessening of the bonds of "surplus repression" is also reflected in the new "culture heroes," the rock stars, Yippie leaders, and antiestablishment movie actors.[25]

Thus, many of the students and faculty in the liberal arts departments of universities, by virtue of their value systems and social philosophy, exist as a subculture "continuous" in some respects with family backgrounds and earlier socialization but "discontinuous" with American culture at large. That is, the values of the campus community do not equip its members for roles in the technological, economic, and political structure of American society.[26] This gap between early socialization and the demands of the larger society results in a social climate approaching "anomie"—the absence of a framework of values and norms within which the individual can integrate role behavior and a sense of self that is syntonic with the culture.[27] This condition, despite the more genuine possibilities for the triumph of Eros in the life of the individual, creates a psychological constellation of isolation, anxiety, and alienation for the students in this subculture. The potential for anomie is enhanced in the large university by its bureaucratic organization and policies of governance which reflect values assimilated from the society. The two major techniques used to resolve anomie and its associated potential for psychological pain are (1) to form strong groups for the purpose of actively maintaining and spreading "deviant" subcultural values—for instance,

---

[25] If nothing else, Jerry Rubin, in his role as clown, dramatizes the relationship between the humorless, repressed quality of the mainstream of American life and the politically repressive climate in America.

[26] This point has been particularly stressed by Zbigniew Brzezinski in *Between Two Ages: America's Role in the Technetronic Era* (New York: Viking, 1970).

[27] The concept of "anomie" was first significantly applied by the French sociologist Emile Durkheim in his study *Suicide* [1897] (Glencoe, Ill.; The Free Press, 1951). The concept has been developed by Sebastian de Grazia in a study of cohesiveness and disintegration of political communities: *The Political Community: A Study of Anomie* (Chicago: University of Chicago Press, 1948). Robert Merton used anomie in accounting for deviant social behavior, stressing the dissociation between the aspirations valued and promulgated in a society and the available channels for achieving these goals. (In Social Structure and Anomie," *American Sociological Review*, vol. 3, 1938, pp. 672–82.)

the radical and militant student movements [28]—and (2) to "drop out" and turn to a world of drug-induced inner experience, sensation, and immediate pleasure. Dropping out represents a fusion of the individual's failure at psychological adaptation and the society's failure to provide meaningful roles for atypical people.

The activism of today's students has a unique form. Beyond the differences in theoretical orientation and organization between the Old Left and the New, there is a fundamental difference in the psychological organizations of individuals in these two generations.

A sense of *immediacy* is characteristic of a significant faction of youth today. This psychological state produces the relatively uncompromising quality of radical and militant demands and tactics, in contrast to the gradualism of their parents' generation. (I do not mean here only Old Left parents but, rather, *all* people over thirty.) This generational difference in rhythm and timing reflects more than the time-honored "impetuousness of youth." We are witnesses to a new adaptive mode.

The formative psychosocial years for the "over-thirty" generation were qualitatively different from the comparable epoch in today's students' lives. The parents of today's students were born in the pre-Depression years, the era of gunpowder, not thermonuclear arsenals. The atmosphere of hope, prosperity, and glamour was all but destroyed by the Depression, but it was renewed in the optimism of the New Deal and the charisma of Roosevelt. The Depression was viewed as an accident, a malfunction of the system that could be and was remedied. In our most destructive childhood and adolescent fantasies, we could not conceive that in a few years 6 million Jews would be murdered in gas chambers, and that one United States bomb would kill almost 200,000 human beings without warning. The Marxists of the 1930's were far more Utopian than today's revolutionaries. There was not the life-death urgency, and there was considerably more faith that the state could lead the way to the light, be it the Russian experiment or the perfection of democracy here.

---

[28] The comprehensive application of the concept of anomie to student radicalism is the subject of a work in progress by Eleanor Laudicina ("The Politics of Anomie: Student Radicalism and Political Deviance").

The relationship of individuals born before World War II to external social movements and political changes is based on what might be described as a "psychosocial time sense," a cognitive function shaped by the symbolic meaning of the social and political climate of the years of their childhood. This generational time sense, which residually continues in the present, affects both the individual's reaction time to events and his expectation of what the tempo of progress and reform should be. Thus, for almost all adults, the psychosocial time sense has become translated into the political position that gradually, through due process, the necessary changes, initiated by the government, will bring equality and justice while the disenfranchised wait patiently.

In dramatic contrast are the roots and tempo of the post-Hiroshima kids, expressed by young Jacob Brackman in a piece called "My Generation":

No, no breather yet for reminiscence, no nostalgia, no wistful catalogue of names and feats. The biggest crop in national history. War Baby boom; Hibakusha, survivors of Hiroshima. Happening now. Our fathers had played out our chances for us. Next time the lamps start going out, no one shall ever see them lit again. Half America under twenty-five, stirring, rumbling, unbuttoned potentially, exquisite and terrible.[29]

The urgency of his prose is synchronous with the content. The prenatal events that shaped the psychic time sense of today's students were Buchenwald and Hiroshima and 20 million killed. In their own lifetimes, this time sense has been reconfirmed by the murders of civil rights workers, the Kennedys, and King.

A few years ago, a brilliant psychotic young man said to me:

I finally realized why nobody was ever allowed to see President Kennedy's body after the original autopsy. The body doesn't exist any more. It was immediately cut up into millions of cubes of LSD and given to all the kids in America.

With poignant eloquence, he focuses on a profound psychohistorical relationship. He speaks of the cultural transmutation of the despair experienced by his generation, growing out of the trauma produced by the assassination of President Kennedy, into a major

[29] J. Brackman, "My Generation," *Esquire*, vol. 70, no. 4 (April, 1968), p. 127.

aspect of the youth drug culture. A repetitive ritual in the drug culture is the LSD "trip." A full "trip" involves a symbolic psychological equivalent of the dissolution of ego boundaries, which some users have called "ego death." This state serves the psychological function of allowing the individual to experience death symbolically while he continues to live. However maladaptive, it provides an active means of mastering the passive state of helplessness in the face of the fearful possibility of real death. The assassination of a young President with whom a great many of the youth could identify was an event of incalculable psychological magnitude, far beyond its political ramifications.

Their lives have already encompassed two wars in Asia, the Cuban missile crisis, and the summers of Watts, Newark, and Detroit. The resultant sense of the tenuousness of life is manifested profoundly in its unconscious aspects. More specifically, it has created a sense of urgency to effect change, so that life can go on. At the time of the Columbia crisis, students felt themselves locked on a conveyor belt moving inexorably from the lawns of Columbia to the jungles of Vietnam. Student activists are frantically grasping for a way to halt the machinery. The years since the assassination of President Kennedy had hardly given them grounds for faith that the state would do it for them.

The disproportionate number of Jews among campus radicals has received attention.[30] In addition to the usual historical-sociological reasons, I believe that the psychological scars of genocide exist in the psyche of every Jew, including those born after 1945, and that the resultant pool of anxiety, fed from suppressed and repressed sources, motivates many to join in the attempt to crush the machines of war and racism. At the same time, it motivates many in the New Left to repudiate the state of Israel—the symbol of the "survivors" and reminder of the horror of the past. Paradoxically, the genocide of Jews is a source of anxiety for blacks that I feel is a significant unconscious factor in black anti-Semitism. The gassed Jew is the horror image of what blacks might come to in their American nightmare.

[30] S. M. Lipset, "The Socialism of Fools: The Left, the Jews, and Israel," *Encounter*, vol. 23, no. 6 (1969); and N. Glazer, "The Jewish Role in Student Activism," *Fortune*, vol. 79, no. 1 (1969).

So we who have been reared in a climate of progressive but gradual improvement, with no fear of immediate death, are out of phase with these students, black and white, with their desperate demand for change *now* and their deep despair over the prospect that the power structure will voluntarily give relief to the oppressed or even perceives the inevitable endpoint of the policies of escalation.

As Robert Lifton has articulated in his discussions of "death symbolism," [31] nuclear death is psychologically different from death by disease or gunpowder. Nuclear death means the annihilation of life on earth and, therefore, the barring of all paths to "symbolic immortality"—a pervasive human need. We are all faced with the possibility of sudden and absolute "termination," but, depending on our age, we psychologically integrate this threat differently. Every semester I ask my undergraduate students if they have been aware in recent years of experiencing anxiety about nuclear death. Whereas many people who entered adolescence before Hiroshima do experience such manifest anxiety, most members of the younger generation do not. It appears that this threat is psychologically overwhelming and has been resolved by both denial of the danger and isolation of the affects of fear and anxiety. This adaptation is akin to the child's reaction to the death of someone close to him. The capacity for responding to a lost love object by experiencing and working through feelings of grief does not develop until adolescence. The young child lacks ability to comprehend conceptually, integrate, and act appropriately on the knowledge of the permanence of the loss. Thus, the affect of grief is denied and isolated, but nonetheless the psychological trauma manifests itself in varying ways in aspects of his future psychological development and behavior. And so with today's youth and the bomb.

Five undergraduates in one of my classes in the spring of 1969 chose as a term-paper topic the effect on their development of having been born in the nuclear era. Allowing for the selective bias in those who picked this topic, I think that the results are compelling in their developmental implications.

---

[31] Lifton, *Death in Life, op. cit.; Revolutionary Immortality: Mao Tsetung and the Chinese Revolution* (New York: Random House, 1968).

The first student, a senor, was a liberal nonactivist who came to Columbia from the "Bible belt." His paper, "The Bomb and I," reads as follows:

When I was a junior in high school I wrote the short story "Last Laugh," in which a respectable man in a small Texas town called Araratsville becomes obsessed with the messianic duty of warning all of a nuclear holocaust. He fails to gain credibility among the townspeople and consequently builds an elaborate shelter, secludes himself in it, and goes mad. I feel now that there are many parts of that short story which illustrate my view of the world as a child of the bomb. . . .

Another factor in the short story is crucial to the personality developed under the bomb; that of a sense of urgency. Needless to say, this too was exploited in the fundamentalist faith by identifying this as the same evangelical urgency St. Paul attempted to implant in early Christianity. But even with this religious factor removed, I can feel a certain dominance of time and related factors in my life that I feel are abnormal. [He here describes aspects of a three-year relationship with his fiancée, during which they were separated much of the time, and goes on to muse] . . . Still, I very often think how ironic it would be for the bomb to kill either me or my fiancée just as our long separation is coming to an end.

. . . Another feeling that is quite incongruous with my general sentiment in relation to a nuclear holocaust is the fact that it might work out to a return to a freer life for the survivors. The yearning to return to the simpler life is not unique to me; there are several friends of mine who have cited this possible good end.

. . . Finally, there is the ever-present feeling that I have been cheated of a certain amount of self-determination in my future. My generation is the first that is subject to this very real threat of an arbitrary end to everything. I feel a resentment at times that this spectre was thrust on me.

The second paper, entitled "Gang Bang," was written by a senior English-literature major from a well-to-do urban family. He occupied a building during the rebellion.

. . . Now I do not necessarily spend every day wondering whether this will be the one on which some loonie, infatuated with his phallic ICBM, will decide to unzip his pants and fuck the world. I do, however, consider that the whole concept of social relations and world society is rendered absurd by the existence of nuclear weapons. That is to say, . . . that the principle of collective decisions being made by those whose lives will be consequently affected can never be reconciled with the existence of a nuclear trigger. The mere potential for nuclear destruction carries me and everyone else in the world, as individuals, to an infinite point on a curve approaching the asymptote of non-existence. For instance, I am reduced, as in a dream a year or so ago, to the absurdity of trying to get a subway train out of New York City when I see enemy planes about to carry out a nuclear attack overhead.

. . . Of course, one consolation is that no one will be left to despair —yet I think it is quite clear that I suffer from a kind of ultimate fatalism, if not despair, which may well be necessary to continue living in this age. Certainly, if some of the phenomena of the culture and consciousness of this younger generation are historically unique for an age group about to or having just matured into consciousness (I think they may well be), then it is tempting to venture that these manifestations of the response to the threat of nuclear holocaust— alienation, despair, desolation, black humor, frenetic and incoherent behavior, escape, etc.

I do not drink, take drugs, sleep around, live chaotically, believe in revolutionary politics, gamble, and avoid planning solely because of the existence of that threat; but I certainly would be willing to wager it has something to do with it, since its images are nearly inescapable in daily life. In any case, it certainly has a lot to do with my view of history, which makes up a significant aspect of my consciousness.

The third student, a junior, describes himself as follows:

Politically I am quite liberal, but not utopian, more realist. I am a practicing Roman Catholic, although I practice religion with respect to what is important to me. My moral guidelines appear to have been set by the Church.

His paper, entitled "Life as a Post-Hiroshima Person," continues:

A favorite question of a person born before Hiroshima to a person born after Hiroshima is, "Do you have any anxiety about the bomb?" I had never really thought about it for any great length of time, so the answer is "No."

. . . The nuclear age is my life. Imagine sitting in your second-grade class when sirens sound and the teacher telling you to file to the basement because this is an air-raid drill. Even though I participated in the drill, I did not know what it was all about, nor did I care. The drill was really only 15 minutes away from the cranky old teacher. As I think about it now, I seriously doubt whether or not I would want to go down in a basement during a nuclear attack. What would there be to come up to?

. . . I am not really conscious of it [the threat of nuclear holocaust], but I act as if it is pressuring me. That is why I say I am being shaped by outside forces. I still have my plans for the future, but I still act in a way that seems to cram everything into the present. That is my world—everything is here, so why not use it?

. . . This is the way life looks to me. There is a threat of annihilation from nuclear war, but that is it—there is a threat. This threat of nuclear annihilation has changed the world in which I live, which in turn has changed me from the people of older generations. This has been my life, nuclear threat from the start. It is part of me. Maybe those absurd air-raid drills made me accept nuclear war as part of my life.

The fourth student, a senior, came from suburbia. He occupied a building during the rebellion. In his untitled paper, he recalled:

In my eighth-grade English class, a student read aloud the best short story of the class. It was about a man who was very afraid of nuclear war. This man, after great calculations, moved his family to the safest spot in the United States. It was in the middle of the desert in the Southwest. He set up food and water-supply stocks and a very safe underground shelter. One day World War III almost came. Last second a compromise was reached but some missiles were in the air. All but one were turned back in time. After a few seconds of panic the one was redirected to a safe spot, the middle of the desert in the Southwest.

The story was very well received by the class. Somehow it seemed very right. There's no sure way to get away. Three years later, in the eleventh-grade there was another assignment to write a short story. Another student, Tom, waved his hands wildly and said he had written a great story. He read it to the class. When the class told him that it was the same story Joe had written in the eighth grade, he was indignant. He was sure he had made it up himself, but everyone else remembered the story from three years before.

I think, in general, . . . the nuclear threat has made me very cynical. The feeling that mankind is very stupid and very suicidal was for me the only possible explanation.

The fifth student, a junior, was a psychology major from suburbia, who was reared as a Roman Catholic and went through an intensely religious early adolescence. He had been active in the radical movement during the previous years and, at the time of the Columbia rebellion, stayed in Hamilton Hall the first night. He left because of fear of violence but played an active supporting role from outside. He called his paper "Retrospective Introspections on My Personal Relationships with the Atomic Bomb."

After describing a recent gathering in which his friends engaged in rather cynical black humor about the bomb, he wrote:

This is not, of course, to say that I hang around with morbid people or that we of the "Pepsi generation" worry perpetually about nuclear Armageddon and genetic mutation. Indeed, quite the reverse is the case. The topic nuclear war seldom comes up in conversations, and there is almost never overt anxiety expressed in that connection. One might say that we have, to use the psychological term, isolated that possibility from its affect. Such, however, was not always the case—at least for me.

The earliest recollections I have of the way in which the bomb has affected me center around a chronic obsession I had, throughout most of my elementary school years, with the prospect of an air raid (presumably nuclear). Though it may be evidence more of a personal neurosis than of generational commonality, I spent a very large part of my waking life worrying about being bombed. I collected (and later read) repetitive masses of pamphlets on what to do in the event of nuclear attack, counted the miles between New York City and my home, and compared that with the radii of destruction of the ever improving bombs and even went so far as to plan out in my head what I would do when the time came. (I still remember that I would have turned on all the water faucets in the house so as to lessen our vulnerability to "fire storms.") I used to dread (and I mean, quite emphatically, dread) going to bed at night, not so much for fear of bad dreams as out of the knowledge that, if the Russians attacked, they would do it while we were all asleep.

After describing his shifting interests, attitudes, and emotions during pre-adolescence and early adolescence, he related his developing interest in creative writing. He went on to say:

The following year, I became editor of the high school literary magazine, and in the hopes of stilling the vocal discontent of what small readership we had, our first decision on editorial policy was to automatically exclude from publication any and all stories concerning the end of the world, nuclear attack, and, less specifically, morbid topics in general. . . . What this meant was that we literally had to refuse to consider the single largest topical interest of all our contributors—and we rejected very large numbers of poems and stories on just that basis. . . . We still found it almost impossible to get any decent story that didn't deal with something morbid. We even went so far as to offer a prize for the funniest story and yet found the school to be incapable of any humor beyond limericks and nonsense poems. . . .

I suppose that here I must jump all the way to the present, and state that I have no emotional concern with the prospect of nuclear war whatsoever. With most of the people I know, I can say that even in discussions that have led to the conclusion that nuclear war would indeed be upon us at some time in the future, the only emotion displayed in the face of such a conclusion has been an ironic laugh.

I will not undertake detailed analysis of these various presentations. For students #1 and #5, nuclear holocaust was the subject of massive anxiety, finally mastered in adolescence. The accounts of short-story writing by the students themselves convey their preoccupation with the theme and their attempt to resolve their fear and anxiety through creative sublimation. They see themselves as different from adults because of their different life experiences with the bomb. Combined with amorphous resentment, there is conscious resignation and acceptance of the destructive potential of the bomb and of their powerlessness to do much about it. Student #1 goes so far as to rationalize that life may even be better for the survivors. Student #3 employs the strongest defenses, recalling no anxiety about the bomb; nevertheless, he clearly intuits its effects in shaping the sense of immediacy that governs his life. It is striking that all disavow manifest anxiety in their current lives caused by the thought of nuclear war, but all convey profound impact in earlier years.

I have recently collected fifteen additional term papers by Columbia undergraduates on the same subject. Because all the students in the class wrote on the topic, the selective bias of the group quoted earlier was eliminated. All but two of the papers followed the same pattern: At a point in pre-adolescence, there was a sudden breakthrough of massive anxiety related to the possibility of nuclear annihilation—probably occurring when the child's conceptual ability was sufficiently developed to permit an integration of three elements: a knowledge of the bomb's destructive potential; an awareness of some of the implications of current political events; and a capacity to conceptualize his own future. Then, following the outbreak of anxiety, there were a few years during which, as a young teenager, the student attempted to master the anxiety by primarily intellectual means, such as reading compulsively about the subject and becoming a factual "expert" on the bomb or writing short stories about it. Upon the achievement of intellectual "mastery," an emotional numbness took over with regard to the prospect of nuclear death. Related to this emotional numbness and intellectual mastery is the awareness of a shift in life view and future plans in the direction of obtaining immediate pleasure and fulfillment while, at the same time, proceeding with preparation for long-term goals, just in case the bomb might not fall. Thus, these students have adapted to a massive threat by employing the defenses of isolation and denial. The threat nonetheless continues to affect psychological integration and produces a markedly altered life view. In addition to the patterns described, there are more socially malignant defense mechanisms, such as reaction-formation, with its urge to "strike first"—the institutionalized paranoia of certain prowar groups.

But it is not sufficient to enumerate individual mechanisms of defense, even though these are widely shared. We must also consider how they become institutionalized in adaptive and maladaptive social movements. Just as there is a spectrum from idealistic to nihilistic radicalism and militancy, so there is a spectrum from activism to "quietism." The embodiment of institutionalized "quietism" was the early "hippie" movement, which, in the core of its ethic, renounced violence and aggression: "Make Love, Not War." Brickman, in an excellent paper,[32] discusses this movement in psychodynamic terms related to the theme of violence from the outside and violent impulses from within and their relation to a psychology of death. As mentioned earlier, the drug-induced psychedelic experience is an adaptive attempt to master the fear of death. I have been impressed by the manner in which the drug mystique, with its preoccupation with "experential transcendence" and its "death" and "rebirth" imagery, represents an attempt to escape the immediate dangers of urban life, the prospect of the draft, and, more generally, anxiety about the bomb.

The drug route, however, fails as a long-range coping vehicle. It involves a compulsive, repetitive ritual that, because it is concerned with symbols that are displacements from the real sources of anxiety, never affects these real sources. It is "autoplastic,"

[32] H. Brickman, "The Psychedelic 'Hip Scene': Return of the Death Instinct," *American Journal of Psychiatry*, vol. 125, December, 1968.

involving change in the self rather than the environment, but, of course, the external dangers remain.[33] In contrast, political actions, radical, liberal, traditional, or even conservative, are "alloplastic" and adaptive in that they involve "action" directed against the perceived sources of trouble or danger. If one is successful in effecting change by one's action, as in a local way at Columbia, the immediate personal gratification is high, as we have seen. But changing the distribution of power at Columbia has little effect on the national and international threats and horrors. Because it is a political reality that control resides with those national forces that support war and racist policies, the liberal-radical struggle is slow and uphill. And, as the horizon seemingly recedes further with every small step forward, many develop the syndrome of "weariness," which Robert Coles has described in his landmark action-studies of Southern civil rights workers. Coles observed:

The symptoms reveal fear, anxiety, and anger no longer "controlled" or "managed." Depressions occur, characterized by loss of hope for victory, loss of sense of purpose, and acceptance of the power of the enemy where before such power was challenged with apparent fearlessness.

I have seen no particular person specially vulnerable to this "battle fatigue." Constant exposure to frustrating social struggle seems to be the critical element in a "syndrome" which affects those with widely different characters and ways of handling stress.[34]

Against less flexible and responsive institutions than universities, the radical movement has had virtually no impact. In fact their vulnerability is a major reason for the choice of the universities as the targets of student action. Continuous frustration in the struggle beyond the campus leads to "weariness," which then tends to drive the individual into either withdrawal or more violent tactics.

Hence, most of Columbia's radicals have today withdrawn from

[33] The terms "autoplastic" and "alloplastic" are used here in the sense suggested by Heinz Hartmann in *Ego Mechanisms and the Problem of Adaptation* (New York: International Universities Press, 1958). Hartmann speaks of adaptation to a stress or challenge by change in the self, including intrapsychic re-equilibration, as "autoplastic"; adaptation by acting upon the environment to change it is "alloplastic."

[34] R. Coles, "Social Struggle and Weariness," *Psychiatry*, vol. 27, no. 4 (1964), pp. 308, 314.

political activism, although they still adhere to radical ideology. A few have left the university and moved to a more militant posture, engaging in confrontations marked by diffused violence. A factor in the rise of violence is that frustration in achieving progress creates demands for new leadership, almost always with magical expectations. Despite the continued presence of certain New Left leaders, there have been new waves of young leaders each season, offering their following more militant tactics, dictated by frustration and as an antidote to weariness.[35] Another aspect of the turn of the movement toward random violence and political nihilism is the fact that the more militant, nihilistic members often possess a Machiavellian skill that enables them to ascend successfully to leadership and control. These individuals then behave in such ways as to repulse and ultimately drive out of the "active" movement the larger body of idealists. The result is factionalism, with some radical groups consisting of a small but active corps of nihilists. It is not, as Feuer suggests, a case of a movement destroying itself, in the sense that all of its members remain active and follow a common motivational pathway to the unsuccessful end. As the elements in a movement become nihilistic, because of the ascendancy of more nihilistic types, factions proliferate, and eventually the number of active followers falls sharply. The response of the larger potential radical following is expressed in an editorial that appeared in the *Columbia Daily Spectator* on May 5, 1969, a year after the original occupation of buildings. The three editors who wrote it had supported the

[35] An imprisoned conscientious objector quoted by Willard Gaylin conveys some of the feeling accompanying the process whereby helplessness and weariness progress to violent political action: "I felt that all along violence was not an intelligent response to a problem. It was an insane or irrelevant kind of response. I still see it as insane or irrelevant, but perhaps the times call for irrationality. The longer I'm in here, the more doubt I have about the effectiveness of write-ins, literature, marches, or any of those things. Perhaps the only effective things in terms of the blacks, the poor whites, even the young—perhaps the only thing—is violence. . . . Before, I believed in dialogue—that you could speak to the system and speak to the people, and it could make a difference. Since then I've learned they don't pay any attention to your arguments." In W. Gaylin, *In the Service of Their Country: War Resisters in Prison* (New York: Viking, 1970), p. 308.

spring, 1968, action. In this piece, they are responding to a brief "occupation" of two buildings in the spring of 1969.

REVOLUTIONARY ADVENTURISM

Last week's occupation of Mathematics and Fayerweather Halls was an occasion for weeping—not because it failed miserably, but because it was from the very start an ugly episode in the corruption of a radical movement. Signs of a tragic but familiar pattern have been accumulating for months. The open and undogmatic attitudes that once characterized many people in SDS have given way to a narrow sectarianism. Within the organization the ideal of participatory democracy has been banished and a small party hierarchy dominated by three leaders has grown up. Secrecy has become a way of life. Locked into a repetitive set of slogans and obsessed with the idea of repeating last spring's revolt, the SDS leadership lost touch with the rest of the campus, including many of those who were arrested last year. Perhaps it is the fate of those who have been agents of history to fancy themselves the main cause, and end by pathetically trying to re-enact their moments of power. In any case, SDS rushed headlong into the buildings this year, only to find that no one was following them any more.

In their weakness and isolation they turned bitter, divided and violent. They carried clubs as a matter of habit in the buildings. . . . The atmosphere inside, in marked contrast to last year when there was mass support, was stifling. . . . But it is not just their failure that is repelling: it is what SDS has become. In its own structure and actions can be discerned more than the outlines of authoritarianism and manipulation. When they fled the buildings, they had to hide their faces because they had already deserted their principles. That is what makes the history of SDS a tragedy and not heroic drama.

As the Columbia movement increasingly lost touch with the needs, perceptions, and aspirations of the larger body of students who had been radicalized during the rebellion, the new leaders, who were responsible for this direction, revealed their lack of the qualities that enable some leaders—for example, those identified by Erikson—to relate rationally and flexibly to their constituency and to inspire it to new levels of consciousness and forms of political action that also happen to be syntonic with the leaders' private motives and unconscious aims.

To understand a revolutionary leader at any point in time, from either a psychological or a political perspective, we must conceptualize his life as a *process* in which current behavior makes

sense only in terms of the "reality" of the leader's past experience
with political oppression, itself the result of a history of radical
commitment. The separation of the young leaders at Columbia
from their followers can be traced in part to the transformation
in their political analysis that inevitably emerges from a long
period of intense involvement in the radical movement. For reasons discussed in Chapter IX, the young leader has, by late
adolescence, consolidated "social consciousness" as a central element in his identity, often with fervent idealism. As he progresses
into his youth at college, his identity progresses to "social activist."
Once deeply committed to the movement, he will very likely live
in a radical cooperative or other quasi-communal arrangement,
which separates him from his fellow students on campus. His
political work brings him in frequent contact with militant representatives of other groups. He may be called upon to house
fugitive revolutionaries. He experiences continuous rebuffs and
frustrations in his attempts to organize a broad-based movement.
Further, the nature of his activities often makes him the object
of disciplinary procedures by the college administration and
harassment by police "red squads." Thus, out of his daily participation in the movement emerges a compelling firsthand experience with political oppression that has no counterpart in the
experience of fellow students who share his sympathies but not
his commitment to activism. In the subjective view of reality
produced by this unique objective experience, the need for political
action is urgent. The tactics dictated by this sense of urgency are
no longer synchronous with the views of the leaders' potential
followers. As at Columbia, the gulf becomes too great for mutual
understanding and collaboration between leaders and followers.

Much has been said about the corruption of "ends" by compromises in "means." Given political realities, the idealized goals
of any revolution always remain to be attained and the struggle
toward attainment is an ever continuing process. When "temporary" deviations from the humanistic tradition (such as ter-
rorism) begin to characterize the tactics used to obtain the ends,
these compromised values become internalized in the psychological organization of the members of the movement, particularly
the younger ones who enter and are indoctrinated at that phase

of the revolution. The corrupted values then are passed on through the generations.

The "immediacy" of youth no doubt has major sources other than the bomb—for example, the psychological impact of advances in transportation and communications. A New Yorker no longer conceives of Paris as 3,000 miles and a week away, but six hours from where he is. And, apart from the much-written-about impact of the fact that events are immediately reproduced on the television tube in one's bedroom or living room, there is also the formative effect of the kind of congnitive activity involved in transmitting the percept into concept.[36] In the era of radio, stimuli were perceived through the receptors in the form of words. The conversion into mental imagery in "picture form" required *active* mental operations. Now, with visual receptors recording the picture images directly, the cognitive experience is much more passive, involving simply a mental reproduction of what has been fed in, in unaltered form. This mental process of immediate visual receptivity becomes an internalized standard and, as such, another contributor to the individual's expectancy of and then demand for immediate achievement.

Associated with this is the whole wave of push-button, electronic labor-saving devices, particularly for the household. Antibiotics offer relatively immediate relief from infection. Patients now walk within twenty-four hours of major surgery instead of healing with the protection of prolonged bedrest.

In these and many other parallel areas, the change in time, space, and energy-expenditure relations over the past generation contributes to the urgency of the demands of youth. But at the base of the feeling embodied in the political tactics and life style of "NOW" is the sense of impending doom. A rock classic called "When the Music's Over," by The Doors, sums up this theme in

---

[36] Marshall McLuhan has stressed how the medium itself profoundly influences our psyches, in *Understanding Media: The Extensions of Man* (New York: McGraw-Hill, 1964). Robert Jay Lifton speaks of the historical tendency of "flooding of imagery," by which contemporary man is overwhelmed by superficial messages and undigested cultural elements transmitted by mass-communication networks, as a contributing force to the development of the identity of "protean man." (*History and Human Survival, op. cit.*)

the recurrent line: "We want the world/And we want it Now!"
Then follow the lines:

> Persian night!
> See the light!
> Save us!
> Jesus!
> Save us!

Epilogue: Reflections on Psychoanalysis, Psychiatry, and Student Radicals

In the course of writing this book, I have become aware of many of the ways in which who I am has determined what I have "seen" at Columbia and has thus influenced the model I have presented for understanding politically committed students. Inasmuch as who I am has been shaped in part by my professional training and affiliations, I feel impelled also to assess where psychiatry—more specifically, the psychoanalytic movement—stands at this time in relation to political movements.

In April, 1968, a few days before the occupation of buildings at Columbia, Anna Freud, herself a pioneer in the application of psychoanalytic knowledge to social problems, noted that today's youth are more concerned with the problem of man against society than with man against himself.[1] She cautioned psychoanalysts not be be lured into chasing after them by changing psychoanalysis to "fit in." This shift in the direction of the concern of the young has been widely observed and now threatens the future of psychoanalysis. I would, however, question Miss Freud's guideline as appropriate for the psychoanalytic movement.

The origins of psychoanalysis were truly revolutionary. With extraordinary courage and sacrifice, in the face of scorn and ostracism, Sigmund Freud exposed oppressive aspects of the social order, not of only Viennese culture, but of all Western society. He then developed therapeutic tactics for releasing mankind from forms of suffering imposed, in part, by the mores of the times. In the process, he generated original explorations and ferment in virtually every area of intellectual and artistic endeavor. Youth were enthusiastically drawn to the movement. As Miss Freud had described, after World War I, they flocked to hear the revelations

[1] Anna Freud, "Difficulties in the Path of Psychoanalysis," Eighteenth Freud Anniversary Lecture, New York City, April 16, 1968.

of psychoanalysis in the lecture halls. She recalls, "The young then avidly received [psychoanalytic principles] and eagerly, often secretly, discussed them as the embodiment of the spirit of change." [2]

In the last decade the pendulum has reversed direction. Not only are proportionately fewer young psychiatrists interested in formal psychoanalytic training, but more and more of those youth who question the existing social order and espouse new forms are renouncing psychoanalysis as their spiritual and intellectual beacon. Increasingly, they charge that psychoanalysis is "irrelevant" or, worse, a handmaiden of the *status quo*, helping people to "adjust" to institutions that should be changed.

We are witnessing the emergence of new forms of individual character organization and ego integration. Such writers as Coles, Erikson, Fromm, Kardiner, Keniston, Lifton, Marcuse, Riesman, Wangh,[3] and the school of cultural anthropologists have encouraged us to abandon the concept of fixed character structure to understand identity as process related to changing historical forces. To embrace this orientation in no way requires abandonment of a classical instinctual theory of personality development. By restraining the free biological unfolding of man, culture and society dictate the vicissitudes of individual lives and, hence, the course of particular civilizations. As Freud indicated, the history of man is the history of his repression.

What is to be repressed is determined by society. The superego

[2] *Op. cit.*
[3] R. Coles, *Children of Crisis: A Study of Courage and Fear* (Boston: Little, Brown, 1964); E. H. Erikson, *Identity: Youth and Crisis* (New York: W. W. Norton, 1968), and *Young Man Luther: A Study in Psychoanalysis and History* (New York: W. W. Norton, 1958); E. Fromm, *Escape From Freedom* (New York: Rinehart, 1941); A. Kardiner, *The Psychological Frontiers of Society* (New York: Columbia University Press, 1945); K. Keniston, *The Uncommitted: Alienated Youth in American Society* (New York: Harcourt, Brace & World, 1965), and *Young Radicals: Notes on Committed Youth* (New York: Harcourt, Brace & World, 1968); R. J. Lifton, *Death in Life: Survivors of Hiroshima* (New York: Random House, 1968), and *History and Human Survival* (New York: Random House, 1970); H. Marcuse, *One-Dimensional Man* (Boston: Beacon Press, 1964); D. Riesman, *The Lonely Crowd* (New Haven, Conn.: Yale University Press, 1950); M. Wangh, "National Socialism and the Genocide of the Jews: A Psychoanalytic Study of a Historical Event," *International Journal of Psychoanalysis,* vol. 45 (1964).

is nothing more than internalized social standards of acceptability
and nonacceptability that have no inherent value. Although certain
forms of behavior have been universally prohibited (for example,
incest), the content of the superego at any given time and place
is significantly influenced by the class in power. And this includes
the internalization of values, often codified as laws, that serve to
perpetuate that power. Thus, the dialectic between instinctual id
and culturally determined superego results in synthesized individual egos that are strongly inclined toward preservation of the
social *status quo.*

Psychoanalysis has moved from its own struggling and radical
youth to respectability. Whereas, eighty years ago, a Viennese
psychoanalyst was jeered off the stage of a medical school for
challenging established thought, today another Vienna-born psychoanalyst is dean of the Yale University School of Medicine.
With respectability has come considerable economic comfort for
psychoanalysts. And with affluence and status has come the motivation for many to "not see" in ways and places that Freud insisted on "seeing." As science and economics have become intertwined, psychoanalytic therapy has become, if not less relevant,
certainly less obtainable for those who are not economically highly
advantaged, which generally excludes the young. Thus, when the
psychoanalyst studies or treats student radicals, he risks opening
Pandora's box. If the contents are given credence in their own
right and not treated as "only" resistance, they can shake the
foundations of many of his own beliefs and practices.

It is not difficult to find behavior on the part of some radicals
and militants that appears to be manipulative, destructive, bizarre,
and inhumane. Since we in America are not at this time approaching a "revolutionary situation," many young revolutionaries will
inexorably move to their own personal destruction; their legacy
may be primarily, as some Old Left critics suggest,[4] a wave of
conservatism, political repression, and compromise of civil liberties. For those who are frightened by conflict, who have vested
economic and status interests in the present organization of
society, or who hate the young because they remind them of their
own irretrievable youth and lost possibilities, it is strongly appeal-

[4] Irving Howe, "The Agony of the Campus," *Dissent,* Sept.-Oct., 1969.

ing to search for psychopathology in dissenters. Such a focus will serve well the masters of the *status quo.*

Meanwhile the blacks, the young men who must die in wars, the "irrelevant" humanities majors on campuses, and more and more women will become angrier and angrier. Their actions will become increasingly desperate. Their violence will paradoxically offer comfort to the establishment because they can then be isolated and labeled "crazies." And the validity of their critique and intent of their social vision for the moment will be lost and discredited. Therefore, psychiatrists and psychologists must not only come to understand the ways in which the structure of their professions perpetuates the inequalities of the *status quo*, but also resist the strong pull to aid the forces of repression and exploitation by allowing themselves and their theories to be used, with an aura of scientific respectability, to quiet those youth who scream out that there is something terrible going on in our country and that it must be changed. For psychoanalysis at this point in its life cycle to remain "safe" and avoid the complex questions of the relationship of man's psyche to the political and social realities of the times, whether out of fear of error or fear of change, is to deny the reality of mankind's present danger.[5] As Norman O. Brown has warned us, "Psychoanalysis, unless it is transformed into a critique of reality, resembles a psychosis in being autoplastic in its aim as well as in its faith in the magic word. But psychoanalysis, thanks to the humanity of Freud, has also within it the possibility of being a new and higher stage of human consciousness." [6]

In facing today's youth, there is the danger, then, that—if the psychoanalytic movement cannot change its methods and concepts to accommodate psychohistorical forces and, hence, new forms of individual character organization and ego integration, without pejoratively labeling them "unanalyzable" (which means resistant to our healing method and therefore, implicitly, mentally ill)—the movement will cease to be a major force for understanding and

[5] This point has been emphasized by Martin Wangh in his discussion of my paper, "Radical and Militant Youth: A Study of Columbia Undergraduates," *The Psychoanalytic Forum* (in press).

[6] N. O. Brown, *Life Against Death: The Psychoanalytic Meaning of History* (Middletown, Conn.: Wesleyan University Press, 1959), pp. 154–55.

helping conflicted people of all generations. As "analyzable" patients get older and older, and fewer and fewer, the analytic movement will move toward obsolescence and irrelevance, while remaining "pure."

Freud well knew that people cannot be cured in the consulting room alone. Man must be studied in the context of his society. Psychological health is an abstraction. To move toward its actualization demands social change. If man is to progress to a state of emotional freedom and begin to live with a sense of trust and community, the psychoanalyst must pioneer not only in bringing people to recognize what they fear—when they have become so "numb" that they do not even know that they are afraid—but also in elucidating the psychological process by which practices and institutions in our society rob us all of part of our humanity. I am speaking of the *subversive* role psychoanalysis should play, both as social commentator and in individual therapy. True psychological liberation requires not only that the patient become aware of repressed instinctual urges and their maladaptive forms of disguised expression but also of the ways in which he has been conditioned to collaborate in his own repression and to accept the social *status quo* instead of to dream of and work for what might be.

The boundaries between "being" political and studying and clarifying those issues that influence people's political behavior seem to have been more clearly defined in past years. Radical and militant youth are explicitly political and seek to change society by political pressure. As scientists, we do not ordinarily attempt to enrich society by political means. However, as nuclear physicists have painfully learned, there is no "pure" science divorced from the ethics of its possible application. The illusion that science can remain value-free and apolitical leads only to self-deceptive silence. And this silence is a political act of covert support of those in power. The student activists at Columbia understood this. They knew that humanitarian education could not be properly pursued in a setting where glaring elements contrary to that ethic existed.

When Einstein asked him, "Why war?," Freud said, "There is no question of getting rid entirely of man's aggressive impulses; it is enough to try to divert them to such an extent that they need not find expression in war." [7] To war we must add racism and the forms of spiritual exploitation to which we are all subjected. If we and our children are to survive, after having created the means of our own destruction on earth, a radical restructuring and redistribution of power and wealth within America and among nations as well as a revolution in consciousness are necessary. This vision will not be realized without radical action, but such action will have to be combined with a commitment to the ideal of using the tools of our disciplines in the service of illuminating social and individual truths.

In Hermann Hesse's *Demian,* Sinclair, the searching youth, says, "For us, humanity was a distant goal toward which all were moving, whose image no one knew, whose laws were nowhere written down." To move toward this ideal, the wisdom and strength of the political activists, the technical expert, the quiet scholar, and the adventurer in new life styles of each generation will have to join, each lending strength to the others.

[7] S. Freud, "Why War?" (1932), in *Collected Papers,* vol. XXII (London: Hogarth Press, 1964), p. 212.

Index